BLUE RIDGE ROADWAYS

Blue Ridge Roadways

A Virginia Field Guide to Cultural Sites

By

M. Anna Fariello

JOHN F. BLAIR
PUBLISHER WINSTON-SALEM, NORTH CAROLINA

Published by John F. Blair, Publisher
Copyright © 2006 by M. Anna Fariello
All rights reserved under
International and Pan-American Copyright Conventions

*The paper in this book meets the guidelines
for permanence and durability of the Committee on
Production Guidelines for Book Longevity
of the Council on Library Resources.*

MAPS BY TONY ROBERTS, THE ROBERTS GROUP
BOOK DESIGN BY DEBRA LONG HAMPTON

COVER
"Blue Ridge Parkway," by Anna Fariello

Library of Congress Cataloging-in-Publication Data

Fariello, M. Anna.
Blue Ridge roadways : a Virginia field guide to cultural sites / by M. Anna Fariello.
p.   cm.
Includes index.
ISBN-13: 978-0-89587-332-3 (alk. paper)
ISBN-10: 0-89587-332-X
1. Historic sites—Virginia—Guidebooks. 2. Historic sites—Blue Ridge Mountains—
Guidebooks. 3. Virginia—Tours. 4. Blue Ridge Mountains—Tours. 5. Automobile travel—
Virginia—Guidebooks. 6. Automobile travel—Blue Ridge Mountains—Guidebooks. 7.
Virginia—History, Local. 8. Blue Ridge Mountains—History, Local. I. Title.

F227.F225 2006
917.5504'44—dc22
                                        2006015746

Contents

2 SOUTH BLUE RIDGE TRAIL   69

3 EASTERN LOWLAND TRAIL   121

Preface

In 1995, the White House Conference on Cultural Tourism defined cultural tourism as "travel directed toward experiencing the arts, heritage, and special character of a place." The landmark conference served as a challenge to communities throughout the nation. "Every place in America can develop cultural tourism," the conference concluded. "Each must discover and value its heritage and decide for itself what kind of tourism and how many tourists it wants to have. Each must tell its own story." At the turn of a new century, many American communities were considering cultural tourism as a viable alternative to industrial development. Rural areas in particular looked to cultural tourism as a diversified and sustainable industry that promised to enhance the quality of life of residents while opening up opportunities to connect them with the outside world on their own terms.

"You have to think in terms of 'sustainable tourism,' tourism that captures the authentic quality of the experience and channels resources back to the community in a way that helps preserve what it is you want to share," said Paul Tyler, then deputy director of the Virginia Commission for the Arts, in a public-radio interview.[1] In areas that sorely need economic investment, cultural tourism can be simultaneously challenging and gratifying. It requires localities to shift from a development perspective that favors manufacturing as a primary economic solution to a diversified entrepreneurial approach. Rather than looking at rural areas as empty spaces that need filling, cultural tourism provides new ways of conceiving of open space as an asset—as something, rather than nothing.

Heritage tourism in particular focuses on existing cultural amenities, rather than new travel products or destinations. Where no single tourist attraction is large enough to have an impact on the regional economy, small community assets are bundled together to form an attractive destination. The partnership approach takes advantage of the decentralized character of rural communities by encouraging projects across county lines. In its instructional guide *Stories Across America: Opportunities for Rural Tourism*, the National Trust for Historic Preservation suggests principles that lead to successful tourism development, including collaboration, authenticity, preservation, and "making sites come alive."[2]

Yet cultural tourism remains a matter of balance. While rural communities promote tourism as a "clean industry," visitation out of balance with community needs can lead to disastrous results. Gatlinburg, Tennessee, is an example of too much of a good thing. Gatlinburg was once a quiet community tucked between high-walled mountain ridges, but the coming of the Great Smoky Mountains National Park and its attendant tourism all but obliterated the local landscape and culture. Early tourism in Gatlinburg was fueled by promoters of a regional craft revival that marketed simple, high-quality, locally made goods to outside visitors. But in the second half of the 20th century, strip-style development brought in chain stores and restaurants. Ironically, today's glitzy downtown Gatlinburg sells mass-produced T-shirts and "souvenir" crafts made in far-off factories. Some imitations mimic Appalachian traditions but undercut opportunities for regional craftsmen. Others use traditional culture to create unflattering humor, turning honest simplicity into ignorance. If rural communities don't take a proactive approach to the type of industries and tourism developed in their midst, they are left open to a manufactured Disney-esque identity.

It was not long ago that outside industrial interests pillaged the Appalachians for lumber and coal. Many of today's distressed Appalachian counties still feel the impact of such "economic development," which served the interests of outside investors at the expense of local citizens. Indeed, some of the most rural—and most beautiful—parts of the region still struggle against a 21st-century version of the coal-baron mentality in fighting mountaintop removal and chip mills.

A primary factor in cultural tourism is identity, developed through the process of "visioning"—that is, the ability to imagine the future. Successful visioning blends an appreciation of the past with an understanding of the present in order to create an effective future. A common trap in heritage-tourism development is the outmoded assumption that economic development is in opposition to preservationist concerns. Either-or thinking doesn't lead to concrete answers. Instead, it keeps communities circling on a merry-go-round of stagnation.

Investment is what brings vision to realization. In cultural tourism, investment doesn't always mean money. Rather, it may take the form of time, effort, cooperation, and compromise. The 1999 Harvard Business School text *The Experience Economy* proposes that experience itself can be thought of as a new economic commodity. "Experiences are . . . distinct from services as services are from goods, . . . [having been] lumped into the service sector along with such uneventful activities as dry cleaning, auto repair, wholesale distribution, and telephone access. When a person buys a service, he purchases a set of intangible activities carried out on his behalf. But when he buys an experience, he pays to spend time enjoying a series of memorable events that . . . engage him in a personal way."[3]

Where tourism has become convenient and predictable, it has lost the glow of adventure. While the nationally franchised hospitality industry can provide a predictable product, homogeneous communities lack a distinctive sense of place. Personal experience and a sense of place, the keys to success in cultural tourism, form the philosophic core that informs this book.

Mapping Community Assets

Blue Ridge Roadways evolved from the final phase of a state-funded cultural inventory conducted under the auspices of the Highland Cultural Coalition, a project of Floyd County. Funded by the Virginia General Assembly, the initiative was promoted by a coalition of state legislators from southwestern counties whose vision for heritage preservation, cultural promotion, and economic development preceded the bandwagon that would become Virginia's tourism trails. Originally planned to occur over three years, the inventory took twice that long, due to the fits and starts of state funding during lean economic times.

The Highland Cultural Coalition study began with a process of asset mapping. Its goal was to produce a comprehensive cultural inventory, the first such systematic study to examine so many rural communities in southwestern Virginia. In conjunction with the Appalachian Studies Program in Virginia Tech's Department of Interdisciplinary Studies, the inventory was organized into a database. In turn, the database was made available via the South Atlantic Humanities Center Digital Library Web site (www.southatlanticcenter.org). This goal enabled counties and localities to direct tourists and residents to information on a Web site that will be maintained by Virginia Tech's digital library.

The inventory was thorough and systematic. Initial data collection began with existing guidebooks, brochures, and literature provided by organizations including the Blue Ridge Travel Association, the National Park Service, the Virginia Association of Bed-and-Breakfasts, the Virginia Association of Museums, the Virginia Department of Historic Resources, and the Virginia Tourism Corporation. Financial contributions and guidance were given by the Blacksburg-Christiansburg Regional Chamber of Commerce, Château Morrisette, Floyd County and its chamber of commerce, the Historic Crab Orchard Museum, the Peaks of Otter Winery, Pulaski County, the Saltville Foundation, Tazewell County, and the towns of Blacksburg, Dublin, and Pearisburg.

A call for participation was put out in the newsletters of arts organizations including the Arts Council of the Blue Ridge, the Association of Virginia Artisans, Cave House, Lynwood Artists, the Southern Highland Craft Guild, the Virginia Commission for the Arts, and the Virginia Mountain Craft Guild. While the project's initial intent was to highlight the studios of individual artists and craftsmen, not enough were accessible to the public at the time to warrant a guide focused on open studios alone. Instead, the project was broadened to include a more generalized inventory. After a tentative mapping of existing sites, project staff began a series of site visits, adding new locations and verifying information.

In the initial development of the project, the Highland Cultural Coalition aimed to highlight public and private enterprises that could interface with its educational mission. Major cultural attractions—Explore Park in Roanoke, the Historic Crab Orchard Museum in Tazewell, the Jacksonville

Center in Floyd, the Mountain Lake Resort in Giles County, and the Piedmont Arts Association in Martinsville—were selected as focal points. The directors of these organizations were invited to serve as advisers to ensure an accurate portrayal of the region. Joining them were representatives from the Virginia Department of Historic Resources, Virginia Tech, and Virginians for the Arts. Together, they analyzed the inventory process and refined the pilot project. Selected members of the advisory committee reviewed the inventory in draft form. A pilot guide, supported by a Virginia Foundation for the Humanities grant, organized parts of three county inventories into a small guidebook. This pilot guide was printed in a limited run and distributed to localities, libraries, historical societies, and museums. Its cover features the colorful wagons and tricycles lining the sidewalk beneath Floyd County's single traffic light where Route 8 and U.S. 221 meet, flanked on all sides by cultural sites.

No such project can be completed without the input of numerous individuals. In their roles as preservationists, the following people contribute every day to the public good. Although some are no longer affiliated with the organizations credited here, they lent their expertise to the initial advisory board and are acknowledged for their contribution to the effort: Jayn Avery of the Jacksonville Center in Floyd; Toy Cobbe, director of the Piedmont Arts Association in Martinsville; Roger Ellmore, director of Explore Park in Roanoke; Lucius F. Ellsworth, director of the statewide advocacy organization Virginians for the Arts; Betty Fine and Anita Puckett, professors in Virginia Tech's Department of Interdisciplinary Studies; John Kern of the Virginia Department of Historic Resources; David Rotenizer of the Carroll County Historical Society; Buzz Scanland of the Mountain Lake Resort; Llyn Sharp, coordinator of the New River Watershed Roundtable; Paul Tyler, deputy director of the Virginia Commission for the Arts; and Ross Weeks of the Historic Crab Orchard Museum in Tazewell. Becky Anderson, who conceived and produced the much-copied *Craft Heritage Trails of Western North Carolina*, created a highly praised model for subsequent projects. I thank her for her encouragement. George Nester, Floyd County administrator, was the fiscal administrator of the Highland Cultural Coalition and the quiet hand behind its development. Susan Nunn, his administrative assistant, processed the paperwork with good humor and attention to detail. Initial research was conducted with the help of Pat Sharkey, Charmagne Dutton, and Kirsten Sparenborg. Contributing their expertise were members of local chambers and historical societies whose efforts at historic preservation cannot be overstated.

Midway through the cultural study, Kate Rubick was hired as project coordinator, assuming a major role in the project's operation and development. She joined me in my position as project director in communicating the mission and aim of the coalition to community members, cultural organizations, and local government representatives. Once the inventory was complete, it was Kate who participated with me in further research, building on the Highland Cultural Coalition study to create this guide. Her diligent research and lucid writing were critical in the development of a user-friendly guidebook. It is Kate Rubick's writing that is woven throughout these chapters in the clear, concise, and complete site descriptions that are a joy to read.

[1] Paul Tyler in Anna Fariello, "Trail Blazing: A Conversation about Cultural Tourism," *Virginia Association of Museums* newsletter (Winter 1999): 3-5.

[2] Suzanne G. Dane, *Stories Across America: Opportunities for Rural Tourism* (Washington, D.C.: National Trust for Historic Preservation, 2001).

[3] B. Joseph Pine and James H. Gilmore, *The Experience Economy: Work Is Theatre and Every Business a Stage* (Boston: Harvard Business School, 1999), 2.

Acknowledgments

Research and editorial assistance:

Kate Rubick

Research and photographic collections:

Château Morrisette
Christiansburg Institute Museum and Archive
Digital Library and Archives, Virginia Polytechnic Institute and State
    University
Federal Highway Administration Web site
Friends Historic Library, Swarthmore College
Lora Robins Collection, Virginia Historical Society
Maps Collection, Library of Virginia
Montgomery News Messenger Photographic Archive
Reynolds Homestead and William S. Rogers Metals
Robert B. Basham Family Collection
Southern Historical Collection, Wilson Library, University of North Caro-
   lina at Chapel Hill
Special Collections, Hunter Library, Western Carolina University
Special Collections, McConnell Library, Radford University
Virginia Department of Historic Resources
Virginia Foundation for the Humanities Folklife Program

How to Use This Guide

Virginia is a state with a wealth of geographic diversity. Its Tidewater region is home to America's first colony, Jamestown, established in 1607. Its loamy Piedmont contributed to an agricultural abundance that ensured its economic power. Virginia's foothills rise farther west, affording views from forested rolling hills leading upward and westward to its highest peaks. Here, in 1768, Thomas Jefferson began to clear the land to build Monticello, his 43-room Neoclassical mansion. At the state's northern border, Virginia's mountains are called the Shenandoahs, a favorite haunt of Herbert Hoover. In 1931, in the waning days of his presidency, Hoover authorized funds to begin construction of Skyline Drive, a road with breathtaking mountaintop views. Virginia's highlands continue in a southwesterly direction, splitting into the two chains that frame the Valley of Virginia. To the east lies the Blue Ridge, its peaks linked by a popular and panoramic federal parkway; to the west lie the Alleghenies, the range that separates Virginia from West Virginia. It is this section of Virginia—the 16-county swath of communities framed by the state's southern upland ranges—that is covered by this book.

Blue Ridge Roadways: A Virginia Field Guide to Cultural Sites is a visitors' guide to places indicative of the culture and heritage of Virginia's Blue Ridge region. It contains five trails that are carefully designed to introduce visitors to the rich contemporary culture and historic significance of the area spanning the Blue Ridge and the Valley of Virginia. These are not trails of a hiking variety; rather, each is a self-guided auto tour that leads visitors off the interstates and onto rural roadways passing through dozens of small towns and rural communities. While general directions are included, this book is intended to be used with a state highway map for specific directions to the communities listed in the text.

Each of the tours in *Blue Ridge Roadways* departs from one of three major transportation arteries—I-81, I-77, or the Blue Ridge Parkway—to circle through the region's hills and valleys. Each trail is designed as a loop that leads visitors back to their original starting point, although a trail may be picked up at any point along the way. Adventurous travelers may want to jump trails or combine them to create their own itineraries. The configuration of these five loops is based on the educational value and the scenic nature of the drives. Periodically, spurs are included to direct visitors to interesting sites located a short distance off trail. Completing each loop at a relaxed pace will take a weekend or a midweek overnight visit.

The trails provide stopping points every 15 minutes, allowing visitors to leave their cars and walk to the suggested sites. Site selection was based on educational merit, authenticity, scenic character, and entertainment value. To be selected for inclusion in the guide, sites had to welcome travelers, studios and storefronts had to maintain regular hours or be willing to open by appointment, and signage had to be visible to approaching visitors. Retail stores, large and small, have been included only if they sell Virginia-made goods. Studio artisans included in this guide display work for sale and often offer interpretive information as part of their displays. The accommodations included here are in historic homes or offer activities based on cultural or agricultural traditions. Antique shops are not covered because there are already books on them; bed-and-breakfasts are included only if they are historic or if they provide activities relevant to regional culture. Likewise, the restaurants in *Blue Ridge Roadways* serve traditional foods or support regional food ways. Where possible, agricultural sites have been included, as have nature-based destinations. The guide describes local historical societies, art cooperatives, museums, and visitor centers throughout the region. Historic sites that are not open to the public have been included with a reminder that they may be viewed from the road. Courthouses and schools that no longer serve their original purposes are described as "historic" to differentiate them from courthouses and schools in use. The site descriptions relate historical information and provide a context for heritage celebration, cultural appreciation, and contemporary understanding. For ease of use, sites are listed alphabetically within each stop. Chambers of commerce, visitor centers, and farmers' markets are listed generically, rather than by specific names. Contact information was accurate at the time of publication.

The trail loops lead visitors off high-speed interstates onto secondary routes, many of them scenic byways.

The Highlands Trail covers the Blue Ridge Parkway and the Blue Ridge Music Center near Galax, circles the southern edge of Grayson Highlands, and accesses the New River Trail at Whitetop and Damascus before leading north to Saltville and a string of towns along the Valley of Virginia, then heads south again to Foster Falls and Woodlawn.

The South Blue Ridge Trail follows the southern end of the Blue Ridge Parkway through Fancy Gap, Meadows of Dan, and Mabry Mill and visits the county seats of Floyd and Hillsville.

The Eastern Lowland Trail winds from Rocky Mount to Ferrum, Stuart, and Martinsville, heads north to sites around Smith Mountain Lake and historic Bedford, and concludes at the Peaks of Otter.

The National Forest Trail begins on I-77 near the West Virginia border and takes in towns and sites near Wytheville before looping north through Pulaski and Giles counties, with spurs leading as far west as Burke's Garden, Tazewell, and Pocahontas.

The North Blue Ridge Trail begins on I-81 and winds through Salem, New Castle, and Paint Bank before heading west along historic Route 42 and into the New River Valley, where it meets the Blue Ridge Parkway to complete the loop to Roanoke.

Each chapter weaves together site descriptions and historic and contemporary photographs to form a collage portraying the particular flavor of the Blue Ridge. Visitors will encounter modern places that are windows into agricultural traditions and historical industrial development. Scattered throughout the tours are short historical sidebars that provide an overview of overland travel on the Warriors Path, the Great Wagon Road, the Wilderness Road, the National Road, the Lee Highway, and the Blue Ridge Parkway—the great roads that have taken travelers through southwestern Virginia for nearly three centuries.

As a field guide to the region, *Blue Ridge Roadways* can be read apart from travel. Its mix of contemporary description, visual images, and historic interpretation conveys a sense of the region. Kept handy on a bookshelf or packed in the car, this guide is meant as a companion and a welcoming introduction to the quiet, beautiful, exciting, and challenging cultural sites of Virginia's Blue Ridge.

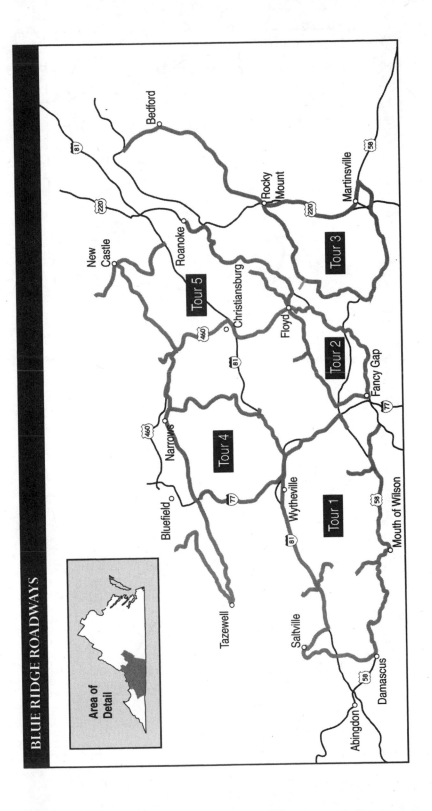

BLUE RIDGE ROADWAYS

Area of
Detail

Bedford

Rocky
Mount

Martinsville

58

220

81

220

Tour 3

New
Castle

Roanoke

Christiansburg

Tour 5

Floyd

460

81

Tour 2

Fancy Gap

77

Narrows

460

Tour 4

77

Bluefield

Wytheville

Tour 1

58

Mouth of Wilson

81

Tazewell

Saltville

Damascus

58

Abingdon

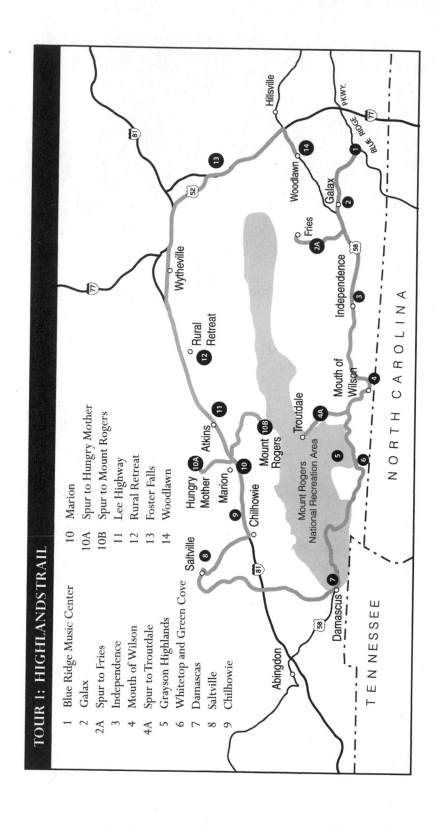

TOUR 1: HIGHLANDS TRAIL

1   Blue Ridge Music Center
2   Galax
2A Spur to Fries
3   Independence
4   Mouth of Wilson
4A Spur to Troutdale
5   Grayson Highlands
6   Whitetop and Green Cove
7   Damascas
8   Saltville
9   Chilhowie
10 Marion
10A Spur to Hungry Mother
10B Spur to Mount Rogers
11 Lee Highway
12 Rural Retreat
13 Foster Falls
14 Woodlawn

Banjos in Barr's Fiddle Shop, Galax. PHOTOGRAPH BY ANNA FARIELLO

Chapter 1

HIGHLANDS TRAIL

The Highlands Trail begins at Milepost 213 of the Blue Ridge Parkway, stopping first at the Blue Ridge Music Center. The trail travels to nearby Galax, where it picks up U.S. 58, a highway that runs the length of Virginia's state line along its southern boundary. The trail loops in and around Grayson Highlands State Park and Mount Rogers National Recreation Area, following U.S. 58 West into Independence, Grayson Highlands, and Damascus. The loop cuts north on Route 91 into Saltville and turns south to Chilhowie on the way to Marion, with spurs to Hungry Mother and Mount Rogers. The trail follows I-81 and the Lee Highway north to intersect with I-77. There, the loop circles south to Foster Falls and Woodlawn.

Blue Ridge Mountains, southwestern Virginia. PHOTOGRAPH BY ANNA FARIELLO

Envisioning a Parkway

The Blue Ridge Parkway started out as a pleasure road, a way to bring Americans from near and far to the scenic beauty of the Appalachian landscape. The idea of a road that would itself be a park was new in the minds of 20th-century Americans. The bicycle was already popular when a brand-new mode of transportation—the automobile—had citizens looking for recreational destinations.

Early in the 20th century, a "Crest of the Blue Ridge Highway" was proposed and begun in North Carolina. It was planned to start in Marion in the heart of the Valley of Virginia. From there, the Crest of the Blue Ridge Highway would climb Whitetop Mountain before descending from the ridge line on the other side. Entering North Carolina, the road would go through Boone and its neighboring tourist destination, Blowing Rock. This parkway predecessor was to make its eventual way to Tallulah Falls in northern Georgia, not far from the southern terminus of what is now the Blue Ridge Parkway. Construction on the first stretch of this road began in 1912 but soon was curtailed by World War I. That first stretch is in the area of Linville, North Carolina. As you travel from Milepost 317.6 to Milepost 318.7 on the Blue Ridge Parkway, you're following the original Crest of the Blue Ridge Highway.

Another parkway, planned but never built, would have connected the Shenandoah Mountains with Natural Bridge, a popular tourist destination even in colonial times. This parkway would have continued south to rail connections in Roanoke. The road would join other routes at Wytheville, then a highly cultured crossroads.

In 1930, Congress proposed the Colonial Parkway, a road to link historic sites at Jamestown, Yorktown, and Williamsburg. Of these early parkways, only the Colonial Parkway was completed.

The construction of the Blue Ridge Parkway was set in motion by a unique set of circumstances. In 1930s America, vision collided with the cold reality that was the Great Depression. In the face of worsening economic conditions, President Herbert Hoover was steadfast in his assertion that the welfare of the country's citizens was "not a function of the government," but belonged instead to church and family. The American electorate disagreed.

In the fall of 1932, Franklin Delano Roosevelt was elected with a promise to give American citizens a "new deal." FDR's New Deal programs were broad, encompassing Social Security and rural electrification. It was the lesser-known Civilian Conservation Corps that built the Blue Ridge Parkway. Within weeks of his inauguration, Roosevelt asked Congress to create a program that would focus on environmental problems and not interfere with normal employment. Already, the nation was aware of human impact on its great wilderness, much of it already despoiled. The Civilian Conservation Corps worked to improve natural sites and also eased unemployment during the nation's worst economic times. The CCC provided training and public-sector jobs to men and boys. The president's plan created what has been called "Roosevelt's Tree Army"—young men in nonmilitary service to their country, working on reforestation, soil conservation, and flood control.

In 1933, the National Industrial Recovery Act was set in motion to identify projects that could put the unemployed to work. Road building, a public good, had the advantage of not producing a manufacturing surplus that might have had an inflationary effect on the economy. Such public-sector employment provided jobs without charity and put money in the pockets of those who needed it most. Moreover, the wages paid—so needed—went immediately into circulation, creating a demand for goods that could prop up the failing manufacturing sector. Other Depression-era public-works programs employed experienced professionals. Among them was the

Fence exhibit, Blue Ridge Parkway. PHOTOGRAPH BY ANNA FARIELLO

Federal Arts Project, which paid artists to create murals for the nation's federal buildings. The CCC had the advantage of providing work for a traditionally underemployed segment of the population, inexperienced young men and boys.

Along the length of the proposed parkway route, men were recruited county by county from relief rolls to form local work teams. More mature men who lived in the vicinity provided an experienced work pool. They were given the acronym LEM, for *local experienced men.* The LEM already possessed the skills needed for road building, as they were competent at wielding axes, shovels, and other tools. Where the parkway went through the Cherokee reservation in North Carolina, work teams were drawn from the Native American population. Otherwise, the LEM were hill people from the same Anglo stock that had moved down the Great Wagon Road 200 years earlier. African-American men were recruited into the CCC, but in the still-segregated South, they were assigned to separate camps.[1]

The CCC provided training to 18- to 25-year-old physically fit males, provided they were unmarried and unemployed. Thousands signed up to work for $30 a month, $25 of that going home for their families or into their savings accounts. Enrollees made their beds, cleaned their barracks and tents, and policed the grounds before reporting at 8 A.M. for transport to work. A veteran of the CCC program reminisced, "The work week was usually eight hours a day, five days a week, with an hour break for lunch, mostly sandwiches, pie and coffee, sometimes a hot meal. After transport back to camp, everyone changed into dress uniforms and presented themselves for the evening meal of fresh vegetables, bread, fruit and dessert. Food was plain and served in large quantities. The first year's ration per man was thirty-seven cents."[2]

In August 1933, President Roosevelt came to the Shenandoah Valley to inaugurate the first Civilian Conservation Corps camp, named in his honor. There, he met the young men who worked on the nation's first federal parkway. By the time the CCC was disbanded in 1942, almost 4,000 men built more than 46,000 bridges, installed 5,000 miles of water lines, planted 45 million trees, and restored almost 4,000 historic structures.

[1] Harley E. Jolley, *The CCC in the Smokies* (Gatlinburg, Tenn.: Great Smoky Mountains Natural History Association, 2001), 9.

[2] Bill Bryant, "The Civilian Conservation Corp," *Parkway Milepost* (Fall-Winter 2002-3): 11.

Stop #1 Blue Ridge Music Center

The late Janette Carter, 2002. Janette was the daughter of A. P. and Sara Carter, Virginia's Carter Family. PHOTOGRAPH BY ANNA FARIELLO

Blue Ridge Music Center

Over a decade ago, the town of Galax donated 1,000 acres to the Blue Ridge Parkway for the purpose of building a cultural center devoted to the interpretation and preservation of old-time music. The partnership between the National Park Service and the Council for Traditional Arts was celebrated by the construction of an outdoor amphitheater to host the bluegrass and gospel music that has made the region famous. In summer, the music center's open-air amphitheater, adjacent to the 3,600-foot Fishers Peak, offers a concert series featuring local and legendary performers. Picnickers enjoy music and dancing in a verdant landscape, the headwaters of Chestnut Creek bubbling in the background. *The center is open seasonally. For more information, call 276-236-5309 or visit www.blueridgemusiccenter.net.*

From the Blue Ridge Music Center, the trail heads north along the Blue Ridge Parkway. Between Mileposts 206 and 207, exit the parkway and head north on Route 608 at Pipers Gap. Follow Route 608 to Route 97 North, drive nine miles, turn north on Route 89, and follow the signs to U.S. 58 and Galax.

STOP #2 GALAX

In 1905, the village of Bonaparte was renamed Galax in honor of the distinctive leaf of a local plant. The tiny village erected its first schoolhouse in 1908 on the site of the present elementary-school building. Just a short time later, a prominent local businessman sponsored the construction of a racetrack and grandstand on a 20-acre lot south of the village center, a site known today as Felts Park. Since 1924, when Galax native Ernest Stoneman went to New York to cut a track with Okay Records, local and regional music has been a focus in Galax. In 1925, the community began hosting the Old Fiddler's Convention. The most famous of the celebrations held at Felts Park, it has contributed greatly to Galax's claim of being "the World Capital of Old-Time Music." Galax is representative of the type of small community along this trail. The townsfolk exhibit a strong sense of pride in their land and heritage. Hometown festivals include the Annual Firemen's Carnival, the Galax Leaf and String Festival, and a juried quilt exhibition. In the fall, a daylong celebration of apple butter and molasses making recalls harvest traditions.

BARR'S FIDDLE SHOP

Owner Tom Barr grew up surrounded by mountain music. As a young fiddle player, he made the acquaintance of renowned musician and fiddle maker Albert Hash. The two played together often. Hash allowed Barr to undertake an apprenticeship. For over 20 years, Barr has handcrafted fine fiddles, banjos, and dulcimers. Many hang along the walls of his shop in historic downtown Galax. *Located at 105 South Main Street, the shop is open daily except Sunday. For more information, call 276-236-2411.*

CHAMBER OF COMMERCE

The Galax Chamber of Commerce provides information on local events and happenings. Two weeks' notice is required for a guided tour. A short video offers clips of local scenery and mountain music. *Located at 111 East Grayson Street, the chamber is open regular business days. For more information, call 276-238-8130.*

CLIFFVIEW TRADING POST

This trading post, adjacent to the 51-mile New River Trail, offers everything an adventurous visitor needs for exploring on horseback. It will arrange lessons, stable rentals, outfitting, tack, and snacks for the day. For those who prefer to be a little closer to the ground, Cliffview also rents mountain bikes. *It is located at 442 Cliffview Road. Horseback excursions are offered on select days seasonally; Sunday trips must be booked in advance. For more information, call 276-238-1530.*

FARMERS' MARKET

Opening early in the morning, the farmers' market is where local farmers and bakers display and sell fresh fruits, vegetables, herbs, and a variety of canned goods. Freshly baked goods include sourdough and whole-grain breads, muffins, and fruit pies. Area artisans offer handcrafted items, seasonal floral arrangements, and potted plants. *Located at 210 North Main Street, the market is open select days seasonally. For more information, call 276-238-8130.*

FRAMER'S DAUGHTER

Taking up two floors of a restored 1920s building in Galax's historic downtown, the Framer's Daughter features the work of untutored and professional regional artists. While it is essentially a gift shop, the gallery includes an extensive collection of paintings and prints by Virginia native P. Buckley Moss, as well as a selection by American painters like Mort Kunstler, who created work for the box-office drama *Gods and Generals*. *Located at 121 North Main Street, Framer's Daughter is open daily except Sunday. For more information, call 276-236-4920.*

Hub Restaurant

Brenda's Hub was one of the first drive-in restaurants in Galax, a real hot spot for local bobby-soxers. Today, the full-service Hub Restaurant features authentic country-style cooking. Breakfast, served until 10 A.M., includes such dishes as biscuits and gravy, hot cakes, omelets, and grits. For lunch and dinner, the Hub offers sandwiches and entrées such as oven-fried chicken and country fried steak. The nightly vegetable special includes local favorites such as pinto beans, boiled cabbage, and fried okra. *Located at 1007 South Main Street, the restaurant is open seven days a week. For more information, call 276-236-6701.*

Matthews Memorial Museum

This museum, founded in 1974, was named for local shop owner Jeff Matthews, who donated its first extensive collection, a gathering of regional Native American artifacts. The museum's collections, spread throughout an 8,000-square-foot building, include North American big-game animals and trophies, Civil War memorabilia, and a display devoted to Kylene Baker, who in 1978 became the first Virginian to win the Miss America title. Two historic structures have been relocated to the museum property from the banks of the New River. One is a restored 14-foot-square cabin dating to 1834, originally constructed by Galax native John Austin and his wife. The second cabin was built by Austin when he returned from the Civil War in the mid-1860s. Both cabins have been refurnished with items authentic to the period. *Located at 606 West Stuart Drive, the museum is open select days seasonally. For more information, call 276-773-3711.*

Cabins at Matthews Memorial Museum, Galax. PHOTOGRAPH BY ANNA FARIELLO

MEADOW CREEK DAIRY

On their 170-acre dairy farm, the Feete family practices sustainable agriculture to produce a wide selection of hormone-free cheeses stamped with the Virginia seal of quality. Jersey cows are raised in open, organic pastures, and their milk reflects the rich and diverse soils of the region. The hand-tended cheeses include the rich, buttery Mountaineer, Appalachian Jack, and the original Meadow Creek Feta. Cheeses are available for purchase from a small shop. If staff members have a free moment, they will conduct short tours of the dairy and plant. *To reach the dairy, turn off U.S. 58 onto Meadow Creek Road about two miles west of Galax; it is seven miles to a sign marking the driveway. The dairy is open seasonally. For more information, call 888-236-0622 or 276-236-2776 or visit www.meadowcreekdairy.com.*

OLD CRANK'S MOTOR CAR MUSEUM

This museum houses a collection of early-20th-century automobiles, including a Stanley Steamer and a Detroit Electric Auto. Also headquartered at the museum is the regional chapter of the Antique Automobile Club of America. The Galax club sponsors an annual antique car show on Memorial Day weekend. At other times, Old Crank's vintage soda fountain offers hand-dipped ice-cream cones in a variety of flavors. *Located at 407 Railroad Avenue, the museum is open weekends and by appointment. For more information, call 276-236-5114 or visit www.oldcranks.com.*

REX THEATER

This historic 450-seat theater hosts a live radio show called *Blue Ridge Backroads* on WBRF (98.1 FM), one of only three radio stations broadcasting mountain music nationwide. The Friday night get-togethers at the theater, open to the public, feature performances by old-time, bluegrass, and gospel groups. *Located at 113 Grayson Street, the theater is open year-round; show schedules vary. For more information, call 276-238-8130.*

ROOFTOP OF VIRGINIA CRAFTS

The Rooftop of Virginia Community Action Program was started in 1965 to support low-income residents. Still operating today, the guild is headquartered in the historic First Baptist Church, built in 1907. Its craft shop features quality products handmade by local artisans. The wide selection ranges from hand-shaped soap cakes to fine quilts to Appalachian folk dolls to crocheted items to locally made

Rex Theater, Galax
PHOTOGRAPH BY ANNA FARIELLO

jams, jellies, and butters. *Located at 206 North Main Street, the shop is open daily except Sunday. For more information, call 276-236-7131.*

The Smokehouse

Located in a historic commercial building, the Smokehouse features authentic pit-cooked barbecue. Its lunch menu includes pulled pork sandwiches and barbecued chicken entrées and side dishes like fried potatoes smothered in cheddar cheese and brisket bits topped with a signature sauce. *Located at 101 North Main Street, it is open seven days a week. For more information, call 276-236-1000.*

From Galax, drive west on U.S. 58, then head north on Route 94 to Fries. The spur to the historic town of Fries is a 15-mile detour off the trail along the New River. Returning to Galax via Route 94, the Highlands Trail continues along U.S. 58 West for about 13 miles to the county seat of Independence.

Spur to Fries

The town of Fries stretches a short distance along the valley floor beside the New River. Entrepreneur Henry Fries, the man for whom the town was named, constructed a 40-foot rock dam across this section of the New River in 1903. His textile mill became the foundation for a bustling town center. The Norfolk & Western line operated through this corridor for most of the 20th century. It brought raw cotton into Fries from other Southern states and shipped out refined textile products. The local landscape retains evidence of such commercial rail traffic in its abandoned brick factory buildings. The commercial Main Street, just two blocks long, is the focal point for citizens, hikers, and river folk alike. A charming waterfall flows in the center of town.

New River Trail Access

The New River Trail is a popular hiking and biking trail constructed in 1986 along the former rail bed of the Norfolk & Western line. Fries, one of six towns along the defunct rail line, is a popular access point at Mile 45.3. *From downtown Fries, follow Route 94 and Riverview Avenue to the river access. Parking is available in the lot adjacent to the town park.*

New River Trail Café

Hikers and travelers alike can find a down-home meal on the New River Trail. This cozy full-service restaurant offers an extensive breakfast menu for all appetites. A typical lunch or dinner may include pepper steak, green beans, mashed potatoes, and a piping-hot dish of baked apples. *Located at 439 West Main Street, the café is open daily except Sunday. For more information, call 276-744-3446.*

Ice jam on the New River near Fries, circa 1917. Courtesy of Norfolk & Western Historical Photograph Collection, Virginia Tech Special Collections

Riversong

Riversong's property fronting the New River is populated with an extensive representation of local wildlife. The cabins take their name from the sounds of pileated woodpeckers and local songbirds like the vireo and the wood thrush. Riversong can arrange guided fishing trips along its stretch of the New. *From Fries, travel north for two miles on Route 94, then drive nine miles on Route 737. Look for the signs. Located at 916 Swinney Hollow Road, Riversong is open year-round. For more information, call 276-744-2217 or visit www.riversongcabins.com.*

From Galax, take U.S. 58 West for about 13 miles to Independence. For the most part a four-lane thoroughfare, U.S. 58 is referred to as "the Grayson Highway" in this region. It runs along Virginia's southern border from the Atlantic Ocean for nearly 500 miles.

Stop #3 Independence

Formed from neighboring Wythe County in 1793, Grayson County was named for William Grayson, one of Virginia's earliest senators. The original county seat was Old Town, near the Grayson County-Carroll County border. In 1850, a dispute festered among Grayson citizens over a newer and more centralized county seat. To solve the conflict, an elected commission hiked to the top of Point Lookout, north of what is now Wytheville, to see if any place captured their attention. A small wooded area at the confluence of five streams was selected as the new seat and named Independence. Like Galax, the town of Independence is largely defined by its celebrations. Famous for its Fourth of July Extravaganza and its Mountain Foliage Festival in October, Independence is a cultural bright spot in the mountains. The locals are not without a sense of humor. The autumn foliage fest features a

Grand Privy Race, for which the Chamber Pot Trophy is the grand prize. Among the attractions are live music, clogging, arts and crafts, and booths of country-style snacks.

Davis-Bourne Inn

This Queen Anne-style home dates to 1865, when its foundation was laid by Colonel Alexander Davis, an officer of the Confederate army. The former residence maintains an elegant façade with decorative shingles, a wraparound porch, a tin-covered turret, and a cupola topped with a traditional weathervane. The bed-and-breakfast offers guests a choice of four distinguished rooms with vintage fixtures. Some rooms have fireplaces and original claw-foot tubs. The inn is surrounded by 10 acres of giant oaks and black walnuts, herb and edible-flower gardens, and regional wildlife. *Located at 119 Journey's End Drive, the inn sits atop the hill behind the contemporary courthouse. It is open year-round. For more information, call 276-773-9384 or visit www.davisbourneinn.com.*

Gallery on Main

Located in a historic commercial building next door to the Historic 1908 Courthouse, this gallery has an interior with original wide-plank floors and an elegant pressed-tin ceiling. One long wall of plate-glass windows illuminates a mix of contemporary handicrafts and antique items. Fine work by local craftsmen and artists in wood, clay, metal, and paper is placed among vintage crocks, washboards, and other traditional items. Interested guests should inquire about local artists who welcome visits to their studios. *Located at 119 East Main Street, the gallery is open select days. For more information, call 276-773-2800.*

Historic 1908 Courthouse

The first courthouse in Grayson County was built at Old Town near what is presently the Carroll County-Grayson County line. After Carroll County was formed from Grayson, a new courthouse was built in Independence in 1850. More than 50 years later, in 1908, a second building was constructed on the original foundation by renowned architect of public buildings Frank P. Milburn. His immense and impressive design in red brick retains several original architectural features, including the cream-colored pressed-tin ceilings. In 1978, it was decided that the courthouse could no longer serve the growing county's needs. At the subsequent public auction, over 1,000 people held hands and encircled the historic building as they waited for a bid that favored preservation rather than a development project that meant destruction. They cheered when Dan Baldwin, a local businessman, secured the building and promised to restore it. Today, the building, listed on the National Register of Historic Places, houses the Grayson County Tourist Information Center, which stocks a variety of brochures and local maps. The hallways showcase vintage photographs of the community and region. *Located at 107 East Main Street, the courthouse is open daily except Sunday. For more information, call 276-773-3711.*

JOURNEY'S END RESTAURANT

Four-star executive chef Will Burrell serves an extensive selection of French provincial cuisine featuring local game, fish, and produce. Specialties include pan-fried mountain trout and herb-encrusted chicken breast. Desserts like crème brûlée and apple feuilletage—caramelized apples atop puff pastry—are offered. The wine list includes both international and Virginia vintages. Guests may choose to dine in one of the Victorian-style dining rooms or on the covered garden patio. *Located at 119 Journey's End Drive, the restaurant sits atop the hill behind the contemporary courthouse. It is open for dinner select days. For more information, call 276-773-9384.*

NEW RIVER CANOE

Located just below the confluence of the North and South forks of the New River, this recreation center organizes unique outdoor adventures, shuttling visitors and canoes (rented or owned) to a put-in site to mark the

Historic 1908 Courthouse, Independence. PHOTOGRAPH BY ANNA FARIELLO

start of a daylong or week-long adventure. Trips can be planned to accommodate families and kayakers yearning for the New's Class II rapids. Camping cabins and tent sites are available. The camp store, which stocks food, supplies, and New River T-shirts, is open seven days a week. Visitors should call ahead to arrange an outing. *The center is located halfway between Galax and Independence off U.S. 58 West at 3745 New River Parkway. It is open seasonally. For more information, call 276-773-3412.*

PEAR TREE

The Pear Tree gallery features the work of late artist Robert Broderson, an educator, figurative painter, and Guggenheim fellow who retired from academics in the mid-1970s. He settled in Independence, where he continued to paint and lived out his days. The gallery's director can answer questions about the painter's life and work. *Located at 122 West Main Street,*

Pear Tree is open select days and by appointment. For more information, call 276-773-2030 or 276-773-2041.

The Treasury

Boasting over 100 contributing artists and artisans and housed in one of Grayson's finest architectural specimens, this shop features contemporary and traditional creations by Appalachian artists and artisans. Items for sale include stained-glass panels, hand-woven baskets, oil and watercolor paintings, earthenware place settings, and books on local and regional history and culture. *Located at 107 East Main Street in the Historic 1908 Courthouse, the Treasury is open daily except Sunday. For more information, call 276-773-2743.*

Vault Museum

This museum takes its name from the clerk's vault, once used to house official court documents. It features exhibits on Grayson County politics, early area industry, pioneer tools and farm implements, and domestic life. An annex room has been converted to highlight 19th-century coverlets and counterpanes by Fannie Halsey Gambill, a talented and prolific Appalachian weaver. An interesting collection of photographs, maps, and other documents sheds light on many of the county's small communities. *Located at 107 East Main Street on the first floor of the Historic 1908 Courthouse, the museum is open daily except Sunday. For more information, call 276-773-3711.*

Virginia House

Situated on a hill overlooking its acreage, this elegant bed-and-breakfast offers a selection of guest rooms with central air and private baths. Amenities include complimentary toiletries and a continental breakfast served in the sunroom. Guests may roam the grounds or settle down with a book in one of the many cozy corners. *From U.S. 58 West about halfway between Galax and Independence, turn north on Virginia House Lane. The Virginia House is open year-round. For more information, call 276-773-2970.*

Sulphur Springs Methodist Church, Mouth of Wilson
PHOTOGRAPH BY ANNA FARIELLO

From Independence, continue on U.S. 58 West for 10 miles to Mouth of Wilson, named for the point where Big Wilson Creek empties into the New River. U.S. 58, lined with wildflowers in season and newly paved, skirts within a mile of the North Carolina line.

STOP #4 MOUTH OF WILSON

Mouth of Wilson's original town center is identified by a green-and-white highway sign at an intersection flanked by early commercial buildings. The Fields Manufacturing Company, with its pressed-tin façade and vintage sign, sits opposite an original local feed-and-seed store. The trail passes a number of other interesting historic structures, including the Sulphur Springs Methodist Church, where horses sometimes graze in the old churchyard. The white frame church with green trim and faded double doors has floor-to-ceiling louvered windows in its chapel.

Duck Roost Inn

Nestled in the historic rural community of Cox's Chapel, this renovated 1906 farmhouse offers guest rooms with luxurious touches like fresh flowers and feather pillows. Breakfast is served family-style in the dining room or on the wraparound porch, weather permitting. The inn will pack box lunches for guests' all-day excursions. Duck Roost's hostess is a local artist who specializes in calligraphy and graphic design. Her studio on the property is always open. *The inn is located off U.S. 58 West about halfway between Independence and Mouth of Wilson; turn off U.S. 58 West to reach 777 Riverbend Road. It is open year-round. For more information, call 888-712-7551 or 276-773-9325 or visit www.ls.net/~duckroostinn.*

Nemeton Meditation and Study Center

Nemet is a Celtic term for a haven where natural resources like fresh water and wildlife are protected. Fred and Bette Inman's 35-acre valley sanctuary welcomes visitors to join them for an afternoon trek with llamas. An affiliate of a national biofeedback and meditation project designed by spiritual teacher Deepak Chopra, the study center invites guests to join educational sessions about llama needs and learning habits. Llamas, like dolphins, are highly communicative with humans. Visitors receive a brief lesson on meditative breathing techniques before picking up a packed picnic lunch and heading out to explore the countryside. *The center is located on U.S. 58 West (420 Virginia Lane); a sign is posted at the entrance. It is open seasonally every day except Sunday. For more information, call 276-579-2449 or visit www.ls.net/~inman.*

Oak Hill Academy

Situated on 400 acres of open meadows and woodlands, this Baptist-affiliated academy dates to 1878. Oak Hill is included on the trail for the benefit of sports enthusiasts. Its boys' basketball program is nationally acclaimed for producing ranked teams and college-caliber athletes. The 180-student school in tiny Mouth of Wilson is invited to participate in commercially sponsored tournaments up and down the East Coast and as far away as California. Famous alumni include Carmelo Anthony of the Denver Nuggets and Jerry Stackhouse of the Dallas Mavericks. Visitors who want to catch a game and glimpse future NCAA talent can call the athletic department for a roster and a schedule. *The academy is located off U.S. 58 West at 2635 Oak Hill Road; a sign is posted. The winter athletic season typically runs November to March. For more information, call 276-579-2619 or visit www.oak-hill.net.*

ONA'S COUNTRY KITCHEN

Conveniently located on the way to Grayson Highlands, Ona's offers hikers and wayfarers a chance to fill up. This full-service down-home restaurant serves three meals daily. The menu includes regional dishes such as eggs with country ham, pinto beans and cornbread, and barbecue. *Ona's is located on Route 16 (4013 Troutdale Highway) at the junction with U.S. 58 four miles west of Mouth of Wilson. It is open seven days a week. For more information, call 276-579-4440.*

Moonshiners Quartet, Poplar Mountain, circa 1950
PHOTOGRAPH BY EARL PALMER, COURTESY OF EARL PALMER COLLECTION, VIRGINIA TECH SPECIAL COLLECTIONS

The Highlands Trail forks off U.S. 58 West and follows Route 16 North for five miles of pleasant country road to the small town of Troutdale. It then returns south on Route 16 to rejoin U.S. 58 and continues west to Grayson Highlands State Park.

Spur to Troutdale

Troutdale boasts the smallest population and the highest elevation (4,016 feet) of any incorporated Virginia town. In the community's early boom days, when the Marion & Rye railway connected it with the bustling county seat of Independence, the local population reached almost 3,000. The busy rail depot was flanked by hotels and storefronts, and enough was happening in town to warrant the creation of a Troutdale newspaper. The first local post office opened in the 1880s. Timber production was the major early industry here. Older residents still recall the commotion of days gone by with pleasure but relish the quiet country life of the village today.

Appalachian Trail Access

The Appalachian Trail crosses the Grayson County-Smyth County line as it winds through open meadows and pastureland. The path is marked by blue-blazed posts. Along the AT, lightly wooded patches are vibrant with rhododendrons and azaleas in June and July. Hikers enjoy mature timber stands as they wind through the gap and across the Holston River heading north or up and across Wilburn Ridge heading south. The Mount Rogers Appalachian Trail Club, based in Troutdale, maintains a 57-mile stretch through the region. *From Troutdale, take Route 603 West for four miles to Fox Creek, where a sign marks the access. The trail is accessible year-round, weather permitting. For information, call 276-628-2601.*

Dove Oaks Farm

Dove Oaks Farm opens its gates to visitors who want to peek into the lifestyle of a Blue Ridge llama farmer. Libby Boyd trains some of her 30 big-eyed llamas to participate in shows, parades, and educational programs and tends to the newborn babies of others. She also spins the llamas' richly colored wool into textured knitting yarn. A farm hand will take visitors on a brief tour of the property. *Follow Route 16 to Hoffman's Store and call for directions. The farm is open regular business days. For information, call 276-579-3078 or visit www.ls.net/~doveoaks.*

Fox Hill Inn

A half-mile drive on a narrow gravel road, wooded on both sides, leads to a hilltop with panoramic views. The Fox Hill Inn is situated on 70 pristine acres populated by wild turkeys, grouse, and white-tailed deer. It offers eight guest rooms surrounded by lush gardens blooming with roses, poppies, day lilies, and bluebells. Among the amenities are a slate patio with hummingbird feeders and a large living room with an oversized fireplace. Breakfast includes fresh blueberry pancakes and eggs cooked to order. A large, airy kitchen is available for self-catered lunches and dinners. *The inn is located a few miles south of Troutdale on Route 16 (8568 Troutdale Highway); signage is posted along the road. It is open year-round. For information, call 800-874-3313 or 276-677-3313 or visit www.bbonline.com/va/foxhill.*

Hoffman's General Store

Hoffman's is a family-run operation three generations in the making. The classic general store was built in 1936 along the newly constructed Route 16. Once the Troutdale post office, the site hosted several local elections in the 1940s and 1950s. The store has high ceilings, wall-to-wall wooden shelves, tongue-and-groove countertops, and glass cases filled with hunting and fishing supplies. Visitors can pick up a fishing license and assorted Southern foodstuffs and browse the selection of handmade Appalachian baskets. This is a rare example of an authentic country store whose wood stove and straight-backed chairs are still used by local residents. *Hoffman's is located three miles north of Mouth of Wilson on Route 16 North (716 Troutdale Highway). It is open daily except Sunday. For more information, call 276-579-6033.*

Little Wilson Trout Farm

Family-owned and operated for three generations, Little Wilson Trout Farm welcomes guests by way of a hand-painted sign sporting a trout. A friendly farm with horses grazing within a picket fence alongside the drive, it invites visitors to grab a pole and find a spot around the spring-fed trout pond stocked with specimens "pan size to trophy size." The right catch may win the season's biggest-fish contest. For those who want fish without fishing, fresh rainbow trout fillets are available for at-home cooking. *From the intersection of U.S. 58 and Route 16 (Troutdale Highway), travel north to 270 Little Wilson Road. The farm is open seasonally. For more information, call 276-579-7154.*

Ripshin

Ripshin is the former home of Sherwood Anderson, author of *Hometown; Winesburg, Ohio; Hello Towns!* and other books about small-town life. Anderson traveled extensively. After spending time in Grayson and Smyth counties, he and his wife purchased farmland along Ripshin Creek four miles from Troutdale. In 1925, he constructed a two-story stone-and-timber Craftsman-style home overlooking the mountain waterway. Anderson bought the Marion Publishing Company two years later and became editor and publisher of two weekly newspapers for Marion and environs. Today, the privately owned home is listed on the National Register of Historic

Turned wooden bowls by Terry Clark, Three Peaks Crafts, Troutdale
PHOTOGRAPH BY ANNA FARIELLO

Places. Anderson's writing cabin still stands in the woods within walking distance of the residence. *In Troutdale, turn east off Route 1 onto Ripshin Road and drive 2.5 miles to its intersection with Route 732 (Laurel Creek Road). The house, immediately to the left over a small bridge, may be viewed from the road year-round.*

THREE PEAKS CRAFTS

Former furniture maker Terry Clark has shifted his attention to wood turning, making decorative and functional bowls, platters, rolling pins, finely detailed bottle stoppers, and cherry-and-brass kaleidoscopes. *Three Peaks is on Route 16 North (9399 Troutdale Highway) a mile south of Troutdale. It is open select days; call ahead to arrange a visit. The number is 276-677-3724.*

From Troutdale, the quickest way to Damascus is Route 603 West off Route 16 through the heart of Grayson Highlands State Park. The Highlands Trail takes a more circuitous route, turning south on Route 16 back to Mouth of Wilson to pick up U.S. 58 West to Rugby, Grayson Highlands State Park, Whitetop, and Green Cove on the way to Damascus.

STOP #5   GRAYSON HIGHLANDS

Grayson Highlands is considered a state treasure for its peaks topping 5,000 feet and its herds of wild ponies roaming the park and the national forest. The park hosts the Wayne C. Henderson Music Festival and Guitar Competition the third Saturday in June. Sites listed here include those in and around the park and those in the community of Rugby.

APPALACHIAN TRAIL ACCESS

A trail-access map is available at the Grayson Highlands State Park Visitor Center, located near the summit of Haw Mountain. From the visitor center,

Trailer camp, 1941
Farm Security Administration photograph,
courtesy of Virginia Tech Special Collections

follow the Rhododendron Trail for a half-mile to the Appalachian Trail. Marked with blue blazes, this portion of the AT is the most frequently used path to nearby Mount Rogers. *The state-park entrance is well marked on U.S. 58 about seven miles from its intersection with Route 16 North. The trail is accessible year-round, weather permitting. For more information, call 276-579-7092.*

GRAYSON HIGHLANDS STATE PARK

The park features an array of hiking trails and bridle paths leading to overlooks and waterfalls, some of which pass a 200-year-old cabin. Some trails follow the overgrown rail beds used in the early 20th century to transport felled trees to the nearby mountain depot. The park's visitor center has historical and ecological exhibits. Interpretive programs include guided day hikes, bluegrass and old-time music performances, naturalist programs, and cultural demonstrations. A homestead site depicting mountain living consists of two reconstructed cabins, a springhouse, and a cane mill. Grayson

Highlands is one of many Civilian Conservation Corps parks in the state. *The well-marked entrance on U.S. 58 is about seven miles from its intersection with Route 16 North. The park is accessible year-round, weather permitting. For more information, call 276-579-7092.*

HAW ORCHARD BAPTIST CHURCH AND CEMETERY

This simply constructed white frame building is representative of mountain churches in the region. Haw Orchard Baptist Church sits in an awe-inspiring location. An evening gospel sing is held on the fourth Saturday of each month. The cemetery is noted for the grave site of renowned fiddler and instrument maker Albert Hash, born in 1917 on Cabin Creek, which runs through what is now Mount Rogers National Recreation Area. Hash had a long and successful career with a variety of old-time bands. He also created custom-made fiddles, no two ever alike. His personal favorite had a peacock on the back with a bird's silhouette on the peg head. Hash was honored with a National Heritage Fellowship in 1981, two years before his death. *The church and cemetery are located on Route 797 (Haw Orchard Road) off U.S. 58 a half-mile west of the entrance to Grayson Highlands State Park. Sunday services are open to the public.*

HENDERSON'S GUITAR SHOP

Wayne Henderson made his first guitar under the tutelage of master fiddler Albert Hash. While still a boy, Henderson converted his family's woodshed into a guitar shop. Today, in the tiny town of Rugby just beyond Mouth of Wilson, he operates a much bigger shop where he builds and repairs instruments. On the walls are guitars and fiddles for sale, as well as a selection of Henderson's recordings. He has played at many famous venues and events, including Carnegie Hall and the Smithsonian Folklife Festival. Henderson also sponsors a guitar competition in nearby Grayson Highlands State Park. *Five miles from the junction of U.S. 58 and Route 16, turn south on Route 725. The shop is at 388 Tucker Road. It is open select days. For more information, call 276-579-4531.*

Wayne Henderson building a guitar in his shop
PHOTOGRAPH BY JON LOHMAN, COURTESY OF
VIRGINIA FOLKLIFE PROGRAM

HISTORIC E. C. BALL STORE

Born in the rural Blue Ridge in 1913, Estil Ball grew up with the mountain music of the Carter Family and Jimmie Rodgers. He and his wife, Orna, had a bluegrass-and-gospel band that was heard on radio stations in Galax, Virginia, and Bristol, Tennessee. Their band also performed at Baptist tent revivals. Ball operated a small general store in Rugby where famed guitarist Wayne Henderson learned to pick. Ball's recordings are available today in specialty record shops. *About five miles from the junction of U.S. 58 and Route 16, turn south on Route 725 (Tucker Road) to reach Rugby. The store may be viewed from the road year-round.*

RUGBY CREEK

Rugby Creek is a 63-acre horse farm and retreat. The farm rescues and rehabilitates all kinds of animals, from miniature ponies and goats to everyday dogs and cats. Guests at Rugby Creek are encouraged to roam the grounds, sign up for a pony ride, and hike down to the farm to meet the animals. The two rustic cottages at the back edge of the property have private baths, covered porches, and decks with grills. The mountaintop cabin features a Jacuzzi-style tub and a great room with a 20-foot window for viewing the adjacent ridge line and pasture. *To reach the farm, continue on U.S. 58 to Volney, where Route 16 heads north to Troutdale. From this intersection, go an additional five miles on U.S. 58 to the first paved road, Tucker Road, then bear right on Rugby Creek Lane; a sign points the way to the farmhouse. Cabins are available year-round. Travelers can make an appointment to visit the property. For more information, call 276-579-4215.*

From Grayson Highlands, the trail continues west on U.S. 58 to the small communities of Whitetop and Green Cove.

Stop #6 Whitetop and Green Cove

These tiny communities in the southern shadow of Whitetop Mountain are located at the intersection of three counties—Washington, Smyth, and Grayson. The village of Whitetop hosts several unique heritage festivals, including the Maple Fest in March and the Molasses Festival in October. Its famous Ramp Festival, held in May, celebrates the ramp, a wild leek that looks like a green onion and tastes like garlic. Festivities include live mountain music and games. Among the mountain fare are bean plates and barbecue served on steaming hoecakes.

Appalachian Trail Access and Whitetop-Laurel Circuit

About three miles west of Green Cove on U.S. 58, turn south on Route 728 to reach the Creek Junction parking lot. From the parking lot, a 10-mile loop marked by white and blue blazes follows a portion of the AT on Straight Mountain and a portion of the Virginia Creeper Trail along Laurel

Creek. The trail is accessible year-round, weather permitting. For more information, call 540-783-5196.

Buchanan Inn at Green Cove

Schoolteacher William Buchanan came to Green Cove just after the turn of the 19th century. He married and later completed a white frame farmhouse for his new wife in 1915. Buchanan then opened a general store, a post office, and a train depot close to the new home. In the same entrepreneurial spirit, his wife, Mary, worked diligently with their daughters to pack fresh boxed lunches for travelers and crew aboard the Norfolk & Western, charging 50 cents apiece. It was not uncommon for train travelers staying over at the Buchanan house in inclement weather to occupy every inch of available floor space. The historic building, completely renovated in period style, offers three bedrooms named for the Buchanan daughters. Dinner may be requested in advance. *About 10 miles west of the entrance to Grayson Highlands State Park, turn southwest off U.S. 58 onto Route 600 (Green Cove Road) and drive a half-mile. The inn is open year-round. For more information, call 276-388-3367 or visit www.thebuchananinn.com.*

Green Cove Station

This early-19th-century railroad depot is one of the few structures remaining along the former rail bed that is today's Virginia Creeper Trail. The 1914 station once served as a post office, general store, and community gathering place. When it closed in the 1970s, most of the contents were left inside. Today, they form an eclectic display that tells the story of the tiny Green Cove community. The renovated depot, currently the trailhead for the Virginia Creeper Trail, offers a wide selection of gifts, souvenirs, and guidebooks. *About 10 miles west of the entrance to Grayson Highlands State Park, turn southwest off U.S. 58 onto Route 600 (Green Cove Road) and drive a half-mile. The station is open seven days a week. For more information, call 276-783-5196.*

Historic Millers Store

Located across the street from the Whitetop Visitor Center, this historic commercial building dating to the early 20th century recalls the days when it provided such things as produce, dry goods, bib overalls, and animal feed to residents of the busy mountain community. *The store is located off U.S. 58 about 10 miles past the entrance to Grayson Highlands State Park on Route 726 (Whitetop Gap Road). It may be viewed from the road year-round.*

Virginia Creeper Trail Access

What began as a primitive Native American footpath eventually became a segment of the Virginia-Carolina Railroad in the early 1900s. The railway hauled passengers and products including lumber and iron through the mountains. Today, the Virginia Creeper Trail is part of a nationwide rails-to-trails project that converts old rail beds to shared-use recreational trails. The Virginia Creeper Trail runs 34 miles from Whitetop to Abingdon through verdant mountain ecosystems and over original railroad trestles and bridges. *The access is located off U.S. 58 on Route 755 almost 10 miles past the entrance to Grayson Highlands State Park. Follow Route 755 about two miles to Route 726 (Whitetop Gap Road). The trail is accessible year-round, weather permitting. For more information, call 276-676-2282 or visit www.southernregion.fs.fed.us/gwj/mr/creeper.html.*

Whitetop Mountain

From 1931 to 1939, Whitetop was the site of a fiddlers' convention that attracted contestants and enthusiasts from far and wide. First Lady Eleanor Roosevelt attended in 1933, casting a national spotlight on the region's music. At an elevation of 5,520 feet, Whitetop has the commonwealth's highest road accessible to automobiles. Visitors may drive to overlooks offering panoramic views of the North Carolina and Tennessee Appalachians. On a clear day, the visibility extends upwards of 40 miles. *The mountain is located on Route 600 North off U.S. 58 West just east of the Whitetop community; ask for directions at the Grayson Highlands State Park Visitor Center. It is accessible year-round, weather permitting. For more information, call 276-773-3711.*

Whitetop Station

The original Whitetop passenger depot was situated at the highest elevation of any station east of the Mississippi. From 1912 until 1957, it

First Lady Eleanor Roosevelt at the 1933 music festival, Whitetop
Courtesy of Southern Historical Collection, Wilson Library, University of North Carolina at Chapel Hill

brought people and goods to this remote community. The station, reconstructed by the National Park Service to accommodate a larger gathering space, sits on the original foundation. It houses exhibits of artifacts and photographs surveying the history of the station and community. Today, the historic depot is a departure point for the Virginia Creeper Trail. *It is located on Route 755 off U.S. 58 almost 10 miles past the entrance to Grayson Highlands State Park. Follow Route 755 about two miles to Route 726 (Whitetop Gap Road). The station is on the left. It is accessible year-round, weather permitting. For more information, call 800-628-7207.*

Caboose Information Center, Damascus
PHOTOGRAPH BY ANNA FARIELLO

From the Grayson Highlands State Park entrance, continue west on U.S. 58 for about 20 miles to Damascus.

STOP #7   DAMASCUS

Pioneers following the Wilderness Trail to Kentucky were attracted to the rich and vigorous mountain atmosphere. When the Mock family settled here and built a gristmill, a small community grew. In the 1800s, the village was named Damascus. It became a stop on the Virginia-Carolina Railroad. Like neighboring communities, its primary export was mountain timber. Today, deforested areas have returned as new-growth woodlands populated by early successional species like paper birch, red and chestnut oak, and tulip poplar. U.S. 58 follows the main street of Damascus, often referred to as "Trail Town USA." The Highlands Trail winds through Mount Rogers National Recreation Area. Several pull-offs allow motorists to explore local creeks on foot or with fishing poles in hand.

CABOOSE INFORMATION CENTER

The forest service operates an information center out of this authentic Norfolk & Western caboose situated in the town park just before Bridge 16 on the Virginia Creeper Trail. The caboose, exactly like those used by the railroad, is open for viewing. Its cozy interior reveals the luxury of early-20th-century travel. The information center is staffed to answer trail-related questions. Light refreshments and restrooms are available. *The center is on U.S. 58 West just over the Beaver Creek Bridge at the end of West Laurel Avenue. It is open select days. For more information, call 276-783-5196.*

DAMASCUS OLD MILL

A century-old gristmill on Laurel Creek has been retrofitted to house an inn and restaurant. Its six guest rooms are named for local trails and topography. Each has access to an upstairs balcony overlooking the river. Dinner guests enjoy a menu offering items such as Laurel Creek trout, certified Angus beef, garlic mashed potatoes, and apple-butter barbecued ribs. A wide selection of desserts is created daily in-house. Local artwork and fine hardwood details set the tone in the dining room, which overlooks the river. In season, dinner is served on an outdoor deck. *To reach the old mill, take Route 1223 off Laurel Avenue. Located at 215 Imboden Street, it is open select days year-round. For more information, call 276-475-3745 or visit www.damascusoldmill.com.*

VIRGINIA CREEPER TRAIL ACCESS

The Virginia Creeper Trail takes its name from the steam locomotives that slowly made their way up the steep grades of this section of the railroad. After the last train ran in 1977, the rail bed was converted to a hiking-and-biking trail that runs 34 miles from the North Carolina line near Whitetop to Abingdon. Scattered throughout Damascus are many outfitters offering shuttle service, bike rentals, and guided trips. *The trail is accessible year-round, weather permitting. Look for signs along U.S. 58 through town.*

VIRGINIA CREEPER TRAIL ACCOMMODATIONS

The streets of Damascus are lined with overnight and weekly accommodations catering to a variety of tastes, from elegant bed-and-breakfasts to back-to-nature cottages on rushing Laurel Creek, where guests may fish for native trout just out the back door or watch for ducks, geese, and other wildlife from the porch. *Look for signs along U.S. 58 through town.*

Pencil drawing by unknown artist of salt makers, Saltville
COURTESY OF NORFOLK & WESTERN HISTORICAL PHOTOGRAPH
COLLECTION, VIRGINIA TECH SPECIAL COLLECTIONS

From Damascus, the Highlands Trail
follows Route 91 North about 20 miles to Saltville.

STOP #8 SALTVILLE

The Saltville Valley was distinguished in its earliest days by a natural abundance of brine springs and ponds. The ponds, known as salt licks, attracted giant prehistoric creatures and became a burial ground for their immense skeletal remains. Thomas Jefferson was the recipient of the region's first excavated fossil in the late 18th century. Land was first patented here, in Smyth County's northwest corner, by Charles Campbell in 1753. Revolutionary War hero William Russell, the man for whom neighboring Russell County was named, made salt from mines near Saltville as early as 1788. At the zenith of production in 1864, the saltworks manufactured about two-thirds of the product required by the Confederacy, which used it to cure and preserve foodstuffs. Today, Saltville's town center lies along a pair of parallel streets. Company houses, evidence of early-20th-century development, are simple in style and construction but exude a sense of balance and symmetry.

Buck's Drive-In

Reminiscent of days gone by, Buck's offers a curbside dining menu with items like hand-cut French fries and soft ice cream. An outdoor picnic area is available during warm-weather months, when a handwritten sign advertises fresh strawberries and custard. *Buck's is located on Route 91 a mile north of its intersection with Main Street. It is open daily except Sunday. For more information, call 276- 496-7291.*

Civil War Overlook

The Civil War Overlook commemorates a skirmish considered to be the largest Virginia conflict west of Lynchburg. Dubbed by locals as "Battlefield Overlook," this site offers views of Saltville, the valley, and Clinch Mountain in the distance. Confederate defensive trenches are still in place. An interpretive marker illustrates details of the Saltville battle. To support an attack on the salt mines in October 1864, the Union government ordered the newly formed Colored Cavalry to join white Federal forces approaching Saltville. In the offensive, wounded African-American soldiers were left behind by their Northern counterparts. Those who could not retreat were killed by Confederates, their bodies dumped into a sinkhole. The event is commemorated annually by a memorial service. *The overlook is located about a mile from the intersection of Route 107 and Route 91 south of town. It is accessible year-round.*

Clinch Mountain Wildlife Management Area

This management area, the second-largest preserve maintained by the Virginia Department of Game and Inland Fisheries, covers 25,000 acres in parts of four counties. Hikers will be able to identify tree species in both low- and high-elevation forests as they climb from the narrow valley floor. This area was heavily logged in the early 19th century; industrial artifacts are occasionally visible. The diverse preserve contains oak and hickory forests, beaver ponds, meadows, and lakes. The Virginia Birding and Wildlife Trail organization recommends this as a prime viewing spot for all sorts of native fauna, including white-tailed deer, cottontail rabbits, and a number of songbirds with colorful names. The management area allows fishing and hunting in season. *From Saltville, go south on Route 91 for a quarter-mile to Route 634 (Allison Gap Road). After about a mile on Route 634, turn onto Route 613 (Poor Valley Road) and drive four miles to Route 747; signs are posted. For more information, call 276-783-4860.*

Elizabeth Cemetery

This cemetery contains markers dating to the late 18th century. Among them are stones belonging to family members of Confederate general Jeb Stuart. The cannon at the cemetery entrance was used to guard the saltworks during the Civil War. The grounds were also the site of a skirmish in which Confederate troops unsuccessfully attempted to keep Union soldiers at the base of Sanders Hill (at the east end of the property) from reaching the river. *The cemetery is located on Route 91 a mile north of its intersection with Main Street. It is accessible year-round during daylight hours.*

Historic Mathieson Alkali Works

A brick commercial structure is what remains of the alkali works, opened in 1892. Factories like Mathieson turned salt brine, mined from the earth, into things as diverse as baking soda and rocket fuel. They made poisonous gas used in World War I and the fuel that sent the Apollo spacecraft to the moon. In its early days, the Mathieson company supplied the community with utilities, medical services, and reasonably priced housing. It also replenished the town budget when the coffers ran dry. In the late 1960s, the Environmental Protection Agency established the Virginia Water Control Board, which mandated new, more stringent standards. The saltworks (then Olin-Mathieson) were not solvent enough to redesign operations to comply with new emissions regulations. During the three months from December 1971 to February 1972, some 900 employees were laid off. The story of Mathieson is bittersweet. While its chemical dumping contributed to river pollution, it also created the foundation for today's Saltville. *Located in downtown Saltville, the facility may be viewed from the road year-round.*

King-Stuart House

This historic two-story log cabin, built by Irish immigrant William King, an early partner in the King Salt Works, dates to 1795. It later belonged to the family of Confederate hero Jeb Stuart. When the Rebel general was killed in 1864, his widow, Flora, converted the first floor into a grammar school that she operated with her sister-in-law, Mary Headen. The cabin is interesting for its pair of side-by-side doors, possibly meant to separate schoolboys from schoolgirls. *The home sits on a hill behind Main Street. Turn onto Stuart Drive less than a quarter-mile past Salt Park on Route 91 South. It may be viewed year-round from the road; tours are available. For more information, call 276-496-5342.*

Madam Russell House and Church

This cabin is a replica of the home built by General William Russell and his wife, Elizabeth, in 1788. The Russells entertained such notable guests as president-to-be James Madison and Mrs. Russell's brother, Patrick Henry. Elizabeth Henry Russell was a respected figure and a religious leader in Smyth County. The Methodist church next door to the cabin was built of local sandstone in 1900. It was named for Madam Russell, whose image is depicted in a glass panel in the sanctuary. Other colored-glass windows are also on display. Directly in front of the house and church is Saltville's Wall of Honor, which pays tribute to local veterans. *Located at 207 West Main Street, the church may be viewed from the road year-round. Sunday services are open to the public. For more information, call 276-496-7971.*

Museum of the Middle Appalachians

The Saltville Valley was once covered by an ancient sea that left behind numerous salt deposits. It is also situated along one of the largest thrust faults in the Appalachian range. These factors and other geological characteristics created a rich area for archaeological research. Showcasing some unique finds is the Museum of the Middle Appalachians, located in the heart of downtown Saltville. Exhibits on the Ice Age highlight fossils from the late Pleistocene epoch. Artifacts on display include a woolly mammoth skull, a giant beaver skeleton, and fossilized bones from a mastodon, a woolly mammoth, and a muskox. Other displays cover Woodland-era Native American life, pioneer settlement, and early industry. An extensive photographic collection documents the history of Saltville from 1800. The gift shop stocks books on local and regional history, souvenirs, casts of fossils, and copies of prints. Digs are held at the adjacent Well Fields for two to three weeks each summer. *The museum, located at 123 Palmer Avenue, is open seven days a week. Admission is charged. For more information, call 276-496-3633 or visit www.museum-mid-app.org.*

Palmer Mill and Playhouse

A mill operated by George Palmer in the 1800s has been reconstructed a short distance from its original location. Historic photographs of the complex guided the raising of a timber building on a foundation of stacked stones. Today's Palmer Mill Playhouse is an accurate reproduction of a working gristmill complete with a 20-foot wheel. The mill is home to the Salt Theater Corporation, a community-based arts organization that strives to preserve the heritage and culture of the region by hosting a variety of musical acts and performances in its 130-seat theater. *Located less than a mile from town at 618 Palmer Avenue, the mill is open year-round. For more information, call 276-496-4900 or visit www.palmermill.com.*

Memorial wall honoring fallen soldiers, Saltville
PHOTOGRAPH BY ANNA FARIELLO

Sander's Salt Park

This park is located on the site of what is said to have been the first hand-dug salt mine in the United States, dating to 1795. At the King Salt Works, cavities were dug to the level of the salt bed. When ground water rose to the surface, brine was drawn and boiled in kettles until the salt crystals could be scooped out with a giant ladle. Dried in loosely woven baskets, the salt was then dumped into long trays sheltered in a frame shed. The park includes a restored mine site, a reconstructed salt furnace with five original kettles, and a steam-driven well pump. Also on the property are a pair of original Smyth County pioneer cabins and the ruins of a salt furnace, encased in a protective structure along the park's rear edge. *Located a mile out of town along Route 91 at King Avenue near the Smyth County-Washington County line, the park is open year-round. For more information, call 276-496-5342.*

Well Fields

According to the Virginia Birding and Wildlife Trail organization, Saltville's Well Fields are the only inland saline marshes in the commonwealth. The wetland system consists of several clear ponds ringed with various types of freshwater and saltwater vegetation. Flanked by cattails and sedge grass, a road winds quietly through the natural area, past resting groups of Canada geese. *From town, follow Palmer Avenue to Lake Drive. The Well Fields are also accessible from Route 91 on the way into Saltville from Salt Park. They are open daily during daylight hours. For more information, call 276-496-5342.*

Stop #9   Chilhowie

Settled by Europeans in 1748, this community was originally called Town House. In 1815, a local businessman opened the Chilhowie Springs Resort. The railroad arrived 40 years later, replacing the old Wilderness Road as the primary connector to the surrounding towns and counties. The town was then renamed Greever's Switch to honor the first stationmaster and the mechanical switching system that allowed freight trains to move off the passenger track to load and unload goods. In 1913, the name was changed to Chilhowie, meaning "valley of many deer." The name honors the area's early Native American history. From the date of Chilhowie's establishment until 1989, a local family grew and distributed apples so successfully that the tiny town became southwestern Virginia's center of apple production. Chilhowie is still known for its three-day Apple Festival in September, held annually since 1952. The festival includes a parade of antique cars, homemade floats, and marching bands; bluegrass competitions; art and craft exhibitions; and vendors offering country-style confections and treats.

Chilhowie Wayside

Around 1750, Samuel Stalnaker constructed a four-room log house on a hill overlooking what is now downtown Chilhowie. A historical marker on U.S. 11 commemorates what was then the settlement located farthest west in Virginia. Stalnaker's cabin along the Wilderness Road served as both a protective fortress and a meeting place for newly arrived settlers. In the 19th century, a post office and a stagecoach inn were added to the property. A second marker gives a brief history of the town's development. *The markers are located a half-mile south of the intersection of U.S. 11 and Route 107 just outside the town center. They are accessible year-round.*

Historic Post Office

This historic building with two front entrances dates to 1915. The structure served a double purpose. The right side was the town's post office, while the left was home to Snavely Dry Goods and Grocery. An internal door connected the two spaces, as the postmaster was also the grocer and clerk. Today, the right side is occupied by the Art Place, a community-based gallery offering space to southwestern Virginia artists and housing select exhibits from the Smyth County Museum. *The old post office is located at 127-131 East Main Street. For more information, call 276-783-3161.*

Old Stage Road

While Chilhowie's Main Street is lined with early-20th-century warehouses and commercial buildings, the Old Stage Road, running parallel to it, recalls earlier days. Located west of Route 107, the road offers a view of the remains of the Town House, the oldest colonial building site in Chilhowie. Once a four-room log cabin with a frame addition, the Town House served as a residence, a stagecoach inn, and a post office. All that remains of the original structure are two 18th-century limestone chimneys encased in wild vines. Turning right off Route 107, the road travels to the

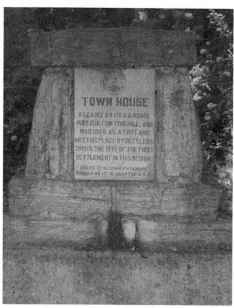

Town House historic road marker, Chilhowie
Photograph by Anna Fariello

Chilhowie Methodist Church, dedicated in 1894. Listed on the Virginia Landmarks Register and the National Register of Historic Places, the late Gothic Revival building has arched doors, stained-glass windows, and an impressive tin roof. *The Old Stage Road crosses Route 107 North just past the Food City complex. Sites along the road may be viewed year-round.*

TOWN HOUSE GRILL

This restaurant, located in a historic 1910 building, is distinguished by its plate-glass storefront, its brick façade, and its pressed-tin ceilings. Originally home to Heninger's Grocery and Dry Goods, Town House Grill offers fine dining in a relaxed atmosphere. The historic photographs of Chilhowie along the walls include views of an 1890s hotel, the Town House, and the original depot station. *Located at 132 East Main Street, the grill is open select days. For more information, call 276-646-8787 or visit www.townhousegrill.com.*

From Chilhowie, the Highlands Trail follows U.S. 11 North along historic railroad tracks toward Marion. That town's revitalized Main Street is lined with Art Deco commercial buildings.

STOP #10   MARION

Organized in 1832, the county was named for General Alexander Smyth, a respected Virginia politician native to this region. In the mid-19th century, the railroad arrived, bringing with it a wave of industrial opportunities. Official Smyth County records cite the prompt establishment of seven sawmills, four furnaces for iron and salt, and two tanneries. Shortly after the county was formed, pioneers began to settle along three forks of the Holston River. The Middle Fork ran right through the center of Royal Oak, a village incorporated in 1849. Royal Oak was later renamed for

Revolutionary War hero Francis Marion, "the Swamp Fox." Marion, the new Smyth county seat, had a rail line and saw significant Civil War action. The town's old-fashioned Fourth of July celebration, held on the courthouse lawn, includes old-time music, games, and a renowned chili contest. The evening culminates with a grand fireworks display at dusk. Marion's colorful history includes a claim to soda-pop fame. Local entrepreneur William Jones created the original recipe for the timeless soft drink Mountain Dew while employed by Marion's Tip Bottling Company.

CHAMBER OF COMMERCE

The Smyth County chamber provides information about sites and activities in the area, including Hungry Mother State Park and Mount Rogers National Recreation Area. *Located at 214 West Main Street, it is open regular business days. For more information, call 276-783-3161 or visit www.swanva.net.*

CIVIL WAR TRAILS

In the December 1864 Battle of Marion, Confederate soldiers were outnumbered four to one. Union forces had been sent to the area to sabotage nearby salt and lead mines and to raid the Virginia-Tennessee railroad. The Confederate brigade held out for two full days. An unlikely hero, the clerk of court, managed to salvage important government documents and county records, stowed in the back of his horse-drawn cart. As local history has it, he was assured escape by a 12-year-old Marion girl who doused the flames Union troops set in the back of the wagon. *Signage is posted along U.S. 11 across from the Bank of Marion near the town's eastern limit. For more information, call 888-CIVILWAR.*

LINCOLN THEATER

The Lincoln Theater was the first major moving-picture house in Marion, following the success of two tiny privately owned cinemas. It was constructed by Marion's wealthiest resident, Charles Lincoln, in the Art Deco style. Popular after World War I, the rich, ornamental style was a synthesis of historic revivals and the dynamic imagery of industrial technology. Lincoln, an industrialist, hired New York's Novelty Scenic Studios to bring its interpretation of Mayan architecture to southwestern Virginia. The theater's interior was decorated in burgundy and gold hues and had stenciled Mayan imagery on the walls, columns, and ceilings. Lincoln died shortly after construction began, but the project was completed by his two sons, who opened the vaudeville and movie house in 1929. In addition to the already elaborate interior design, Lincoln's sons commissioned six giant murals depicting historical scenes and figures including Christopher Columbus, Daniel Boone, Washington's surrender at Yorktown, and Smyth County's cattle industry. Hailed as one of the finest playhouses in southwestern Virginia during the 1930s and 1940s, it hosted such entertainment legends as Roy Rogers, Minnie Pearl, and Bill Monroe. The historic landmark has since undergone a complete physical restoration. *It is located at 117 East Main Street. Tours may be arranged by telephone on regular business days. For more information, call 276-783-6092 or visit www.the-lincoln-theater.org.*

LITTLE'S QUICK CHECK

Serving the community of Seven Mile Ford, Little's Quick Check offers gas, groceries, and a lunch counter complete with a diner-style grill. Checkerboards are set out on tables beneath the original tin ceilings. Bins of Vidalia onions flank the entrance, and the smoky scent of barbecue wafts during hot afternoons. *Little's Quick Check is located on U.S. 11 North (896 Lee Highway) a few miles east of Chilhowie at Seven Mile Ford. It is open daily except Sunday. For more information, call 276-646-5300.*

MARION COLLEGE

Marion Female College was founded in 1873 by a regional Lutheran organization. Accepting both day and boarding students, the college offered instruction in primary and collegiate subjects. Preparatory courses were offered for girls who wished to become schoolteachers, while artistic students were challenged with music, painting, and drawing. Known as Marion College today, the stately academy with brick-columned portico and rotunda sits on a well-proportioned lot surrounded by oaks and sycamores.

Located at the corner of West Main and College streets a short distance from the town center, it may be viewed from the road year-round.

Marion Passenger Station

This fancy, shingled Queen Anne–style passenger station is trimmed with yellow and green wood above a stone foundation. Built in the late 19th century, the station is listed on the National Register of Historic Places. During the 1930s, Whitetop Music Festival promoters recommended the Hotel Lincoln and the Hotel Marion as accommodations for the event. In its heyday, Marion was a transportation hub served by the rail line coming from Bristol and Abingdon. Today, Route 16 winds north and south through the mountains, providing easy access to summer vacation spots. *Located at 651 North Main Street, the station may be viewed from the road year-round.*

R. T. Greer & Company Historic Herb House

Two forward-thinking entrepreneurial cousins from Watauga County, North Carolina, arrived in Marion in 1904. The Greers founded an industry that required a knowledge of traditional mountain culture, as they supplied top-grade herbs, roots, and barks to vendors across the nation. Sherwood Anderson wrote in *Hello Towns!* that one cousin, Tom Greer, used to gather shonny haw and pipsissewa in the North Carolina mountains and sell the bunches to a little country store six miles from home. The historic 1924 building is listed on the National Register of Historic Places. *Located off Main Street at 107 Pendleton Street, it may be viewed from the road year-round. For more information, call 276-783-4062.*

Rosemont

Rosemont Industries was established in the 1920s as a cottage industry producing colonial-style weavings. Following World War I, the market for wool was depressed, leaving area farmers with a surplus on their hands. Laura Copenhaver, a local entrepreneur, gathered a group of women at Rosemont, her family home, where they made coverlets, spreads, and hooked rugs in an attempt to promote these woolen goods to a broader market during the early-20th-century handicrafts revival. *The site of Rosemont Industries is to the rear of the Marion Volunteer Fire Station on Main Street.*

Round Hill Cemetery

Author Sherwood Anderson is buried in Marion's Round Hill Cemetery, tiered into a hillside on the outskirts of town. His easy-to-spot sail-shaped tombstone is adjacent to the Lincoln family tomb along the backside of the cemetery loop. His marker, carved by Wharton Sherick, bears the inscription, "Life not death is the great adventure." Anderson was prolific, publishing eight novels, four collections of short stories, and countless poems, plays, and articles. He retired with his fourth wife, Eleanor, to Marion, where he purchased two weekly papers, one Democratic and one Republican. He wrote for and edited both. Upon his wife's proletarian urging, Anderson became involved in regional labor disputes. The cemetery also contains the markers of Confederate war heroes and Virginia politicians. *To find it, leave town on Main Street, turn onto Park Street, head to the top of the hill, and make a sharp right onto Cemetery Street. The cemetery is accessible year-round during daylight hours.*

Smyth County Courthouse

The county's first courthouse was built in 1834. Seventy years later, the structure was torn down and prominent architect Frank Milburn was hired to rebuild on the foundation. During the second courthouse's construction, the Francis Opera House on Main Street hosted court business. Milburn chose brick and limestone in a unique salt-and-pepper pattern to create a dramatic design featuring an eight-columned portico. Inside, marble stairs lead to the second floor. Beneath the central rotunda, daylight flows in through a stained-glass interior dome. By 1905, Smyth County had incurred a public debt of $54,000, a staggering amount at the time. Almost the entire sum was attributed to construction costs of Milburn's Beaux-Arts building. Today, the original 1834 courthouse bell is on display in the lobby. *Located at 109 West Main Street, the courthouse is open regular business days. For more information, call 276-782-4044.*

Smyth County Courthouse, Marion
PHOTOGRAPH BY ANNA FARIELLO

SMYTH COUNTY HISTORICAL SOCIETY AND MUSEUM

Located in a historic school building dating to 1838, the Smyth County Museum was created in 1961 in an attempt to preserve local social, economic, and agricultural history. Collections include artifacts and photographs from 1808 to 1965. Guests can visit a re-created country store and enjoy exhibits on the life and times of author Sherwood Anderson and the development of local industry, including the railroad and saltworks. The museum is staffed entirely by volunteers. *Located at 105 East Strother Street, it is open select hours. For more information, call 276-783-7286 or visit www.smythcounty.org.*

STALEY COLLINS HOUSE

In the early 1900s, Marion was home to two lieutenant governors, B. F. Buchanan and Lewis P. Collins. The Staley Collins House was home to the latter and his family. Currently the headquarters of the Smyth County Historical Society, it houses exhibits detailing Collins's political career and lifestyle. *Located at 109 West Strother Street, the house is open by appointment and for special occasions. For more information, call 276-783-7067.*

From Marion, the Highlands Trail takes a detour,
following Route 16 North for eight miles
to Hungry Mother State Park.

Spur to Hungry Mother

Hungry Mother is a 2,000-acre state park with nine miles of hiking trails winding through the beautiful alpine forests of the Brushy Mountains.

Hungry Mother Lodge and Restaurant

Hungry Mother Lodge was built by the Civilian Conservation Corps in the 1930s. The recently renovated hand-hewn log cabin sleeps up to 15 people and includes a full kitchen, a fireplace, and a gas grill. Guests may dine at the restaurant at Hungry Mother, an original CCC building. The menu offers casual and gourmet dishes, from fried green tomato sandwiches for lunch to salmon zinfandel served atop a Parmesan and scallion potato cake for dinner. *The lodge is eight miles north of Marion on Route 16 North (2854 Park Boulevard). It is open seasonally. For more information, call 800-933-7275 or 276-781-7400 or visit www.dcr.state.va.us/parks.*

Hungry Mother State Park

The park gets its name from a story that dates to when Native Americans traveling through the area destroyed several European settlements along the New River at what is now the park's southern boundary. A local woman, Molly Marley, and her young daughter were among several residents captured. They escaped to wander in the great forest for a period of time, the legend goes. When a rescue party came upon them, the mother was dead and the young girl had only two words to say to them: "Hungry, Mother." Today, visitors can follow Molly's Knob Trail or a path along Hungry Mother Creek. Recreational opportunities include boating, swimming, and fishing on the 108-acre lake, guided canoe trips, nature and nighttime hikes, and educational programs for children and adults. In July, Hungry Mother hosts an arts-and-crafts extravaganza. *Located eight miles north of Marion on Route 16 (2854 Park Boulevard), it is open year-round. Activities are offered seasonally. For more information, call 276-781-7400 or visit www.dcr.state.va.us/parks.*

The main trail loops back to Marion on Route 16 South. A spur to Mount Rogers National Recreation Area follows Route 16 South for about 10 miles.

SPUR TO MOUNT ROGERS

Mount Rogers was named for William B. Rogers, the 19th-century scientist who first expressed interest in Virginia's unique geological development. A half-mile trail from the visitor center to the summit offers views of the surrounding landscape. The recreation area, covering more than 100,000 acres, encompasses a number of diverse ecosystems.

MOUNT ROGERS NATIONAL RECREATION AREA AND VISITOR CENTER

At 5,729 feet, Mount Rogers is the highest peak in Virginia and the home of the northernmost naturally occurring Fraser fir stand in the state. Acres of rhododendrons and wild blueberries are within the park's boundaries, as are hiking trails suitable for every level and 50 miles of stocked streams for fishing. A 60-mile segment of the Appalachian Trail passes through the park.

Hikers should watch for the wild Wilburn Ridge ponies that populate remote sections of the park. The visitor center has information for bird watchers, wildlife seekers, and mountain bikers. The park offers interpretive programs in summer. *From Marion or Hungry Mother, follow Route 16 South for about 10 miles. The entrance is on Route 16 three miles south of Sugar Grove. The park is open seven days a week seasonally. For more information, call 800-628-7202 or 276-783-5196.*

State Trout Culture Station

This station hatches and raises trout to stock ponds and waterways throughout Virginia. Guided tours are available by appointment. *It is located on Route 16 two miles south of Marion. For more information, call 276-782-9314.*

Early-20th-century roadside cottages, Lee Highway
PHOTOGRAPH BY ANNA FARIELLO

Driving the Lee Highway

Between 1915 and 1925, thanks to the popularity and availability of automobiles, America's enthusiasm for road building accelerated. During the early years of highway building, it was not uncommon for roads to be constructed by private sponsorship.

Lee Highway commemoration, Christiansburg, 1926
FROM *REFLECTIONS*, CHRISTIANSBURG BICENTENNIAL BOOKLET COMMITTEE,
COURTESY OF THE *MONTGOMERY NEWS MESSENGER* PHOTOGRAPHIC ARCHIVE

Hundreds of organizations—including the American Automobile Association, the Daughters of the American Revolution, and associations formed for the specific purpose of building roads—raised funds for the nation's highways. Roads were constructed here and there without an overall plan, resulting in a confusing system of named roadways. To identify highways, telephone polls were sometimes painted in brightly colored bands, much like the blazes on trees that marked earlier paths through the wilderness. But where several highways shared a route, an entire pole might be striped in a confusing array of colors.

The Lincoln Highway, built in 1915, was the nation's first coast-to-coast roadway. Four years after its construction, it was inaugurated with an official convoy of dignitaries and road enthusiasts. The 1919 convoy traveled 3,200 miles cross-country as part of the commemoration. An inscription celebrating the event is engraved on a diminutive monument in the District of Columbia. Dubbed "the Zero Milestone," the marker recognizes "the starting point of [the] first transcontinental motor convoy over the Lincoln Highway." In that convoy was a young brevet lieutenant colonel, Dwight D. Eisenhower. The significance of the event was not lost on the man who, much later as President Eisenhower, signed legislation to initiate the United States interstate system in 1956.

In 1920, Congress authorized funds to construct the Zero Milestone with the idea that there would be an official milestone in every American city from which to provide standardized road measurements. Such a plan was never realized, although some states, including Tennessee, have their own official Zero Milestones. The milestone was modeled after an ancient counterpart in the Roman Forum that linked the most remote provinces of the Roman Empire to the capital, giving currency to the maxim, "All roads lead to Rome." The United States Zero Milestone was constructed in the nation's capital along an axis formed by the White House and the Ellipse. Built from pink granite mined in North Carolina, it was designed by architect H. W. Peaslee and created by sculptor James E. Frazer. The granite pillar is topped with a bronze disk and an engraved compass rose. The rose, an ancient navigational symbol found on the earliest world maps, was made up of radial lines extending to all parts of the then-known world. Their convergence formed a motif that resembled the petals of a rose. In 1923, the United States Zero Milestone was dedicated at a nationally celebrated ceremony presided over by President Harding. In the crowd were 6,000 guests and more automobiles than had ever been assembled in America in any one place.[1]

In the same year that the United States witnessed the first transcontinental convoy over the Lincoln Highway, a group of auto enthusiasts met at the Hotel Roanoke to form an association to lobby for a complementary north-south highway. A number of names were suggested, including the Battlefield Highway, the Valley Highway, and the Lee Highway. The country's first major east-west road having been dedicated as the Lincoln Highway, the symmetry of names was not lost on the group. They opted for the Lee Highway to honor Confederate general Robert E. Lee, Abraham Lincoln's foe during the Civil War.

According to the July 1923 edition of the *American Motorist*, the avowed purpose of the association was to determine the "proper location, construction and maintenance . . . of a great National Highway . . . along the Great Appalachian Valley," claiming there was "no such thing as a continuously improved road" where the Lee Highway is now. The article went on to explain the poor transportation situation: "From some of the larger cities the pavement extended a short distance in either direction toward the next [town] . . . but for the most part there was no road at all, [but only] a primitive wagon trail [or] graded earth road." In 1925, a delegation again converged at the Zero Milestone in the nation's capital and headed south to officially measure and mark the route of the Lee Highway.[2]

The symbolic meaning of the north-south Lee Highway was not lost on President Harding, who officiated at the site of the Zero Milestone. Harding declared that the milestone marked the "meeting point of those sections which once grappled in conflict, but now are happily united for all time in the bonds of national fraternity, of a single patriotism, and of a common destiny." For some, the Lee Highway was a 20th-century symbol of national unification.

To commemorate the completion of the last section of the Lee

Highway, a marble block was laid in the town square of Christiansburg, Virginia. Its demarcation was a dubious distinction, however, having resulted from squabbling between state and federal officials. At the time, the head of the commonwealth's highway department was Brigadier General Jimmy Anderson, a graduate of the Virginia Military Institute. In a Federal Highway Administration article titled "US 11 and I-81 Location Difficulties in Virginia," Anderson was quoted as asking, "Who are the feds to be telling us how to build our highways in Virginia anyway?" The article painted the disagreement as a 20th-century battle in an ongoing War Between the States.

In spite of the political posturing, the Lee Highway was celebrated by Virginia citizens in 1926 as a great success. In Christiansburg, the 1909 Montgomery County Courthouse was covered in swags of red, white, and blue fabric, and a temporary arch was erected over the town square. An estimated 200,000 people showed up for the November 1926 dedication, presided over by governor-elect Harry Byrd.[3]

Today, much of the historic Lee Highway has been displaced by high-speed interstate. Running parallel to the Blue Ridge, the Lee Highway—marked as U.S. 11—shares the valley floor with I-81. If one is willing to travel at moderate speeds, the Lee Highway offers a glimpse of life in towns along the north-south route of a historic 20th-century byway.

[1] Lee Highway Association, Inc., *Lee Highway* (Washington, D.C.: Lee Highway Association, 1926), 5-7.

[2] Richard F. Weingroff, "Zero Milestone, Washington, D.C.," *U.S. Department of Transportation Federal Highway Administration*, http://www.fhwa.dot.gov/infrastructure/zero.htm (accessed June 1, 2005); *Lee Highway*, 35, 104.

[3] John T. Greenwood, "US 11 and I-81 Location Difficulties in Virginia," *U.S. Department of Transportation Federal Highway Administration*, http://www.fhwa.dot.gov/infrastructure/us11i81.htm (accessed June 1, 2005).

The Highlands Trail picks up again, returning to U.S. 11 via Route 16 North from Mount Rogers. The trail travels 14 miles along U.S. 11, passing abandoned service stations and vintage roadside accommodations before turning south on Route 90 for Rural Retreat.

Stop #11 Lee Highway

In the early 20th century, before the establishment of the interstate highway system, there were two roads that traveled the length and width of the United States. The Lincoln Highway went coast-to-coast, and the Lee Highway went from Washington, D.C., through the South. Today, what remains of the historic Lee Highway can be found along U.S. 11.

Appalachian Trail Access

The Appalachian Trail can be accessed seven miles east of Marion where it passes under I-81 at Exit 54 near Groseclose. This portion of the trail is noted for its dramatic summertime floral displays of rhododendron and azaleas and for its snowfalls between October and May. *Drive east on the Lee Highway for seven miles or depart I-81 at Exit 54. The trail is accessible year-round, weather permitting.*

Davis Valley Winery

This vineyard planted its first grape seeds in 2000. Today, beautifully manicured vines line every inch of available hillside. Each long row of grapes is marked with a plaque that denotes the variety and year of planting. A welcome center with impressive stacked-stone columns sits atop the hill overlooking the property. The winery offers tastings and guided tours. Davis Valley also hosts several musical events; call ahead for a schedule. *To reach the winery, exit I-81 at Groseclose and follow the signs embellished with a cluster of grapes. Located at 1167 David Lane, it is open seven days a week. For more information, call 276-686-8855 or visit www.davisvalleywinery.com.*

OLD STONE TAVERN

One of Smyth County's oldest buildings, this two-story stone tavern dates to the late 18th century and is listed on the National Register of Historic Places. Once known as Cullop's Tavern, it was a place of merriment offering rooms at a moderate price. During the first half of the next century, it served as a stop along a stagecoach route. Today, it is home to a traditional tinsmith who exhibits work by members of the Blue Ridge Highland Artisan's Guild. *Located along U.S. 11 (5392 Lee Highway) near the intersection with Nick's Creek Road, it may be viewed from the road year-round. Call ahead for a guided tour; the number is 276-781-0084.*

SETTLERS MUSEUM OF SOUTHWEST VIRGINIA

This museum includes an 1890s schoolhouse and farm, an exhibition hall, and a visitor center. It uses original maps and artwork to chart settlement by Scots-Irish and German pioneers. A farm lane runs through

Settlers Museum of Southwest Virginia, Atkins
PHOTOGRAPH BY ANNA FARIELLO

orchards and flax fields to the front door. A restored farmhouse and outbuildings, a kitchen garden, a granary, a root cellar, and a farm all offer interactive experiences. The 1894 Lindamood School is a good example of the type of school that operated in southwestern Virginia at the end of the 19th century. In Smyth County in 1885, there were 67 schools, almost all of them one-room facilities like this one. Visitors may participate in 19th-century lessons and games and talk with the many costumed interpreters tending crops and livestock on the 67-acre farm. An interpretive brochure available at the visitor center identifies 11 outbuildings and a wellhouse. *Located at Exit 54 off I-81 (1322 Rocky Hollow Road), the museum is open seasonally. Admission is charged. For more information, call 276-686-4401.*

> **The Highlands Trail continues north on U.S. 11 or I-81. From either route, it then departs on Route 90 South to Rural Retreat.**

STOP #12   RURAL RETREAT

Originally called the Mount Airy Depot, this community was renamed Rural Retreat in 1866 and incorporated as such in 1911. In 1871, local farmer H. A. Effort shipped his first load of cabbage to Chattanooga, Tennessee, for two and a half cents a pound. After the turn of the 20th century, thousands of pounds were exported. In 1878, an academy for males and females opened under Lutheran supervision. Early programs of study included English, classics, and modern languages. Today's town center is a mixture of early-20th-century buildings, barns, and industrial structures. Among the highlights are the old stone walls and the vintage tin Sunbeam Bread sign above the porch of the old Frye Grocery, situated up the hill above the historic depot. Several 19th-century churches dot the downtown. A short way down Baumgardener Avenue is the Hotel Sprinkle, dating to the mid-1900s. The three-story frame building's striking double-decker porches and corner turret are evidence of Rural Retreat's sophisticated heyday.

Cedar Springs Fish Farm

Visitors can pay for a day of fine fishing along a stretch of Cripple Creek in Rural Retreat. The Hilton family stocks the creek with prizewinning brook, golden, brown, and rainbow trout and allows fishermen to take home up to five fish daily. *From the town center, take Cedar Springs Road south for about six miles to the T intersection near the county line. Go left on Trout Farm Road to 333 Hilton Lane. The farm is open seasonally. For more information, call 276-686-4505.*

Loading cabbages, Rural Retreat, circa 1934
COURTESY OF NORFOLK & WESTERN HISTORICAL PHOTOGRAPH
COLLECTION, VIRGINIA TECH SPECIAL COLLECTIONS

Historic Rural Retreat Drug Store

The tiny town of Rural Retreat has a national claim to fame. In 1885, Wade Morrison took a job at Pepper's Drug Store downtown. In charge of the soda fountain, Morrison became known for his trial-and-error pop flavors. One recipe combining over 20 flavored syrups was popular with customers young and old. Legend has it that young Morrison disagreed with his employer, possibly over matters of love involving the employer's daughter, and headed for Texas. When he arrived in Waco, he decided to pursue his popular recipe and named the drink after his old boss, Dr. Charles Pepper. The period was dropped from the abbreviation in the 1950s, and consumers were left with the unique Dr Pepper. The famous drugstore, lost to a fire in 1999, was located in the grassy lot next to the Rural Retreat

Historic train depot, Rural Retreat
Photograph by Anna Fariello

Historical Society. Dr. Charles Pepper is buried beneath a six-foot monument in Rural Retreat's Mountain View Cemetery. *The drugstore site, at the intersection of North Main Street and Railroad Avenue, is accessible year-round. For more information, call 276-686-6347.*

RURAL RETREAT DEPOT STATION

Paint peeling and vines growing at the corners, this Italianate gem of a historic structure is made of white clapboard trimmed in blue. The station is bounded by a series of old brick commercial buildings. Across the lot is a red vintage Norfolk & Western caboose. Down the tracks is an operating mill. *The station is located at the intersection of North Main Street and Railroad Avenue. It may be viewed from the road year-round. For more information, call 276-686-6347.*

RURAL RETREAT HISTORICAL SOCIETY

Staffed by a local couple and their daughter, the historical society operates out of a historic brick building just above the depot. In 1969, the Virginia National Bank donated Heritage Hall to the town for the purpose of collecting and preserving its history. *Located on Main Street, the historical society is open select hours and by appointment. For more information, call 276-686-6347.*

RURAL RETREAT LAKE

This 90-acre lake surrounded by a hardwood forest boasts excellent fishing for bluegill, catfish, and largemouth bass. Fishermen may be lucky enough to catch a glimpse of a great blue heron, osprey, or bald eagle. Camping facilities are available. Across the entry road, the bandstand and track host several events in the summer, including a rodeo competition and a tractor pull sponsored by the Mountain Empire Antique Tractor and Small Engine Club. In August, the Wythe County Fair is held on the grounds surrounding the lake. *To reach the lake, travel south on Main Street (Route 749) to Rural Retreat Lake Road (Route 677). It is open seasonally. For more information, call 276-686-4331.*

The historic village of Foster Falls
PHOTOGRAPH BY ANNA FARIELLO

WYTHE COUNTY RACEWAY

Established in 1970, this half-mile dirt track hosts stock car, dirt bike, and vintage car races. Fans have access to concessions and can pay extra to visit the pits. The raceway is a community organization designed to promote interest in racing sports and to encourage amateur drivers. *It is located about a mile outside town off Radio Drive; call for directions. The raceway is open year-round. Admission is charged. For more information, call 276-228-3118 or 276-686-4261 or visit www.wytheraceway.com.*

The Highlands Trail returns to U.S. 11 or I-81 through Wythe County for another 15 miles. The town of Wytheville and environs are included in chapter 4, the "National Forest Trail." To conclude the present loop, pick up I-77 South from I-81 East at Exit 24. Follow the signs to the historic Shot Tower and New River Trail State Park.

Stop #13 Foster Falls

Foster Falls prospered in the mid- to late 1800s as a mining and railroad community. The population of nearly 200 supported a hotel, a sawmill, a gristmill, an iron furnace, and a general store. A flood in 1914 destroyed the railroad bridge. Five years later, the furnace closed. Today, the restored rustic community includes examples of its original establishments. An easy four-mile drive along Route 608 passes vintage farmsteads, log cabins, and agricultural outbuildings.

Historic Foster Falls Village

Within New River Trail State Park is the industrial section of Foster Falls. Several buildings are identified with interpretive panels stating the date of construction and the structures' original function. Period photographs are also posted. An outstanding example of a 19th-century iron furnace is preserved on the site. Constructed in 1880 by the Fosters Falls Mining Company, it employed between 70 and 80 people. *From Exit 24 off I-77, follow the signs to the New River Trail State Park entrance. Admission is charged. The structures are accessible year-round.*

New River Adventures and Horse Livery

This outfitter can arrange a variety of river and trail experiences for visitors of all ages and abilities. It rents bikes, canoes, and inner tubes and shuttles guests to a number of locations up and down the river. Kayaks are available for tackling the New's multi-class rapids. The livery will also arrange horseback trips. *Located within New River Trail State Park, it is open seasonally. Call 276-699-1034 for canoe and bike rentals or 276-699-2460 to schedule a trip on horseback.*

New River Trail State Park

Headquartered in the historic village of Foster Falls, the New River Trail is part of the national rails-to-trails program. Formerly owned by Norfolk Southern Railway, the 57-mile section of rail bed stretches along the New River for 39 miles, connecting Claytor Lake State Park with Mount Rogers and Grayson Highlands State Park. Accessed at points in Ivanhoe, Fries, Galax, Cliffview, Draper, and Pulaski, the trail passes through two rail tunnels and crosses a number of original bridges and trestles. For the physically handicapped, the park offers a three-wheel electric vehicle that operates within a 25-mile radius. In summer, guided tours of Foster Falls are offered. Brochures are available at the visitor center. *To reach the park, depart I-77 at Exit 24 and follow the signs to Route 608 North and the park. The entrance is located at 176 Orphanage Drive. The park is accessible year-round; the visitor center is open seasonally. Admission is charged. For more information, call 800-833-PARK or 276-699-6778 or visit www.dcr.state.va.us/parks/newriver.html.*

Orphanage Drive

The upper section of the historic Foster Falls village is home to three original structures. The 1887 hotel, constructed by a mining company, served for a period as an orphanage, likely affiliated with the neighboring church. The church parsonage, built four years after the hotel, is a typical Victorian farmhouse. It is adjacent to the turn-of-the-20th-century Foster Falls Methodist Church. *Orphanage Drive cuts left off Route 608 North. The structures may be viewed from the road year-round.*

Shot Tower Historical State Park

Built high on a limestone bluff overlooking the New River almost 200 years ago, the Shot Tower is considered a mechanical-engineering landmark. Situated amid a 254-acre preserve, the 75-foot stone tower was constructed to make shot pellets. Built by Thomas Jackson, a self-made miner, mechanic,

Shot Tower, Wythe County, circa 1950
Photograph by Earl Palmer, courtesy of Earl Palmer Collection,
Virginia Tech Special Collections

and ferryman of English descent, it housed a sieve that ran from top to bottom and a shaft that ran another 75 feet underground to a kettle of water. Lead was transported from the nearby Austinville mines to the tower, melted at the top, and poured 150 feet through the sieve and shaft to cool, which broke the hot metal into the shot pellets used by pioneers, hunters, and traders. For a brief period during the Civil War, the Shot Tower was the South's chief domestic supplier of lead. Today, it is one of three such structures in the country. Visitors may access the grounds on foot and climb the restored tower stairs for a dramatic view from the old kettle room. *To reach the park, take Exit 24 off I-77 and go 1.5 miles north on U.S. 52. It is accessible year-round. For more information, call 276-699-6778.*

Stop #14   Woodlawn

Out-of-the-way Woodlawn is home to two sites that showcase authentic regional culture. In September, it hosts a music festival, Fiddlin' on the Lot.

Front Porch Gallery

A native of Appalachia, pencil artist Willard Gayheart operates a studio and gallery showcasing his work and that of other regional artists. Gayheart's drawings aim to preserve mountain culture in their depiction of traditional Appalachian scenes. Some sketches have an old-time spirit, while others portray a more contemporary vision of mountain life and culture. The gallery displays and sells Gayheart's original drawings and prints. His son and daughter are on hand to assist with custom matting and framing, making this a true family business. *Depart I-77 at Exit 14 and take U.S. 58 West. In the tiny village of Woodlawn, turn right on Coalson Church Road. The gallery is housed in the rear of the old Heritage Shoppe. It is open daily except Sunday. For more information, call 276-236-3034.*

Harmon Museum

Visitors enter this museum through the Harmon Boot Shop. The expansive and unassuming space features a unique regional collection of artifacts from the Revolutionary War, the Civil War, World War I, and World War II. It also has a large antique-rifle collection. One end of the rectangular interior space is devoted to pioneer farm tools and domestic objects. An extensive display on the historic Baldwin-Felts Detective Agency, investigators of the infamous 1912 Hillsville courthouse shooting, is housed in glass cases alongside historic photographs and personal ephemera. *The museum is in Woodlawn on U.S. 58 (5122 Carollton Pike). Signs are posted along the road. It is open daily except Sunday. For more information, call 276-236-4884.*

To complete the Highlands Trail loop,
follow U.S. 58 East back to I-77.

Tool display, Harmon Museum, Woodlawn
PHOTOGRAPH BY ANNA FARIELLO

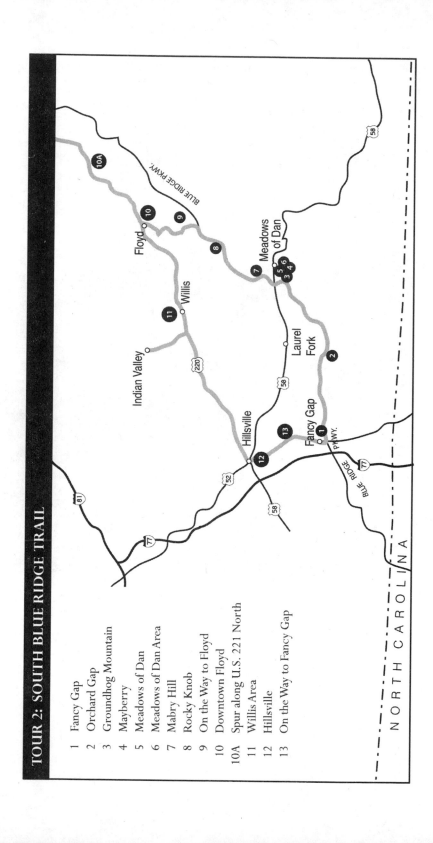

TOUR 2: SOUTH BLUE RIDGE TRAIL

1   Fancy Gap
2   Orchard Gap
3   Groundhog Mountain
4   Mayberry
5   Meadows of Dan
6   Meadows of Dan Area
7   Mabry Hill
8   Rocky Knob
9   On the Way to Floyd
10 Downtown Floyd
10A Spur along U.S. 221 North
11 Willis Area
12 Hillsville
13 On the Way to Fancy Gap

Sidna Allen home. Photograph by Anna Fariello

Chapter 2
South Blue Ridge Trail

The South Blue Ridge Trail begins in Fancy Gap, accessible from either the Blue Ridge Parkway or I-77. From the parkway, take U.S. 52 from Milepost 199.5. From I-77, take Exit 8. The Blue Ridge Parkway is shared by North Carolina and Virginia. Half of its 469-mile length is in the commonwealth; Virginia's section begins at Milepost 217. The South Blue Ridge Trail heads northeast to cover sites along Virginia's southern section of the parkway, from Fancy Gap to Floyd. It passes through parts of Carroll and Patrick counties before leaving the parkway at Route 8. In the heart of Floyd County, the trail picks up U.S. 221 South into Willis before circling through the Carroll County seat of Hillsville to return to Fancy Gap.

Road opening, Fancy Gap, 1928
COURTESY OF SOUTHWEST
VIRGINIA IMAGES
COLLECTION, VIRGINIA TECH
SPECIAL COLLECTIONS

STOP #1 FANCY GAP

Long before this section of I-77 was completed in 1977, the Appalachian Trail followed Fancy Gap through the Blue Ridge. Legend has it that this spot was named by a young boy who drove a team of horses across the mountains and, overwhelmed by their natural beauty, declared the pass a "fancy gap." The boy, Ira Coltrane, would grow up to become a Confederate military hero and the designer and builder of the Carroll County Courthouse. A gateway to the Blue Ridge Parkway, the town of Fancy Gap offers shopping for fresh fruits and vegetables at a variety of farmers' markets and "junking" at the many roadside antique stores.

Southwestern Virginia bottom land
PHOTOGRAPH BY ANNA FARIELLO

Viewing the Land

Among the important transportation arteries of Virginia's Blue Ridge are two interstates, several state highways, and a federal parkway that together form a diverse and efficient network through this section of the commonwealth. Some routes, like I-81, are for the most part laid out along valley floors. Others, like the Blue Ridge Parkway, are true ridge roads, meandering along the crest of a great mountain range. Still others are uniquely constructed. I-77 enters from West Virginia via a tunnel cut through the Alleghenies. Emerging from the other side, it crosses I-81 before heading down off the Blue Ridge plateau into the North Carolina Piedmont. Today, Virginia has almost 100,000 miles of roads, including over 1,000 miles of high-speed interstate. Roads large and small lead travelers into rural villages, small towns, and metropolitan areas. These ribbons of asphalt may appear as the most modern of construction, but beneath their paved surfaces lies a story of human migration that dates back 1,000 years.

Archaeology has revealed evidence of a human presence in the area that became Virginia as far back as 10,000 years ago. While little is known of those earliest inhabitants, a more focused picture begins to emerge from the material remains of Woodland people who lived in

The Appalachian range. PHOTOGRAPH BY ANNA FARIELLO

the valley from 1000 B.C. onward. By 700 A.D., Mississippian traditions included settlements fortified by palisades—walled stockades constructed from long, sharpened sticks driven upright into the ground. Native Americans living in the region eventually broke into autonomous and economically self-sufficient groups. They were a settled people who farmed the green valley, practiced plant propagation, and hunted the abundant game with triangular projectile points. Small game—otters, beavers, bobcats, raccoons, foxes, and minks—provided meat for nourishment and fur for clothing and shelter. Larger mammals like mountain lions, bears, and elk are found in ever-decreasing numbers today. Such large animals require a more expansive habitat than can be found in today's populous Eastern states. But before human settlement carved up their territory, even larger mammals made their homes in the Appalachian Mountains. Buffalo roamed the region until hunted to near-extinction by the end of the 18th century.

The Appalachian Mountains form an upland swath of rugged forested ridges and valleys that stretch the full length of the continental United States, about 1,500 miles of relatively unbroken wilderness. The range begins in southern Quebec and fans out in a southwesterly direction to northern Alabama, where it is barely perceptible as a mountain chain at all. In Upstate New York, the Appalachian Mountains are about 100 miles across; in the South, they widen to 300 miles. At several points in Virginia, they make up the Eastern Continental Divide, where waters on one side flow into the

Gulf of Mexico and waters on the other flow into the Atlantic Ocean. North of the New River, Buffalo Mountain in Floyd County is the Blue Ridge's highest peak, measuring 3,971 feet above sea level. Farther south, on the Smyth County-Grayson County line, Whitetop Mountain reaches 5,520 feet. Its neighbor Mount Rogers claims the title of Virginia's tallest peak, measuring 5,729 feet.[1]

Even modern vehicles are challenged by the mountainous sections of the commonwealth. Eighteen-wheelers chug up Christiansburg Mountain along I-81, barely able to maintain the speed limit. Families hold their breath coming off the Blue Ridge plateau, cutting back and forth on switchbacks along Route 8 into Stuart and on toward Martinsville, or from Fancy Gap toward the North Carolina line. Before modern-day roads, it is no wonder that travelers chose to go around steep mountains via passes through gaps in the rugged terrain.

In Virginia, several regional ranges make up the Appalachians. The Shenandoahs occupy the mountainous north. In southwestern Virginia, the Appalachians split into two distinct parallel chains. Along Virginia's western boarder lie the Alleghenies. Running east of the Alleghenies is the famed and beloved Blue Ridge. There are several stories that tell how the Blue Ridge got its name. One of the earliest commentaries came from Virginia's William Byrd, who, while surveying the state's boundary in 1728, recorded a description of "Ranges of Blue clouds rising."[2] Paintings and poetry describing a veil of blue mist blanketing the hills have given the Blue Ridge an air of mystery and romance. Between the two parallel ridge lines is the lowland known as the Valley of Virginia, a fairly level trough of bottom land extending along the entire north-south axis of the state. Its steep sides culminate in the Alleghenies to the west and the Blue Ridge to the east. Historically, the valley served as a primary transportation corridor for native peoples before the region was settled by Europeans seeking to build a life in the New World.

[1] Ted Olson, *Blue Ridge Folklife* (Jackson: University Press of Mississippi, 1998), xiv.

[2] Harley E. Jolley, *The Blue Ridge Parkway* (Knoxville: University of Tennessee Press, 1969), 4.

DEVIL'S DEN NATURE PRESERVE

This 280-acre preserve is located along the bed of the original Fancy Gap Mountain Turnpike, laid out by engineer Ira B. Coltrane. The preserve overlooks the North Carolina Piedmont to the south and west and backs up against the Blue Ridge plateau. It is home to a unique fault cave called the Devil's Den, the entrance of which is marked by a pair of 50-foot-tall boulders. Visitors who want to explore the cave system or enjoy a semi-rigorous hike should sign up for a guided tour at the visitor center. Throughout the property are walking paths for bird watchers and wildlife seekers that have been included in the *Virginia Birding and Wildlife Trail Guide*. The guide recommends that explorers keep watch for migrating songbirds, ruffed grouse, box turtles, and red foxes. The preserve includes a picnic area, a horseshoe pit, and a historic farmstead that dates to the late 1890s. In summer, Devil's Den sponsors a number of recreational and educational programs and events. *Take the Fancy Gap exit (Exit 8) off I-77 South and follow U.S. 52 underneath the Blue Ridge Parkway. Turn right on Route 608 (Old Appalachian Trail) and drive about a mile to Cemetery Road and the parking area. Signs are posted. The preserve is open seasonally. For more information, call 276-728-2494.*

MAYBERRY STATION GRILL & MARKET

This grill offers old-fashioned hamburgers, hand-cut French fries, fried pies, and unique "Mayberry-style" porkchop sandwiches. Customers can eat at the lunch counter or order to go. The diner-style counter is framed on all sides by Mayberry memorabilia, including photos and posters of Andy and Barney from the popular television series. The door is flanked by an old squad car. *Mayberry Station is located off U.S. 52 on Chances Creek Road at the Exit 8 ramp off I-77. It is open daily except Sunday. For more information, call 276-728-0500.*

OLDE HOMESTEAD GENERAL STORE

This collection of frame buildings in a rustic setting includes the original Fancy Gap post office and a springhouse used by Confederate soldiers. The items sold here include jams, cheeses, and fudge. Area craftsmen and artisans also exhibit and sell their work. *Located just south of Chances Creek*

Mayberry Station Grill & Market, Fancy Gap
PHOTOGRAPH BY ANNA FARIELLO

Road on U.S. 52, the store is open seasonally. For more information, call 276-728-5886.

PINES 'N' NEEDLES

These twin shops feature traditional and country-themed gift items. Locally made foods such as jams, jellies, and fried apple pies are available, as are culturally indigenous gifts including quilts, folk art, dolls, pottery, candles, soaps, lotions, and a wide selection of country, religious, and mountain music. *Located on U.S. 52 (7001 Fancy Gap Highway), Pines 'n' Needles is open seven days a week; hours are seasonal. For more information, call 276-728-9818.*

Blue Ridge Parkway
PHOTOGRAPH BY ANNA FARIELLO

The trail continues north from Fancy Gap to connect with the Blue Ridge Parkway. Sites in Orchard Gap fall between Milepost 195 and Milepost 193. (Note that the parkway milepost numbers decrease heading north; Milepost 193 is north of Milepost 195.)

STOP #2 ORCHARD GAP

The Blue Ridge Parkway passes through some of Virginia's highest elevations. At Mileposts 167 and 170 are, respectively, Rocky Knob at 3,572 feet and Grassy Knoll at 3,480 feet. Buffalo Mountain stands 3,970 feet.

Between the parkway's high peaks are a number of natural gaps in the ridge line. From south to north, these include Pipers Gap, Fancy Gap, and Orchard Gap.

Inn at Orchard Gap

Perched on a hilltop spanning seven acres, this Colonial-style inn has four guest rooms and two cottages. Each of the guest rooms has a private entrance and bath, hardwood floors, and antique and reproduction pieces. The downstairs guest room is handicapped-accessible. *Exit the parkway near Milepost 195 at Route 608. Located at 4549 Lightning Ridge Road, the inn is open year-round, though accommodations vary seasonally. For more information, call 276-398-3206 or visit www.bbonline.com/va/orchardgap.*

Levering Orchard

Cherries, apricots, peaches, nectarines, plums, pears, and apples are ready for picking June through November at this orchard, established in 1908. Visitors can also enjoy outdoor drama held in the Cherry Orchard Theater on summer weekends. A fruit tree might be a good spot to read one of the books written by owners Frank Levering and Wanda Urbanska about the orchard's history and small-town life. *Exit the parkway between Mileposts 194 and 193 at Orchard Gap Road (Route 691). Follow Orchard Gap Road for two miles down the mountain to 163 Levering Lane. The orchard is open seasonally. For more information, call 276-755-4837 or 336-789-7400 or visit www.leveringorchard.com.*

Lonesome Pine Cabins

These cabins offer modern conveniences in a rustic setting with views of Buffalo Mountain and the North Carolina Piedmont. They come equipped with Jacuzzis and bedside fireplaces. In keeping with the regional theme, a restored chicken house serves as a single-level guesthouse, while the "Schoolhouse" cabin is constructed in traditional Appalachian style. Supplies are available from the nearby Orchard Gap Market. *Exit the parkway between Mileposts 194 and 193 at Route 608. Located at 64 Lonesome Cabin Lane, the facilities are open year-round. For more information, call 888-799-9214.*

Orchard Gap Market and Deli

This country store offers picnic supplies and a variety of freshly baked goods including breads, coffeecakes, focaccia, cookies, and brownies. Local produce is available in season. Handmade crafts and local products like quilts and homemade preserves are also available. *Exit the parkway between Mileposts 194 and 193 at Route 608. Located at 1113 Dusty Ridge Road, the market is open seven days a week. For more information, call 276-398-4200 or visit www.orchardgap.com.*

Volunteer Gap Inn

Situated on a hilltop with views of Buffalo Mountain and the Blue Ridge, this log-sided inn offers eight guest rooms with kitchenettes and private baths. A few rustically furnished cottages are situated along the creek. Guests have access to fully stocked ponds and are free to roam the grounds and linger under the fruit trees. *Exit the parkway between Mileposts 194 and 193 at Route 608. Located at 579 Volunteer Road, the inn is open year-round. For more information, call 276-398-3689 or visit www.volunteergapinn.com.*

> The trail continues north along the Blue Ridge Parkway. Sites along this stretch of the trail lie between Milepost 192 and Milepost 188 through Volunteer Gap on the way to Groundhog Mountain.

Stop #3 Groundhog Mountain

The construction of the parkway was meant to bring the public close to nature and to provide majestic views from the Blue Ridge range. Begun in the 1930s, the parkway was completed 30 years later.

Bluemont Presbyterian Church

Bluemont is one of seven rock churches constructed in Floyd, Carroll, and Patrick counties by Robert Childress, a Presbyterian minister raised in a small community at the foot of Buffalo Mountain. Childress turned to religion to combat lawlessness in the region. Four of his rock churches are on this trail. The second-oldest of the seven, Bluemont was completed in early 1924. *It is located between Mileposts 192 and 191. Sunday services are open to the public. A map locating Childress's churches is available at the Rocky Knob Visitor Center.*

Groundhog Mountain Picnic Area

This picnic area includes a pioneer cemetery, 26 picnic sites with tables and shade trees, and a trailhead for a short, easy hike to an observation tower with an elevation of 3,030 feet. The Blue Ridge plateau and the North Carolina Piedmont are visible from the tower. Surrounding the tower are examples of traditional rural fencing styles, including post and rail, picket, buck, and snake fences. An interpretive panel details the history of each. *Located between Mileposts 189 and 188, the picnic area is accessible year-round.*

Pilot Mountain Overlook

Just a short distance north of the Groundhog Mountain Picnic Area is Pilot Mountain Overlook. Its elevation of 2,950 feet allows a view of the

Bluemont Presbyterian Church, Blue Ridge Parkway
Photograph by Anna Fariello

unique profile of Pilot Mountain in North Carolina. *Located at Milepost 189, the overlook is accessible year-round.*

Puckett Cabin

Midwives aided in the births of countless babies in rural areas during the 19th and early 20th centuries. Their training was based on observation and experiential learning. Through proximity and social intercourse, midwives were in a position to learn families' medical histories. "Aunt" Orlean Hawks Puckett (1835-1939) was such a midwife. After all of her own 24 children died in infancy, she became a midwife at age 50 and successfully delivered over 1,000 babies. A roadside exhibit located at her historic home explains other aspects of her life. *Located at Milepost 190, the cabin is accessible year-round.*

Puckett Cabin, Blue Ridge Parkway
PHOTOGRAPH BY ANNA FARIELLO

To access the historic community of Mayberry, exit the Blue Ridge Parkway between Mileposts 181 and 180 at Route 634 to reach Mayberry Church Road, a quiet country lane running parallel to the parkway.

STOP #4 MAYBERRY

The Mayberry community takes its name from Mayberry Creek, which crosses the parkway. Located at the geographic midpoint of the parkway, Mayberry was an important center for mountain commerce. Patrick, Floyd, and Carroll counties all lie within a 15-mile radius of this historic "Heart of the Blue Ridge."

BLUE RIDGE NATURE CRAFTS

This local gallery displays polished rocks, shells, bead jewelry, and original watercolors of local landmarks. Visitors can call in advance for rock-grinding and polishing demonstrations. *Located at 211 Mayberry Church Road, it is open seven days a week. For more information, call 540-593-2273.*

MAYBERRY PRESBYTERIAN CHURCH

In 1924, the Meadows of Dan Sunday school was held in a two-room school building that stood across from the present church site. It was in the Sunday-school building that the Reverend Robert Childress held a revival so effective that it inspired citizens to organize and build a church. The original wooden structure was completed in 1925. In keeping with the tradition of Childress's other churches, it was encased in stone in 1948. *It is located at 1127 Mayberry Church Road. Sunday services are open to the public. For more information, call 276-952-2155.*

MAYBERRY TRADING POST

In operation since 1892, this trading post is a cluster of white-painted

Mayberry Trading Post, Mayberry
PHOTOGRAPH BY ANNA FARIELLO

buildings at the edge of the parkway. The two-story frame store still has the original tulip poplar countertops and mail bins from its earlier days as a post office. Prior to the chestnut blight that struck the area in the early 20th century, shop employees gathered nuts in the fall to be shipped to cities. In winter, dances and social gatherings were held on the store's upper level. Legend has it that bluegrass musicians Bill and Charlie Monroe gave their last ensemble performance at the trading post. One of the best sites on the parkway for culturally indigenous goods, the store features locally made jellies, books, and mountain crafts. Apple-butter- and molasses-making demonstrations are held weekends from Labor Day through October. *Located at 883 Mayberry Church Road, the trading post is open seven days a week. For more information, call 276-952-2155.*

Round Meadow Creek Loop Trail

Visitors can park at the pull-off and enjoy the view or take an easy half-mile walk through a deciduous forest with a stream running along the bottom. The path rewards hikers with glimpses of lowland oaks and poplars. Delicate pink lady's-slipper blossoms from mid-May to mid-June, and mountain laurel blooms white, rose, and pink in early summer. *To access the trail, exit the parkway between Mileposts 180 and 179; signs are posted. It is accessible year-round.*

Continue north on the parkway to the intersection
with U.S. 58 just past Milepost 178.

Stop #5 Meadows of Dan

Many Virginia counties formed prior to 1776 bear names that evidence allegiance to the Crown, while counties established after the Revolutionary War have names honoring colonial patriots. Patrick County was formed from Henry County in 1791, just after the war. The two counties were named in honor of Patrick Henry, whose "Give me liberty or give me death" speech inspired many to fight the British. Henry's 20,000-acre plantation spanned both counties that bear his name. Patrick County's 469 square miles butt up against the North Carolina border to the south and the Allegheny Mountains to the west. Its topography is much like that of neighboring Floyd County—a rolling surface broken by several small mountain chains and numerous streams and rivers. The community of Meadows of Dan is located on what was originally the Danville-Wytheville Turnpike. This section of U.S. 58 is also known as the Jeb Stuart Highway and is the town's principal street.

Blue Ridge Restaurant

This country-style eatery serves lunch and dinner. The menu features down-home specialties such as liver and onions and barbecued pork sandwiches. Desserts include bread and rice puddings. An interesting touch is the topographically correct mural of local mountain ranges circling the main dining room. *Blue Ridge Restaurant is located under the bridge on U.S. 58 at 2309 Jeb Stuart Highway. It is open seven days a week. For more information, call 276-952-2201.*

Evie Shelton's Store, Floyd County, circa 1950
PHOTOGRAPH BY EARL PALMER, COURTESY OF EARL PALMER COLLECTION,
VIRGINIA TECH SPECIAL COLLECTIONS

GREENBERRY HOUSE

Leslie Shelor carries on her family's creative tradition by using a number of antique and modern spinning wheels to spin luxury Angora yarns. The raw fiber comes from her German and hybrid Angora rabbits, which she clips every three months. Shelor also sells colored and white long-haired bunnies, with or without pedigrees, as pets or "woolers." She designs crocheted items and creates baskets and rugs from vintage linen yarn. *The studio is in the upstairs of the old family homeplace, located 200 feet from the intersection of U.S. 58 and the parkway. The address is 12206 Squirrel Spur Road; use the first driveway on the left. It is open by appointment. For more information, call 276-952-1079 or visit www.greenberryhouse.com.*

HISTORIC MEADOWS GENERAL STORE

This store began as a two-story frame building with an entrance located on what was then the main thoroughfare, the Danville-Wytheville Turnpike. A few years later, U.S. 58 was built opposite the turnpike and the entrance was shifted to face the new highway. A front porch was added to welcome highway travelers. The business was purchased in the 1940s by brothers-in-law Taylor Cock and Tom Agee, who operated what they dubbed Cock & Agee No. 2. They sold a bit of everything, including Depression glassware, shoes, groceries, and feed, and accepted produce in trade from local customers. To make use of all available space, the partners hung bridles and overalls from the ceiling. A fixture of the store was the great potbelly stove located at its center. Almost as permanent a fixture in a rocking chair next to the stove was storyteller Len Reynolds. An area native, Reynolds was known for his tales from generations past. The frame building was torn down in the 1950s. The current brick structure was erected alongside the original foundation. The store, currently called Meadows Edge Knife Shop and Antiques, specializes in antique, custom, and Randall knives. *Located near the intersection of the parkway and U.S. 58 (2554 Jeb Stuart Highway), it is open seven days a week. For more information, call 276-952-2500.*

MEADOWS MUSIC

This is a working shop where a family of artisans builds and sells handcrafted traditional musical instruments, including bowed psalteries, hammered dulcimers, and fretted dulcimers, a version indigenous to the Appalachians. Classes are offered in construction and playing techniques for several instruments. *Located at 10 Concord Road in Meadows of Dan, the shop is open select days; visitors should call ahead, as teaching and performing schedules may have the owners out of town. Call 276-952-4865 or visit www.meadows-music.com.*

MOUNTAIN HOUSE RESTAURANT

This locally owned restaurant offers authentic Southern cuisine in a casual atmosphere. The menu features items such as honey ham, chili beans, and homemade pies. A wide range of specials is offered daily. *Located on U.S. 58 (2639 Jeb Stuart Highway), it is open for lunch and dinner daily except Sunday. For more information, call 276-952-2999.*

Nancy's Homemade Fudge

Situated less than a mile from the parkway, this confectionary features over 50 flavors of original-recipe fudge, including Rocky Road and raspberry cheesecake. Visitors may observe the fudge-making process through viewing windows and browse numerous candy cases filled with a large selection of hand-rolled truffles and freshly made chocolates. Nancy's specialties include hand-pulled nut brittles and chocolate-covered graham crackers. *Located at 2684 Jeb Stuart Highway, it is open seven days a week. Guided tours of the work area are offered Monday through Thursday. For more information, call 276-952-2112.*

Poor Farmer's Market and Sandwich Shop

An old-fashioned country store, this market features uniquely Appalachian products including handmade quilts, books by local authors, and regional music. Fresh fruits and vegetables are available, as are mountain honey, homemade apple butter, and fresh-cut flowers in season. Visitors can put together a picnic lunch or play checkers and eat ice cream on the porch. *Located on U.S. 58 East (2616 Jeb Stuart Highway), Poor Farmer's Market is open seven days a week. For more information, call 276-952-2670 or visit www.poorfarmersmarket.com.*

Visitor Center

Visitors can pick up brochures on local attractions at the Patrick County Blue Ridge Visitor Center. Complimentary county maps are also available. *Located at 2577 Jeb Stuart Highway, it is open seven days a week during parkway season. For more information, call 276-694-6012.*

STOP #6 MEADOWS OF DAN AREA

BLUE RIDGE PASSAGE RESORT

The original Cockram's Mill building was constructed in 1884 to handle large-scale production. The gristmill was unique because it was designed with two turbine wheels rather than the typical single overshot wheel. In the 1930s, a Meadows of Dan merchant wished to open an ice-cream parlor down the street from Cockram's Mill. A wire was run from the mill-pond to supply electricity to the parlor and most of the businesses along the street. Today, Blue Ridge Passage includes a pizza parlor and an ice-cream shop. The *Dan River Queen*, a newly constructed riverboat, offers rides, bluegrass music, and dancing. The restored Cockram's Mill, adjacent to the site, is listed on the Virginia Landmarks Register. Appalachian-style log cabins can be rented year-round. *Located on U.S. 58 (4037 Jeb Stuart Highway), Blue Ridge Passage is open select days and weekends; music and carousel rides are offered on Saturdays. For more information, call 276-952-3456 or visit www.blueridgepassageresort.com.*

HILLTOP CAFÉ

In the 1930s, this café was a general store and service station. Famous for its ice cream and milk shakes, it became a gathering place for the nearby communities of Vesta and Meadows of Dan. It was sold in 1950 to a businessman intending to capitalize on the soda-fountain success of the previous owner. Today, it is Patrick County's oldest restaurant. The present "Southern eclectic" menu features items such as the "Vestaburger," farm-fed catfish, pit-cooked barbecue, batter-dipped okra, and yam sticks. *Located three miles east of Meadows of Dan on U.S. 58 (6168 Jeb Stuart Highway), the café is open select days. For more information, call 276-952-2326.*

Lovers Leap overlooking the Dan River Valley, circa 1893
COURTESY OF HARRY TEMPLE COLLECTION, VIRGINIA TECH SPECIAL COLLECTIONS

LOVERS LEAP OVERLOOK

Lovers Leap takes its name from Indian legend as a spot from which couples would leap to their fate to avoid separation, or where one lover would depart this world to meet his or her partner in the next. The leaping point, a large rock at an altitude of 3,000 feet, is now surrounded by fencing for viewers' safety. Visitors can still navigate a narrow ascent to enjoy a view of five counties. The picnic area is furnished with tables and barbecue pits. Just beyond the park entrance is the original site of the Lovers Leap Tavern and stagecoach stop. *Located on U.S. 58 (Jeb Stuart Highway), the overlook is accessible year-round. For more information, call 276-694-3917.*

POOR FARMER'S FARM

This farm offers fresh mountain fruits and vegetables in season. Its open-air theater hosts local bands for dancing on Sundays in summer. Other seasonal festivities include the Apple Butter Festival in October and the Cabbage Festival in August, which features homegrown fried cabbage served with pinto beans and cornbread, three kinds of homemade fried pies, and a hearty portion of bluegrass music. *Located about four miles outside Meadows of Dan on U.S. 58 East (7958 Jeb Stuart Highway) in the community of Vesta, the farm is open seven days a week. For more information, call 276-952-2560.*

Château Morrisette Winery, Floyd County
COURTESY OF CHÂTEAU MORRISETTE

The South Blue Ridge Trail continues north along the Blue Ridge Parkway. Sites in this stop are located near Mabry Mill between Mileposts 177 and 170.

STOP #7 MABRY MILL

Mabry Mill is such a picturesque tourist spot that several states use it on postcards representing country life. One of the most visited sites along the parkway, it is popular during any season.

CHÂTEAU MORRISETTE WINERY

Founded in 1978, this winery produces more than 150,000 gallons annually. Tours of the timber-frame production facility are offered daily at two-hour intervals. Visitors can stroll the beautiful grounds, mingle with the family's signature Labrador retrievers, and taste the distinctive award-winning wines of Château Morrisette. They may also dine at the winery's gourmet restaurant, which features organically grown Floyd County vege-tables, free-range meats and poultry, and freshly baked bread. The winery hosts an outdoor jazz concert series during the summer. The gift shop offers unique wine-related items. *Located between Mileposts 172 and 171 on Route 177 (287 Winery Road), the winery is open seven days a week. The restaurant is open on select days for lunch and dinner. For more information, call 540-593-2865 or visit www.chateaumorrisette.com.*

Eagles Nest Bed-and-Breakfast

Situated on five wooded acres, this rustic country house offers five guest rooms with private baths. Visitors have access to a cozy sitting area and two large covered porches. The full Southern breakfast served daily includes freshly baked bread and biscuits, sausage gravy, country-cured ham, and eggs cooked to order. Accommodations for disabled guests can be arranged. *Located three miles from Milepost 174 on Route 799 (2983 Connor Grove Road SW), Eagles Nest is open seasonally; visitors should call ahead. Call 540-593-2107 or visit www.eaglesnestbandbva.com.*

Mabry Mill

This mill was established by fifth-generation Virginian Edwin B. Mabry and his wife, the former Lizzie DeHart. Intent on becoming a miller, Mabry purchased land, acquired water power, and constructed an extensive flume system for his sawmill and gristmill. Both mill buildings have been renovated by the National Park Service. The grounds include other interpretive sites designed to explain mountain industry and pioneer culture. Visitors can walk the half-mile Mountain Industry Trail, which features frontier exhibits including a whiskey still, a wheelwright and blacksmith shop, and a log cabin. Demonstrations include basket making, chair caning, spinning, weaving, blacksmithing, and woodworking. On Friday, Saturday, and Sunday, the mill grinds cornmeal to demonstrate the milling process. In the fall, visitors can see sorghum molasses and apple butter being made. Old-time music is performed Sunday afternoons from May through October. The Mill Restaurant offers a taste of mountain fare, serving authentic stone-ground corn and buckwheat cakes, country ham, and homemade desserts. *Mabry Mill is located a mile north of Meadows of Dan between Mileposts 177 and*

Mabry Mill, Blue Ridge Parkway
PHOTOGRAPH BY ANNA FARIELLO

176. The mill's self-guided trail and outdoor museum are accessible year-round. The restaurant is open seven days a week; call 276-952-2947. For information about programs and demonstrations, call 276-745-9660.

MEADOWOOD BED-AND-BREAKFAST

Situated high on a hill overlooking the mountains, Meadowood offers spacious rooms with private or shared baths. A full breakfast is served each morning in the formal Williamsburg-style dining room. The grounds consist of 20 acres of fields and woods, home to a variety of birds, deer, and other wildlife. Guests also enjoy the split-rail fences, the spring-fed streams, the park benches, the walking trails, and the catch-and-release fishing in the stocked pond on the property. *Exit the parkway at Milepost 174 onto Route 758 West (6235 Buffalo Mountain Road). Meadowood is open year-round. For more information, call 540-593-2200 or visit www.blueridgebedandbreakfast.com.*

MOCKINGBIRD NEST

This shop features locally made gifts and crafts, including baskets, pewter, needlework, and dough bowls. *Exit the parkway at Milepost 172 onto Route 726 (3576 Black Ridge Road). The shop is open weekends seasonally and by appointment. For more information, call 540-593-3328.*

Rocky Knob Cabins

These seven cabins were built more than 50 years ago by the Civilian Conservation Corps to house workers while they constructed this portion of the Blue Ridge Parkway. Located in a secluded glade, the concessionaire-run cabins are fully furnished and have stocked kitchens and linens. Guests use a centrally located bathhouse. *Exit the parkway between Mileposts 174 and 173 at Woodberry Road and follow the wooden signs to the office and cabins. Rocky Knob is open seasonally. For more information, call 540-593-3503.*

Slate Mountain Church

Before building the Slate Mountain Church, the Reverend Robert Childress conducted services at the local school. The Slate Mountain congregation was said to have been his favorite, thanks to the outgoing personalities and musical talent of the parishioners. Equally fond of him, the congregation wanted to honor Childress with a spiritual venue of his own. Childress worked with the Slate Mountain folk to fashion a stone church in 1932. In 1951, the church was enlarged and a bell tower was added. Altogether, Childress built seven rock churches in the shadow of Buffalo Mountain. *Exit the parkway between Mileposts 172 and 171 at Route 726 and follow it to Rock Church Road. Sunday services are open to the public.*

Villa Appalaccia Winery

This Tuscan-style country house is situated above Rock Castle Gorge National Forest at an elevation of 3,500 feet. Depending on the season, wines, breads, pestos, meats, and local cheeses are served on either the Tuscan-inspired tasting deck or in the Italian-influenced indoor tasting area. The outdoor deck features views of the vineyards and forest; the indoor tasting area is surrounded by potted olive trees. Visitors may play a game of bocce on the landscaped grounds or arrive for live music on Sunday. A mile away, the vineyards of Villa Appalaccia include four acres of vines bearing a variety of grapes including Cabernet Franc, Malvasia, and Primitivo. Watch for the flying Tuscan banner. *Located at Milepost 170 at the Floyd County-Carroll County line on Route 720 East (752 Rock Castle Gorge), the winery is open select days. For more information, call 540-593-3100 or visit www.villaappalaccia.com.*

Touring automobiles, Whitetop Mountain, 1929
COURTESY OF NORFOLK & WESTERN HISTORICAL PHOTOGRAPH
COLLECTION, VIRGINIA TECH SPECIAL COLLECTIONS

Touring the Parkway

Construction of the yet-unnamed ridge road that would become the Blue Ridge Parkway involved more than the men and money required to build it. Political rivalries shaped the road as certainly as did shovels and dynamite. Determining the route of the parkway was a three-way struggle among Virginia, North Carolina, and Tennessee. While both North Carolina and Tennessee pursued their share of the route aggressively, Virginia played a more passive role. Ironically, in the end, Virginia wound up with half the mileage, while none of the parkway passes through Tennessee.

In the earliest stages, citizens and politicians in Carroll County, Virginia, argued that the parkway should pass by the Pinnacles of Dan, an impressive natural feature. Craig and Giles counties petitioned for a different route. Their proposal had the parkway passing through their jurisdictions on the way to Pulaski, Bland,

Wythe, Smyth, and Grayson counties before entering Tennessee. Understandably, this more westerly route found favor with Tennessee politicians, who argued for a third of the parkway to fall within their state's borders.

But such an alliance proved unsuccessful. In the sometimes-heated negotiations, Tennessee may have lost out because of the belligerence of one of its United States senators, Kenneth McKellar, whose "unseemly conduct" was disruptive enough to make it into the official record.[1] In Virginia, negotiations were hampered by the fact that the officially appointed state delegation could not agree on a route. Such internal disagreement compromised their position and weakened Virginia's chances of placing the parkway squarely within its borders. In 1934, a federal delegation was dispatched from Washington, D.C., to examine several proposed routes. It visited, among other places, Mountain Lake and Whitetop Mountain in southwestern Virginia. With such beautiful sites in contention and no clear-cut choice, the process remained torn by political rivalries.

The political struggle between Knoxville, Tennessee, and Asheville, North Carolina, was most vociferous. Each state claimed that tourism was essential to its economy. Letters and editorials filled the towns' papers. Finally, taking a bold step, a contingent of Asheville citizens appealed directly to the president, sending him an album of enlarged scenic photographs. Bound in red Moroccan leather, the album had *Franklin Delano Roosevelt* engraved on its cover.

The culmination of the yearlong debate came at a meeting held at the Department of Interior in September 1934. The official delegations from Tennessee and North Carolina each had an opportunity to present their case as to why the parkway should be located in their state. Virginia senator Harry Byrd was asked why he didn't weigh in on the project. After all, some have credited Byrd with planting the idea for the parkway in the president's mind when Roosevelt dedicated the Civilian Conservation Corps camp in what would soon become Shenandoah National Park. In a letter to Virginia's highway commissioner, Byrd defended his diplomatic approach of staying out of the pitched battle between two neighboring states.[2]

Tennessee and North Carolina officials both had persuasive

arguments for building the parkway in their states. On the Tennessee side was the fact that construction would be less costly and the scenery more diverse. On the North Carolina side was the scenery itself—the lofty elevations and unending views of the highest elevations of the Appalachians. But the overwhelming support shown by western North Carolina citizens probably carried the day. They sent 18 Pullman cars of enthusiasts to Washington, along with a special car for the governor and other officials. Upon their arrival, each North Carolinian was given a large white nametag to wear. A sea of white badges greeted the committee in the packed auditorium. Along with its sheer numbers, the North Carolina delegation also came prepared with talking points and visual aids, including a diorama. In the end, the route was awarded to North Carolina. But Senator Byrd's state did not lose out, as half of the 469-mile parkway would lie within Virginia's borders.

After the route was settled upon, work on the parkway was delayed numerous times. It was six months from the day the first rocks were blasted from the mountains in September 1935 until the first shovel hit Virginia soil. Construction on the parkway was piecemeal for a number of reasons. Delays were caused by the acquisition of land, which was not as easy a task as planners had hoped. States were accustomed to the necessity of acquiring a right of way, but the notion of a scenic easement was a new concept. A scenic easement called for restrictions to prevent the development of land that motorists might see from the parkway—what today's National Park Service refers to as the road's "viewshed." This type of easement was less understood than a physical easement, which allowed for direct access or provided land for a wide-shouldered roadbed. In Virginia, other delays were caused by the state's concerns about the collection of gasoline taxes and other jurisdictional issues that had to be ironed out. Finally, an eight-mile section of Virginia's part of the parkway was begun in 1936 near Adney's Gap south of Roanoke, on a day celebrated only every four years—February 29.

Before its official name was adopted, the Blue Ridge Parkway bore a number of tentative names, including the Park-to-Park Highway, the Appalachian Scenic Highway, the Roosevelt Parkway, and the very cumbersome Shenandoah National Park to Great

Historic rural farmstead
PHOTOGRAPH BY ANNA FARIELLO

Smoky Mountains National Parkway. Planned to employ 4,000 out-of-work men for two years, the parkway took two decades to complete. Its final cost approached $100 million, a far cry from the estimated $6 million at its inception. But the cost was put into perspective by parkway superintendent Sam Weems in 1962, when he remarked that over the 25 years of its construction, the parkway's cost to the individual taxpayer was a mere two cents per year.[3]

[1] Harley E. Jolley, *The Blue Ridge Parkway* (Knoxville: University of Tennessee Press, 1969), 65. According to Jolley in *The CCC in the Smokies*, Senator McKellar later leveled charges against park superintendent Ross Eakin and led the successful movement to disband the Civilian Conservation Corps in 1942.

[2] Jolley, *The Blue Ridge Parkway*, 86.

[3] Jolley, *The Blue Ridge Parkway*, 121.

The trail continues north along the Blue Ridge Parkway
to the vicinity of Rocky Knob. The sites at this stop are located
between Milepost 169 and Milepost 167.

STOP #8   ROCKY KNOB

BUFFALO MOUNTAIN OVERLOOK

This overlook is situated in a "saddle" of the parkway looking east across the Blue Ridge plateau and lowlands and west toward Buffalo Mountain. Walking trails depart from the parking area and weave along the rim of the valley amid dense rhododendron and mountain laurel. *Located at Milepost 168, the overlook is accessible year-round.*

ROCK CASTLE GORGE LOOP

This loop trail running between the visitor center and Rocky Knob Campground covers a strenuous 11 miles at elevations ranging from 3,572 feet at Rocky Knob to 1,700 feet at Rock Castle Creek. From the campground, the trail descends three miles to the creek, revealing evidence of homesites abandoned by mountain folk in the early 1900s. Rock Castle was once an active mountain community. A number of mills were located along the creek, and apple orchards grew on the hillsides. The gorge loop follows the creek for three miles, offering glimpses of unusual cove trees like black maples and additional remnants of frontier homesites. It then begins its winding ascent to Grassy Knoll and parallels the parkway on its return to the campground. Rock Castle Gorge takes its name from the area's crystalline quartz formations. *Located at Milepost 167, the loop is accessible year-round.*

VISITOR CENTER

This converted gas station offers a 72-site camping area and trailheads

Buffalo Mountain
PHOTOGRAPH BY ANNA FARIELLO

for both the Rocky Knob Picnic Loop and the Black Ridge Trail. The Rocky Knob Picnic Loop, an easy one-mile loop through a second-growth forest, is excellent for bird-watching. The Black Ridge Trail is a moderate three-mile loop that passes along a seldom-used gravel road, then across the parkway to join the Rock Castle Gorge Loop for its return to the visitor center. At the overlooks, lucky hikers may witness migratory hawks in spring and fall. The Rocky Knob Visitor Center provides information on National Park Service naturalist programs, campfire talks, and guided hikes. Visitors can seek out a ranger, browse the small bookstore, and explore mini-exhibits on regional wildlife and foliage. *Located at Milepost 169, the visitor center is open seven days a week in season. For more information, call 540-745-9660.*

Continue north on the parkway from Rocky Knob to the
intersection with Route 8 at Milepost 165. To continue the
South Blue Ridge Trail, depart the parkway for Route 8
North and travel eight miles into Floyd.

Stop #9   On the Way to Floyd

Route 8 runs from the Virginia lowlands north, cutting across the Blue Ridge through Tuggle Gap. Sites included at this stop are located in and around Tuggle Gap and along Route 8 on the way to the town of Floyd. Prior to 1896, Floyd was known as Jacksonville, named for President Andrew Jackson. A few sites retain the historic name.

Jacksonville Center

This historic dairy complex, also known as "the Old Jacksonville Barn," has been resurrected and remodeled to serve as a community center for arts and culture and as a visitor center providing information on Floyd and the region. The center has an art gallery. *Located on Route 8 (220 Parkway Lane South), it is open regular business days and weekends seasonally. For more information, call 540-745-2784 or visit www.jacksonvillecenter.org.*

Old Jacksonville Cemetery

This cemetery contains graves dating to 1833, including the unmarked tomb of Patrick Henry's son, Nathaniel. Another interesting feature is a rare tomb table, an impressive slab of native stone raised on four legs. Locally mined and sawn soapstone, a mineral form of talc that is often yellow or gray in color, was used in a great deal of construction in Floyd. *Located off Route 8 on Baker Street, the cemetery is accessible year-round.*

Rakes Millpond

This site is named for local grist miller Jarman Rakes, who was noted

Newt Hylton playing clawhammer banjo, circa 1950
PHOTOGRAPH BY EARL PALMER, COURTESY OF EARL PALMER COLLECTION, VIRGINIA TECH SPECIAL COLLECTIONS

for an inventive entrepreneurial scheme—he charged customers a small fee to fish in the millpond while they waited for their flour. What remains of Rakes Mill is the stone facing of the milldam. It dates to the early 19th century. Today, the site is maintained by the National Park Service. It is a popular spot for picnics and wildlife viewing. *Located at Milepost 164, the site is accessible year-round.*

TUGGLES GAP RESTAURANT AND MOTEL

In the mid-18th century, the Reverend Tuggle built one of the area's earliest homes near what is now the intersection of the Blue Ridge Parkway and Route 8. This old-fashioned motel located near Tuggle's early cabin is a parkway landmark offering seven handicapped-accessible rooms, each with a private bath. The Tuggles Gap Restaurant serves traditional mountain fare like griddlecakes, homemade biscuits and gravy, country ham, and freshly baked pies. It will also pack picnic lunches upon request. *Located at Milepost 165 (3351 Parkway Lane South), it is open year-round. For more information, call 540-745-3402.*

To reach Floyd from the Blue Ridge Parkway, follow Route 8 North from Milepost 165 for eight miles to the town center, located at the intersection with U.S. 221.

Stop #10   Downtown Floyd

Prior to the creation of Floyd County in 1831, the 383 square miles that comprise the region were referred to as "the Little River area." Settlement along this crest of the Blue Ridge followed the competitive surveying of the area by the Woods River Land Company and the Royal Company of Virginia. In downtown Floyd, visitors will find a balance of traditional influences and contemporary flair. Main Street is a mélange of shops, studios, eateries, and historic sites. Floyd's history of craftsmanship is visible in its architecture. Master brick mason Henry Dillon designed and built several structures that stand today. The Tazewell Headen House on Main Street is a massive Georgian Revival home surrounded by wrought-iron fences and original outbuildings. Dillon was also responsible for the rebuilding of the Floyd County Courthouse in 1851. Other Floyd buildings are made of native Appalachian soapstone, including the 1914 Floyd Press Building and the 1912 Brown Howard law office. With its single stoplight and multitude of historic buildings, Floyd encapsulates the tradition and culture of southwestern Virginia.

Blue Ridge Restaurant

Established in the late 1800s as a bank, this restaurant has a walk-in cooler located in the original bank vault. A restaurant since 1931, the popular Blue Ridge serves generous portions of home-style cooking in a small-town atmosphere. The menu features country dishes like biscuits and gravy, mashed potatoes with creamery butter, and homemade pies made with farm-fresh eggs. *Located at 107 East Main Street, the restaurant is open seven days a week. For more information, call 540-745-2147.*

Chamber of Commerce

Here, visitors can pick up brochures on local businesses and attractions, as well as a pamphlet describing a self-guided walking tour of downtown Floyd. The chamber is staffed at midday to answer questions; brochures are available at other times. *Located south of the stoplight on Route 8 (210-B South Locust Street), it is open regular business days. For more information, call 540-745-4407 or visit www.visitfloyd.org.*

County Records

County Records is a major distributor of bluegrass and old-time music. The business dates to 1965, when there was no single place in the region to purchase such recordings. County Records' selection of more than 5,000 tapes, records, albums, books, and videos is housed in the historic Floyd Theatre, which dates to 1834. County Records also stocks the Floyd Country Store with a selection of authentic mountain music. *Located at 117-A West Main Street, down Talley's Alley, it is open daily except Sunday. For more information, call 540-745-2922.*

Earth Dance

This rock, gem, and jewelry shop features the work of local craftswoman Pat Sharky. In addition to gem and fossil jewelry and carvings, customers can choose from a large collection of geological specimens, fossils, and meteorites. Earth Dance also has an exhibit of local rock finds. *Located on Route 8 South (211 South Locust Street), it is open select days. For more information, call 540-745-7961 or 540-651-4819 or visit www.earthdance.swva.net.*

Farmer's Supply

Founded in the early 1900s, Farmer's Supply was originally located in the white frame building that now houses the Floyd Country Store. In the 1920s, the business was purchased by the grandfather of present manager Jack Lawson and relocated to a storefront that dates to 1897. At one time, Farmer's Supply was an agent for Ford automobiles. The business changed hands several times before it was put up for public sale in the early 1980s.

Wagons assembled in front of Farmer's Supply, Floyd
PHOTOGRAPH BY ANNA FARIELLO

Lawson's grandfather bought his old business back, and it has since remained in the family. Today, Farmer's Supply survives as the oldest active business in Floyd. It offers general merchandise, old-time hardware, kitchen accessories, oil lamps, seeds, and lawn, garden, and pet supplies. For the kids, the store stocks a full line of Radio Flyer wagons, displayed along the sidewalk across from Floyd's one traffic light. *Located at 101 East Main Street, Farmer's Supply is open daily except Sunday. For more information, call 540-745-4455.*

FLOYD COUNTRY STORE

This shop was established in 1913 as Cockram's General Store. Music on Friday evenings has drawn young and old, strangers and friends for the past 20 years. From its beginnings in the early 1980s, when a local band practiced in the store on Friday nights, the Friday Nite Jamboree has evolved into a traditional-music extravaganza. Usually starting at 6:30 P.M. with country and gospel, the evening progresses with livelier late-night musical performances. A nominal admission fee gets you five bands back to back and access to the dance floor for "flatfooting" to bluegrass beginning at 7:30 P.M. *The Floyd Country Store is located just south of the stoplight on Route 8 (206 South Locust Street). For more information, call 540-745-4563.*

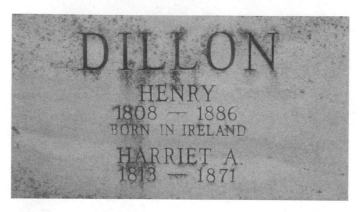

Gravestone of builder and stonemason Henry Dillon, Floyd
PHOTOGRAPH BY ANNA FARIELLO

FLOYD COUNTY COURTHOUSE

The original courthouse was constructed in 1834 by James Toncray, the most prolific architect of southwestern Virginia courthouses before the Civil War. After the structure deteriorated, it was replaced with one built by popular brick mason Henry Dillon in 1851. The contemporary courthouse is the third on this site, as Dillon's was razed in 1951. It features traditional brickwork and stone casings and houses historical records and genealogical resources. Visitors or residents can stop here to pick up a fishing license. *Located at 100 East Main Street, it is open regular business days. For more information, call 540-745-9330.*

MARCELLA'S BOUTIQUE

Floyd County native Jeanie O'Neill has converted her grandfather's brick medical office into a studio, gallery, and boutique featuring her original paintings, handbags, garments, and unique furniture. A lively collaged mural hangs on the brick exterior. *Located at 418 East Main Street, it is open select days. For more information, call 540-745-4327 or visit www.jeanieoneill.com.*

NEW MOUNTAIN MERCANTILE

Located in the historic Roller Mill Building, this shop features the work of over 150 local and regional artists specializing in Appalachian, contemporary, and Native American design. Items for sale include hand-wrought jewelry, pottery, stained glass, weavings, woodwork, folk-art dolls, children's toys, natural-fiber clothing, and bent-willow furniture. *Located south of the stoplight on Route 8 (114-A South Locust Street), it is open seven days a week. For more information, call 540-745-4278.*

ODDFELLAS CANTINA

Located next door to the historic Odd Fellows Hall, this building with its early plate-glass windows was once a meeting house for the Masons. Inside, the original tin ceilings have been beautifully restored. Now a full-service restaurant, Oddfellas specializes in Appalachian-Latino cuisine. The eclectic menu features Floyd-produced organic vegetables, Floyd County beef, and breads baked in a wood-fired brick oven. Live music is performed nightly; traditional mountain music is offered on Thursdays. The restaurant also serves as a gallery for local artists. *Located on Route 8 (110-A North Locust Street) north of the stoplight, it is open daily except Monday. For more information, call 540-745-3463 or visit www.oddfellascantina.com.*

OLD CHURCH GALLERY

This 30-year-old organization emphasizes local history and features art exhibits that run the gamut from the untutored to the professional. The gallery houses a regional archaeological collection and photographic archive. The members are currently compiling an extensive oral history of the Little River area complete with interviews from local tradesmen and craftsmen. *Located off U.S. 221 North (110 Wilson Street), it is open weekends seasonally and by appointment. For more information, call 540-763-2338.*

SCHOOL HOUSE FABRICS

Established in 1971, this shop is located in the former Floyd Elementary School building, which dates to the 19th century. Three floors of fabrics and supplies draw customers from miles around. Each room is arranged according to fabric—linens, wools, bridal silks, and tulles. Draperies and quilts are for sale, as is an extensive selection of laces, trims, and notions. An extra building in the back contains large reels of upholstery fabric, tapestries, and quality remnants. *Located on Route 8 a mile north of Floyd, it is open daily except Sunday. For more information, call 540-745-4561.*

WINTER SUN

Winter Sun was founded in 1983 by an art-school graduate from North Carolina. The inspiration came from a visit to Ecuador that led the founder to create a company producing hand-batiked natural-fiber clothing for women. Winter Sun seeks to promote fair trade, social responsibility, and cultural awareness. It also sponsors two internationally inspired bands that perform in the warehouse community room. Solazo is a group of Central and South American musicians; the Kusun Ensemble travels the world from Ghana, Africa. *Located in a historic commercial brick building on Route 8 (302 South Locust Street), Winter Sun is open seven days a week. For more information, call 540-745-7882 or visit www.wintersuninc.net.*

From the intersection of Route 8 and U.S. 221 at the stoplight in Floyd, turn north on U.S. 221. Return to the loop trail by backtracking along U.S. 221 South and continue into the heart of Floyd County.

SPUR ALONG U.S. 221 NORTH

Just north of Floyd was the site of the former Jacksonville Academy (or Floyd Institute), founded in 1846. The highly respected academy drew elite young men from neighboring counties, among them future Confederate general Jeb Stuart. The original buildings were torn down in 1913 during the construction of Floyd County High School. In the process, workmen discovered a quart-sized antique stoppered bottle in a corner of a basement. The black bottle contained pages from a New York newspaper that bore copies of the Declaration of Independence, as well as a slip of paper listing the trustees and supporters present at the dedication of the school in 1847. Not far from the brick boys' academy was a frame building with an immense fireplace. Simply called the Female Academy, it was staffed entirely by women, save one male Lutheran minister who taught during the Civil War. The schools were combined sometime after the war.

Eagle's Wings Estate Bed-and-Breakfast

Situated on 150 acres, this restored Colonial-style home is surrounded by walking trails and authentic split-rail fences. Eagle's Wings offers four guest rooms, each with access to the home's library with fireplace, parlor with baby grand piano, three seasonal porches, and fishing pond. The Royal and Rose suites feature antique beds. A buffet breakfast is served in the dining room on Saturday and Sunday mornings. *Located off U.S. 221 on Route 615 (1384 Christiansburg Pike), it is open year-round. For more information, call 540-745-4174.*

Phelps Pottery Studio

Tom Phelps's studio features a wide variety of functional stoneware pottery and ornamental pieces for the home, including unique face pots and wall hangings. *Located off U.S. 221 about eight miles outside Floyd at 636 Stagecoach Run SE, it is open by appointment. For more information, call 540-745-3145 or visit www.potterystuff.com.*

Wheel-thrown salt-glazed face jug by Tom Phelps, Floyd
COURTESY OF THE ARTIST

Pine Tavern Lodge, Floyd
PHOTOGRAPH BY ANNA FARIELLO

PINE TAVERN LODGE

This family-owned landmark offers seven guest rooms and a private cottage, all furnished with family antiques. The guest rooms have hardwood floors, small breakfast nooks, and back porches. Some have private baths. The cottage includes a full kitchen and full bath. *Located 1.5 miles from the Floyd stoplight on U.S. 221 North (585 Floyd Highway North), it is open year-round. For more information, call 540-745-4428.*

PINE TAVERN RESTAURANT

Since 1927, the Pine Tavern has hosted speakeasies, country dances, jukebox nights, and dinner theater. The wood beams and floors and the pine woods surrounding the restaurant create a rustic atmosphere. The menu features country food and fresh homemade desserts. Many dishes have been adapted from the culinary repertoire of the owner's grandmother, Mama Nell. *Located 1.5 miles from the Floyd stoplight on U.S. 221 North (611 Floyd Highway North), it is open select days. For more information, call 540-745-4428 or visit www.thepinetavern.com.*

SEVEN SPRINGS FARM

This farm's slogan is "Organically grown in accordance with nature."

The 125-acre Seven Springs Farm has a community-supported agricultural garden with over five acres of vegetables in cultivation. It also runs an apprenticeship program that teaches the workings of organic farms to would-be farmers. Guests may participate in this program or simply tour the property. The Seven Springs shop and catalog stock all-natural pesticides, cover crops, and organically grown flower and vegetable seeds. *About 10 miles north of Floyd, turn west off U.S. 221 North onto Route 661. The farm is on Route 661 (426 Jerry Lane); at the Seven Springs sign, follow the country drive down to the barn. The farm is open seasonally. For more information, call 540-651-3228 or visit www.7springsfarm.com.*

Staples Farm Petting Zoo

This working farm and local attraction invites guests to tour the grounds and greet an array of unusual animals. Whether llamas, emus, horned Dorset sheep, potbelly pigs, or peacocks, there's an animal for everyone. For those traveling with children, Staples offers hayrides and pony rides. For adults seeking an authentic glimpse of mountain agriculture and industry, there are spinning and weaving demonstrations in season. Visitors may arrange with the farm for a wiener roast. *About nine miles north of Floyd, turn west off U.S. 221 North onto Route 665 (1667 Kings Store Road NE). Hours vary with the season. For more information, call 540-651-3274.*

Vitroyoyo Glass Studio

Founded by master glass artist Timothy Burke, the Vitroyoyo Glass Studio is housed in a rustic wooden structure that was a cattle barn and mountain grocery before its conversion to gallery space in 2000. Visitors are welcome to browse the nearly 300 works on display and to observe the artist and his apprentices as they create hand-blown glass. Commissioned works, sculptures, blown vessels, glass castings, and architectural lighting are but a few of the offerings at Vitroyoyo. *About 13 miles north of Floyd on U.S. 221, turn west onto Route 665. After a mile or so, turn right on Daniels Run Road to reach the studio at 1365 Shawsville Pike. It is open by appointment. For more information, call 540-651-3652 or visit www.vitroyoyo.com.*

Woodland Wonders

Woodland Wonders offers natural jewelry created from bracket fungi, a relative of the woodland mushroom. Designer Penny Lane dries the fungi, either leaves them natural or colors them with vibrant permanent inks, and then adorns them with feathers, fairies, nymphs, and rosebuds. She also sells a variety of earrings, necklaces, brooches, and barrettes. *Located about six miles outside Floyd at 298 Turtle Rock Drive, the shop is open by appointment. For more information, call 540-745-5550.*

To continue the South Blue Ridge Trail, turn onto U.S. 221 South at the traffic light in Floyd and head toward the community of Willis. A spur off U.S. 221 South onto Alum Ridge Road leads to Indian Valley before the trail continues on U.S. 221 to Hillsville.

Stop #11 Willis Area

The following sites are located just outside Floyd along U.S. 221 South and in Willis, a neighboring community.

Ambrosia Farm Bed-and-Breakfast and Pottery

This restored farmhouse is situated on rolling pastureland dotted with streams and wildflowers. The landscape, the sunset views, and the local wildlife make for country living at its finest. Guests have their choice of three bedrooms and a loft, each with original hardwood floors and antiques. They also have access to two large covered porches and an upstairs study for reading and relaxing. Breakfast featuring fresh seasonal produce is served daily. The menu changes but always emphasizes whole foods and sustainable organic farming. An original outbuilding has been converted into a studio and gallery showcasing Caroline Gammarino's clay sculpture and pottery. *Five miles from Floyd on U.S. 221 South, take Canning Factory Road*

(Route 807) to reach the farm at 271 Cox Store Road. It is open seasonally. For more information, call 540-745-6363 or visit www.ambrosiafarm.net.

Canning Factory

Shelor's Mill, a turbine-powered gristmill on Howell's Creek, was purchased by S. B. Huff in the early 1900s. Huff built the Canning Factory and several outbuildings and used the original mill building for storage. In the factory's heyday from the 1930s until the 1950s, it was a major employer, drawing laborers from Floyd and the surrounding counties. The factory canned gallon drums of Old Dominion brand beans, tomatoes, peaches, and original-recipe sauerkraut as provisions for the armed services heading into World War II. Huff began trucking in produce from as far south as Florida. He also made arrangements with local growers. When the factory ceased operations in the 1950s and the parcel was put up for public auction, Herb Shelor bought his family's old homeplace and the remaining

Canning Factory, Floyd County
Photograph by Anna Fariello

factory buildings. *Located at the intersection of U.S. 221 and Route 807 (Canning Factory Road), the factory may be viewed year-round from the road. For more information, call 540-745-2835.*

COSTELLO SCULPTURE

This studio features one-of-a-kind wood-and-stone kinetic sculptures inspired by Eastern cultures. The husband-and-wife owners combine polished soapstone pieces with mahogany, cherry, walnut, and oak to make unique pendulum-like creations. *From U.S. 221 South, turn onto Route 750 North (Alum Ridge Road), drive four miles, then turn west on Route 730 to reach 2226 Duncan's Chapel Road. The studio is open by appointment. For more information, call 540-763-3433.*

GREASY CREEK OUTFITTERS

Founded by Virginia Tech professor Michael Smith, author of *Fishing in the New River Valley*, Greasy Creek offers a variety of tour packages throughout the summer. Guests can book a single night or a long weekend of stream or river fishing for trout, walleye, and smallmouth bass. Also available are canoeing trips on the upper New River and fly-fishing in the Dan River Gorge. Smith hosts the tours and often cooks the catch of the day with fresh garden vegetables for the group's lunch or dinner. The lodging accommodations for overnight packages are at local bed-and-breakfasts. *Located on U.S. 221 about 11 miles southwest of Floyd, Greasy Creek is open seasonally. Call 540-789-7811 to schedule an excursion or visit www.greasycreekoutfitters.com.*

WILD GEESE INN

Situated on 105 acres, this three-story cedar-shingled inn offers walking paths through the woods to the top of Mystic Peak and down to Indian Creek. Three guest rooms are available, each furnished with oak antiques and equipped with a private bath and a patio. Guests have access to a library filled with classics and out-of-print editions. A full breakfast is served in the rustic dining room, paneled in oak and chestnut rescued from old barns on the property. *From U.S. 221 South, turn onto Route 750 North (Alum*

Ridge Road) and drive four miles to the inn, located at 319 Mystic Lane; watch for the signs. The inn is open seasonally. For more information, call 540-789-4889.

WILLIS BAPTIST CHURCH

This was the last of the Reverend Robert Childress's rock churches. It was constructed in 1954, just a few years before he retired. The church's present congregation is Baptist, but older residents of the Slate Mountain area recall attending Presbyterian services with Childress at the pulpit. *The church is located at the intersection of U.S. 221 and Route 799 (Connor Grove Road). Sunday services are open to the public.*

To reach Hillsville, follow U.S. 221 South for 25 miles from Floyd to the intersection with U.S. 52. Turn onto U.S. 52 North, which becomes Main Street and enters the Hillsville Historic District. Brochures for a walking tour are available at the Carroll County Historical Society Museum at 307 North Main Street.

STOP #12 HILLSVILLE

Originally known as Cranberry Plains, Hillsville has its roots in trade and agriculture. The county seat of Carroll County, it is situated in the midst of hardwood forests and mountain streams at an elevation of 2,570 feet. During its beginnings as a trading post along a stagecoach road, the town exported agricultural products including rye, wheat, and corn. Today, the region produces dairy goods, livestock, and field crops. The Hillsville Historic District encompasses five acres along Main Street. In addition to Nuckolls Drug Company, which has served Hillsville for over a century, the street is lined with two- and three-story brick commercial buildings dating to the 1930s and 1940s. Hillsville hosts several cultural festivals throughout the year, including Old Mountain Home Week in October. The Labor Day Flea Market transforms the quiet town into one of the largest retail venues in the Southeast, with over 3,000 vendors of antiques, guns, and country treats like barbecued chicken and kettle corn.

CARROLL COUNTY COURTHOUSE

The original courthouse was located in what is presently the center of Main Street. The second courthouse was erected by Confederate hero Ira Coltrane in 1872 and is now listed on the National Register of Historic Places. The building is best known for the March 14, 1912, shootout between county officials and members of the Allen family. Sensationalized in the Northern press, the incident contributed to the region's reputation as a place of violence and lawlessness. Five people were killed, including the presiding judge, the commonwealth's attorney, and the county sheriff. Four people were subsequently imprisoned, and two were executed. Remodeling has since eradicated every trace of the gunfight save one bullet hole outside the building, on the south staircase riser under the portico. Exhibits about the shootout are on display in the courthouse. *Located at 515 North Main Street, it is open regular business days. For more information, call 276-728-7751.*

CARROLL COUNTY HISTORICAL SOCIETY MUSEUM

The site of the original Hillsville post office, this museum has displays and exhibits on pioneer tools, Civil War uniforms, local settlement, and local military, natural, and cultural history. The large exhibit on the courthouse tragedy includes folk-art dioramas and illustrations. Visitors may pick up a brochure for a self-guided walking tour of Hillsville's historic downtown or sign up for a guided tour with museum staff. *Located at 307 North Main Street, the museum is open select days. Admission is charged. For more information, call 276-728-4113.*

CARTER HOUSE

Named after its most recent owner, this Federal-style brick residence was designed and constructed by a large Carroll County landowner, Fielden Hale. Hale sold the two-story home and 16 acres to entrepreneur James Wilkinson in 1880. Wilkinson is said to have operated a store out of the right side of the basement and a post office from the left. It was in

Wilkinson's store that railroad and coal magnate George Carter took his first job. Carter married the owner's daughter. He is credited with establishing the Carroll County Bank on Main Street in 1906, the same year he and his wife inherited the Wilkinson home. They spent over $250,000 adding a third floor, a two-story wraparound porch, and stucco. *Located at 405 North Main Street, the home may be viewed from the street year-round.*

CARTER HYDRAULIC RAM

Hydraulic rams were manufactured in Europe during the late 18th century. Using power from a rapidly flowing stream, they were designed to pump water to locations an appreciable distance from the source. Hillsville's 1920s ram system was constructed by industrialist George Carter to supply water to the Carter House and nearby residences and establishments. In the 1930s, five other tiny Virginia communities, Damascus included, continued to use the system. Carter's hydraulic ram was eventually replaced by an electric model in the mid-20th century. Today, the town's water-supply system is listed on the National Register of Historic Places. *The site is located off Pine Street in downtown Hillsville. For more information, call 276-728-3331.*

HILLSVILLE DINER

Said to be the oldest diner in Virginia, this classic streetcar-style eatery was brought to Hillsville in 1946 from Mount Airy, North Carolina. The diner serves traditional country food at a short-order counter. The menu features griddlecakes, corn muffins, egg custard, and coconut cream pie. The American streetcar diner dates to the 1800s, when a market developed for mobile lunch wagons set up outside factory gates. By the 1920s, wagon-based restaurants appeared on small plots of land while business was good. When business slowed, the wagons were simply rolled to other locations. *Located at 525 North Main Street, the diner is open daily except Sunday. For more information, call 276-728-7681.*

NORTH END CEMETERY

Carroll County was home to a significant Quaker population in the

Hillsville Diner, Hillsville
PHOTOGRAPH BY ANNA FARIELLO

late 1700s. Their original monthly meeting, organized in 1801, was held on a seven-acre site dubbed Mount Pleasant. At least three other meeting houses in the county served as outposts for the central meeting. One of the smaller meeting houses was located within the boundaries of what is now North End Cemetery. Although little of the building's foundation remains, visitors can explore the graves of several Revolutionary War veterans and other early stones dating to 1812. *The cemetery is located off U.S. 52 on Route 886; turn onto Pine Street. It is accessible year-round during daylight hours.*

NUCKOLLS DRUG COMPANY

In 1931, a fire destroyed much of Hillsville's commercial district, including the original Nuckolls frame building, the attached bank, and the post office. The drug company, rebuilt in brick, is reputed to be the longest continuously operating business in Hillsville. Founded by Chester B. Nuckolls, Sr., a general physician, it was later run by his son, Chester Jr. *Located at 510 North Main Street, it is open daily except Sunday. For more information, call 276-728-2643.*

Old Hillmont Hotel

A surviving landmark of days gone by, the Hillmont dates to the early 1930s. In its heyday, the hotel was frequented by many travelers. It offered elegant dining and hosted evening dances open to the community. The hotel is included in the Hillsville Historic District. *Located at 528 North Main Street, it may be viewed from the road year-round.*

The South Blue Ridge Trail leaves Hillsville via U.S. 52 South to complete the loop to Fancy Gap.

Stop #13 On the Way to Fancy Gap

J. Sidna Allen Home

This eight-room Queen Anne-style house is listed on the National Register of Historic Places. It is also a Virginia Historic Landmark. It has local historical significance as the home of J. Sidna Allen, one of the figures in the 1912 Hillsville courthouse shootout. Though Allen and other family members gained national notoriety as outlaws who engaged in a deadly gun battle with law-enforcement officials, the home reflects their respected position in the community. *The home is on the east side of U.S. 52 South leaving Hillsville. It is open on weekends in the summer and may be viewed from the road year-round. For more information, call 276-728-2594.*

Mountain Plains Fabric

For over a decade, this family-run business has specialized in quilting supplies, draperies, and upholstery fabrics. Its selection of over 10,000 ceramic buttons—the largest in the region—includes letters, figures, and

The Cana Volunteer Fire Department's historic fire truck, Carroll County
PHOTOGRAPH BY ANNA FARIELLO

ornaments. *Located on U.S. 52 (4505 Fancy Gap Highway), it is open daily except Sunday. For more information, call 276-728-7517.*

SUNNY SIDE GENERAL STORE

Founded in 1923, this store continues to be run by the founder's family. Still in its original building, Sunny Side bears the mark of years past with a retro Dr Pepper logo painted on its side. Its merchandise includes outdoor clothing and gear, housewares, ceramics, fabrics, and country furniture. *Located on U.S. 52 (2788 Fancy Gap Highway), it is open daily except Sunday. For more information, call 276-728-2033.*

The trail continues along U.S. 52 South into Fancy Gap, where visitors can pick up I-77 or the Blue Ridge Parkway.

Historic mill, Floyd County
PHOTOGRAPH BY ANNA FARIELLO

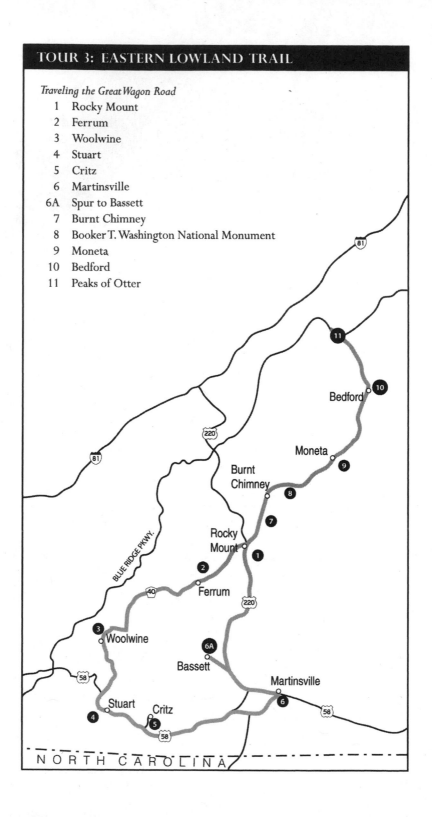

TOUR 3: EASTERN LOWLAND TRAIL

Traveling the Great Wagon Road

Tobacco barns, Franklin County, circa 1952
COURTESY OF VIRGINIA COOPERATIVE EXTENSION COLLECTION,
VIRGINIA TECH SPECIAL COLLECTIONS

Chapter 3

EASTERN LOWLAND TRAIL

The Eastern Lowland Trail begins at Rocky Mount, located 20 miles south of Roanoke on U.S. 220. The trail lies east of the Blue Ridge Parkway in the lowlands at the base of the plateau. From Rocky Mount, it travels through Franklin County and into Patrick County to the county seat of Stuart. There, it picks up U.S. 58 East, crosses into Henry County, and visits Martinsville. Heading north on U.S. 220, the trail passes Philpott Lake on its way to connect with Route 122 North in Rocky Mount. Following U.S. 220 North, the trail travels into the Smith Mountain Lake basin to sites in Burnt Chimney and Moneta, including Booker T. Washington National Monument. Route 122 leads into the historic community of Bedford before taking off for the Peaks of Otter.

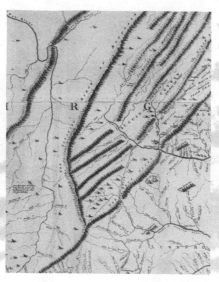

Map of the Great Wagon Road, circa 1750
COURTESY OF THE LIBRARY OF VIRGINIA MAPS COLLECTION

Traveling the Great Wagon Road

With 20,000 inhabitants, Philadelphia was the largest and most cultured city of colonial America. All roads converged at its center. A port city, Philadelphia was a profitable place to bring goods for trade or to purchase finished products fresh from ships arriving from Europe. Leaving Philadelphia, traders headed west to Lancaster, Pennsylvania, before turning south into the Valley of Virginia. There, they traveled a traditional migratory trace long followed by Native Americans, a well-trodden route known as the Warriors Path. In 1744, a treaty was struck that gave title of this roadway to colonists, and the Great Wagon Road was born.

Beginning in the 1750s, members of the Moravian religious sect migrated along this route from settled Northern colonies to establish Bethania and Salem, the latter part of present-day Winston-Salem, North Carolina. Others were also attracted by the lure of available land in the Carolinas. Given this direct route to North Carolina through the Valley of Virginia, the Great Wagon Road was sometimes called the Old Carolina Road.

In 1775, while America was still a colony, the road through the valley appeared on a map. It was described as spanning 435 miles from

Philadelphia to the Yadkin River in North Carolina.[1] Although much of the northern end of the road was wide enough for horse-drawn wagons, migration was primarily on foot. Traders led long lines of packhorses tethered together and loaded with goods, while families walked beside carts and buggies. Some families were better equipped. Pioneer Anne Catherine Antes traveled the road in 1759. "It was not a long journey," she wrote in her journal, "only one month, for our big wagon was drawn by six horses, and we had others for riding."[2]

As the road moved farther and farther from established settlements in Pennsylvania, it became narrow in places, a mere horse path through the woods. In 1779, the Virginia legislature authorized improvement of the road along its entire length through the commonwealth. At key points, the route diverged to connect to other paths leading west into West Virginia and Kentucky. But always the spine remained the Great Wagon Road through the Valley of Virginia, the overland transportation backbone of a nascent American infrastructure.

Knowing that danger faced immigrants in settlements encroaching on Native American territory, Virginia dispatched 50 men to provide security for the crew working on the road.[3] During the next decade, Virginia continued to improve its portion of the route, creating a passage wide enough to accommodate large wagons. The state also ordered that a ferry across the Potomac remain operable, thus guaranteeing travel from coastal colonies across the river and into the valley. In 1794, Congress passed a law that created the United States mail system, authorizing a number of post offices and a complementary series of post roads. It made sense to utilize the already-improved Great Wagon Road as a main point of access, and the act did just that. It designated that a post road begin from Philadelphia and go by way of Lancaster to Pittsburgh.[4]

Heading from Philadelphia into Lancaster County, the Great Wagon Road crossed several rivers. It extended beyond the Potomac at a point called Watkins' Ferry and crossed the James at Looney's Ferry in what is now the town of Buchanan, Virginia. One branch of the road cut west from Buchanan into what are now West Virginia and Kentucky, both part of Virginia at the time. Continuing south from Buchanan, the road followed the valley and dipped into Roanoke, where it forked again. One prong headed in a southeasterly direction via the Staunton River Valley through Rocky Mount and into the Carolinas. The other continued southwest to join the Wilderness Road, which led eventually to Kentucky through the Cumberland Gap. The road's northern terminus was so undisputed that many simply called the route the Great Philadelphia Road. But the southwestern end was shrouded in mystery. Its terminus was wilderness, a tangle of unmapped and unsettled territory.

To accommodate ever-increasing loads of goods through the valley in the mid-18th century, a larger wagon was manufactured in the Conestoga Valley of Lancaster County, Pennsylvania. It took its name from its place of origin. The Conestoga had sides that sloped upward, providing stability to heavy loads transported on rough overland trails. The body of the wagon was built of hardwood—usually hickory, white oak, or poplar—and was topped with a canvas awning stretched over a series of iron hoops. Along its sides were feed boxes for horses. Some even had hinged tailgates to allow easy loading. The Conestoga weighed up to 3,500 pounds and required a team of six strong horses to pull it. Such wagons carried salt, sugar, rum, medicine, and gunpowder, necessities that pioneers could not produce for themselves. Freight-hauling wagons that operated from town to town on fixed schedules were called "liners," a name that was adopted later by seagoing "ocean liners."[5] Though sometimes used by individual families, the Conestoga was primarily a mover of goods for sale. As individuals traversed the territory in smaller farm-made wagons, the Conestoga must have appeared like a tractor-trailer to small-car travelers driving through the same valley today.

Immigrant families and entrepreneurs flooded the road, forming the moving village so richly described by Sharyn McCrumb in her novel *The Songcatcher*:

Just west of Philadelphia a great river of canvas-covered wagons flowed south-southwest toward the backcountry where tall mountains and trackless forest walled out the fainthearted. The wagons headed off to their promised land in a procession like that of the children of Israel on their journey in the Book of Exodus, led by Moses and escorted by the cloud of Jehovah—only the cloud that escorted this exodus was much less exalted in origin: It was Pennsylvania dust, stirred up by hoofs and wheels and the running feet of the restless children. I could barely hear myself think for all the commotion on that well-worn track: Dogs barking as they dodged the dinner-plate hoofs of lowing oxen, babies wailing, wagons creaking, a cacophony of chickens, cattle, goats, and sheep, and above it all, like a grace note in a howling gale, the sound of a lone fife, piping out a spritely tune to cheer us on our way. Why, the road itself was a village.[6]

[1] William O. Steele, *The Old Wilderness Road: An American Journey* (New York: Harcourt Brace, 1968), 24.

[2] Park Rouse, *The Great Wagon Road from Philadelphia to the South* (New York: McGraw-Hill, 1973), 80.

[3] Thomas Speed, *The Wilderness Road: A Description of the Routes of Travel by Which the Pioneers and Early Settlers First Came to Kentucky* (Louisville, Ky.: J. P. Morton & Company, 1886), 29.

[4] Speed, *The Wilderness Road*, 66.

[5] Rouse, *The Great Wagon Road*, 94, 164-65.

[6] Sharyn McCrumb, *The Songcatcher: A Ballad Novel* (New York: Penguin Books, 2001), 136.

Drover crossing the tracks in front of the post office, Cambria
COURTESY OF EARL PALMER COLLECTION, VIRGINIA TECH SPECIAL COLLECTIONS

Stop #1 Rocky Mount

Franklin County, established in 1789 and named for Benjamin Franklin, is the seventh-largest county in Virginia. Its altitude varies from 900 feet in the lake basin to more than 3,200 feet at Cahas Knob along the Blue Ridge Parkway. When the county was formed, it elected as its county seat Rocky Mount, a sleepy village in the shadow of Bald Knob. A log courthouse was constructed in 1786 on land belonging to a local iron master and a gentleman by the name of Hill. Adjacent to the courthouse, the two men built a tavern, a business office, and a dairy. When approached by would-be town administrators, the pair refused to lease even an inch of their property. Citizens hotly contested the pair's control of their community and established a new village, Mount Pleasant, nearby. The two villages grew side by side in an atmosphere of antagonism and rivalry until 1873, when they were incorporated together as Rocky Mount. After the Franklin & Pittsylvania and the Norfolk & Western rail lines arrived, a commercial town center developed. Today, Rocky Mount, the industrial and commercial center of Franklin County, boasts a National Historic District.

Bethel A.M.E. Church

An outstanding example of architectural preservation, this one-story frame building with an original tin roof was constructed in 1913. It is the county's oldest African-American church building still in use. *The church is located at 100 Hale Street. Sunday services are open to the public. For more information, call 540-489-3045.*

Blue Lady Bookshop and "The Grove"

Known as "The Grove," the Greek Revival home constructed in 1854 for a local businessman and his wife became the center of John Hale's tobacco plantation, which covered much of what is presently downtown Rocky Mount. Within the contemporary parcel are several original outbuildings, including two frame storage buildings, an office, brick slave quarters, a smokehouse, and a kitchen. The office accommodated Confederate general

Jubal Early's law practice prior to the Civil War. The Grove's notable residents have included statesman Edward Watts Saunders, but its most intriguing guest may be the Lady in Blue, an apparition who haunts the home, according to local lore. Named for the legendary apparition, the Blue Lady Bookshop is housed in Early's 1850 law office. It is operated by writer and artist Ibby Greer, who stocks an extensive selection of works by regional writers, Appalachian and Civil War histories, and new fiction. *Located at 50 Floyd Avenue, the bookshop is open regular business days. For more information, call 540-483-3692.*

Chamber of Commerce

The Franklin County chamber's offices are on the street level of a historic brick commercial building. The chamber is dedicated to enhancing opportunities for local cultural, educational, and commercial organizations to work with each other and with the community. *Located at 261 Franklin Street, it is open regular business days. For more information, call 540-483-9542.*

Claiborne House

This bed-and-breakfast is an excellent example of the popular Queen Anne style, with its dainty turrets, decorative trim, and wraparound porch. This architectural style appeared in southwestern Virginia communities between 1880 and 1910. The 1895 Claiborne House is surrounded by landscaped grounds, gardens, and orchards. Guests enjoy coffee service and breakfast; lunch and dinner are available upon request. *Located at 185 Claiborne Avenue, it is open year-round. For more information, call 540-483-4616 or visit www.claibornehouse.net.*

Dairy Queen

From the outside, Rocky Mount's Dairy Queen does not look much different from thousands of other ice-cream parlors, but this one is a hub of local talent. A free bluegrass concert and jam session are held every Thursday. *Located on Route 40 (995 Franklin Street) south of town, it is open seasonally. For more information, call 540-483-7754.*

Farmers' Market

An open-air wooden shelter was erected in 1998 at Citizens Square to provide a venue for agricultural sales and to create a community setting for special events. The farmers' market sells cut flowers, homemade condiments, baked goods, and fresh local produce in season. It also hosts Dairy Day in June, Folklife Fridays in October, and seasonal holiday concerts. *Located at the intersection of Franklin and East College streets, it is open seasonally; hardy farmers seem willing to stay into December. For more information, call 540-483-0907.*

Franklin County Courthouse

The first Franklin County Courthouse was a log structure built at Rocky Mount in 1786. Constructed of locally produced red brick in 1831, the second courthouse served for almost a century. The only remnant of that structure is an allegorical painting of Justice that hangs at the front of the present-day courtroom. In 1910, the brick courthouse was demolished to make way for a grander design. Roanoke architect H. H. Huggins, rumored to have had one wife and family too many, constructed the current white-and-cream building, which stands on the foundation of the second courthouse. The building is a medley of architectural styles, including Beaux-Arts and Italianate. Its distinctive features include a hip roof, a cupola with an open belfry, and a three-bay portico. The courthouse has hosted many bootleg trials; Franklin County continues to live down its nickname, "the Moonshine Capital." On the grounds are historic markers, Confederate monuments, and a bicentennial time capsule sealed on December 31, 1976. *Located at 275 South Main Street, it is open regular business days. For more information, call 540-483-3065.*

Franklin County Historical Society

The historical society was chartered in 1968 to document and preserve local history. It operates a small museum on the second floor of the Retail Merchant's Association Building. Oil paintings and photographs from private collections hang along the walls above displays of early agricultural implements, personal artifacts, and railroad memorabilia. Staff members

Franklin County Courthouse, Rocky Mount. COURTESY OF LOCAL HISTORY COLLECTION, VIRGINIA TECH SPECIAL COLLECTIONS

are available to answers questions and to steer those wishing to pursue historical or genealogical research. The gift shop stocks books on area history, some interesting reprints of period journals, and the locally authored 1935 *Virginia Housekeeper's Guide. Located at 95 Floyd Avenue, it is open select days. Visitors should call in advance; call 540-483-1890 or visit www.franklincountyhistoricalsoc.org.*

GRASSY HILL NATURAL AREA PRESERVE

This 1,222-acre property, owned by the commonwealth of Virginia and maintained as a natural area, has a unique ecological story. It is a testament to the historical land-use method that facilitated forest development through fire. According to local Native American history, indigenous tribes used fire to enhance hunting conditions, burning the green, brushy understory and leaving stands of stick-straight white pines, thus eliminating hiding places for wild game. Today, without the periodic application of fire, the forest is mostly mixed hardwoods with patches of Virginia pines, all bounded by open meadows. The preserve is home to endangered flora like Carolina thistle and Menge's flame-flower. *The preserve is located off North*

Main Street on Route 919 (Grassy Hill Road). Parts of the park are closed periodically for resource protection, so please call ahead; the number is 540-265-5234.

HIGH STREET CEMETERY

This large, triangular green was originally the property of one of Rocky Mount's most prominent early families, the Taliaferros. The site of hand-carved monuments dating to 1885, the cemetery holds the remains of prominent citizens like Edward Watts Saunders, who from 1887 to 1920 served as Franklin County's representative in the Virginia House of Delegates and as a United States congressman. Some markers feature colorful inscriptions, like that of Dr. Williams, remembered as "A Shouting Methodist, A Rampant Prohibitionist, and Democrat." *Located at the intersection of High and North streets, the cemetery is accessible year-round. For more information, call 540-483-9542.*

HISTORIC LEE M. WAID SCHOOLHOUSE

In 1915, the Pigg River Baptist Association constructed the Booker T. Washington Normal and Industrial Institute, a two-story building with classrooms and dormitory space for faculty and boarding students. A decade later, a four-room frame building was added with the aid of local funds and a grant from a philanthropic organization headed by Sears & Roebuck president Julius Rosenwald to support school construction for blacks. Also known as the Franklin County Training School, the institute was later renamed for Lee Waid, an African-American businessman and Rocky Mount civic leader. The last graduate of the segregated Lee M. Waid School marched across its stage in 1970. *Located at 332 East Court Street, the school may be viewed from the road year-round. For more information, call 540-483-5736.*

HISTORIC PEOPLES NATIONAL BANK

Constructed in 1928, this brick-and-stone bank has retained several original architectural features. Art Deco scroll-and-spiral designs frame the front entryway. A striking touch is the image of a winged Indian-head nickel carved in low relief above the doorway. *Located at 369 Franklin Street, the bank is open regular business days. For more information, call 540-489-6940.*

Mary Bethune Park

Mary McLeod Bethune was born in 1875 on a rice and cotton plantation in South Carolina. Following the example set by her parents, she sought education as a means to rise above social and cultural limitations based on race. The intelligent and talented Bethune, one of the most successful African-American women of her time, served as an adviser to Presidents Calvin Coolidge, Franklin Roosevelt, and Harry Truman. Among her accomplishments as a social activist and educator, she founded the National Council of Negro Women and the Bethune Women's Club, which initiated the movement to designate Booker T. Washington's homeplace in nearby Hardy a national memorial. Mary Bethune Park, organized by the club in 1941, is maintained by the town of Rocky Mount. *Located at the end of East Street, it is accessible year-round.*

Rocky Mount Post Office

Constructed in 1936, this one-story Colonial Revival building has a handsome mural commissioned by the Depression-era Works Progress Administration. Roy Hilton's 1938 depiction includes three Franklin County scenes—images from the local textile, furniture, and agricultural industries. Here, as in many American towns, the post-office mural is the community's major public artwork and documents a portion of the region's history. *Located at 20 East College Street, the post office is open regular business days. For more information, call 540-483-1530.*

Rocky Mount Presbyterian Church

Built of handmade bricks and influenced by the Gothic tradition, this 1877 church was designed with pointed-arch windows and exterior buttresses. The church is unique for its distinctive proportions, reaching skyward like the cathedrals of Europe from a very narrow foundation. Although the original bell tower no longer exists, the first iron bell hangs in the dooryard. *The church is located at 175 Floyd Avenue. Sunday services are open to the public. For more information, call 540-483-4889.*

Rocky Mount United Methodist Church

The Gothic Revival-style Rocky Mount United Methodist Church was built in 1926. The sanctuary was designed in three sections with an elaborate bell tower separating the church offices from the main chapel. The church is ornamented with arched stained-glass windows on either side of the main vestibule, and the bell tower has pointed-arch ventilation slats. *The church is located at 35 North Main Street. Sunday services are open to the public. For more information, call 540-483-5338.*

Trinity Episcopal Church

This stone-clad structure has a traditional Episcopal Gothic-arched red door. A covered promenade links the vestry and sanctuary and encloses a small garden and walkway. *The church is located at 101 Church Street NE at the corner of South Main Street. Sunday services are open to the public. For more information, call 540-483-5038.*

Visitor Center

The historic Franklin County depot has been renovated to serve as a community and tourist information center. The late-19th-century frame building with an overhang supported by heavy beams was constructed lengthwise along the train tracks. Glass display cases preserve railway artifacts including an 1897 adding machine, lanterns, train tickets, and original rail schedules. Positioned along the exterior walls are larger relics of rail history like vintage cross-arm signals and a dispatcher's desk. Complimentary brochures, maps, and local newspapers are available. For visitors interested in the county seat's architectural history, the center offers a pamphlet outlining a self-guided walking tour. *Located at 52 Franklin Street, the center is open seven days a week. For more information, call 540-483-0948.*

Waid Recreation Area

This 512-acre tract offers hiking and biking trails, picnic shelters, wildflower areas, fishing opportunities, and a wetlands preserve. It is also home to a historic bridge and a preserved section of the 18th-century Great Wagon

Road; along the walking path are remnants of pioneer structures. The Virginia Birding and Wildlife Trail organization recommends that hikers watch for Eastern bluebirds in the park's open areas and white-throated sparrows in the wooded sections. *Follow Route 40 about one mile south from Rocky Mount, turn west on Route 640, and drive about two miles to the junction with Route 800. From there, signs lead to the park entrance. The recreation area is accessible year-round. For more information, call 540-483-9293.*

WASHINGTON IRON WORKS

Built on the banks of Furnace Creek directly across from the granite deposits in Scuffland Hill, this 1777 furnace was fired by a paddle-wheel-powered bellows. The intact 30-foot stone furnace has hearth and bellows openings at ground level. There were once eight lucrative furnaces in Franklin County. One of the oldest furnaces in Virginia, the Washington Iron Works is listed on the National Register of Historic Places and the Virginia Landmarks Register. The furnace is on private property, but the owners are willing to grant permission to visit if contacted by telephone. *The site is located south of Rocky Mount off Route 122; ask for directions. It is accessible year-round with permission; call 540-489-1304.*

The Eastern Lowland Trail leaves Rocky Mount via Route 40 West. Ferrum is located about eight miles southwest of Rocky Mount on Route 40 along the Norfolk & Western rail line.

STOP #2 FERRUM

Local history has it that during a survey at Summit Cut, located off what is now Route 40 on the Norfolk & Western Railway, a surveyor's detector began to spew erratic results. He is purported to have hollered, "Ferrum!" which means iron in Latin, inadvertently naming the community. Progress came to this quiet Appalachian town on wings of steel. The railroad generated commerce, and the local population increased accordingly. The

Rail depot, Ferrum, circa 1917
COURTESY OF NORFOLK & WESTERN HISTORICAL PHOTOGRAPH COLLECTION,
VIRGINIA TECH SPECIAL COLLECTIONS

Ferrum Training School, established in the early 20th century, eventually became Ferrum College, a regional center for folklife and culture.

BLUE RIDGE INSTITUTE FARMSTEAD

This site is dedicated to preserving and promoting the traditional life and culture of the Blue Ridge Mountains. It includes a number of log buildings set amid a working agricultural landscape that re-creates a German-American farmstead from around 1800. Costumed interpreters use period tools and equipment to demonstrate early-19th-century farming methods. They grow crops, prepare food, and perform household chores in keeping with early traditions. *The farmstead, located on the west side of the Ferrum College campus, is open on weekends in summer; call for the current schedule. Group tours may be arranged at other times. Admission is charged. For more information, call 540-365-4416 or visit www.blueridgeinstitute.org.*

BLUE RIDGE INSTITUTE MUSEUM AND GALLERY

Located on the Ferrum College campus, the museum and gallery have been designated the state's Center for Blue Ridge Folklore. The gallery presents rotating exhibits that highlight Virginia folkways past and present. The

Quilt, southwestern Virginia
PHOTOGRAPH BY ANNA FARIELLO

museum sponsors cultural events including the annual Blue Ridge Folklife Festival and the Draft Horse and Mule Show. The gift shop offers folk art, books, recordings of traditional music, and other items related to the region's rich cultural history. *The museum and gallery are located at the intersection of Route 40 and Museum Drive. The exhibit galleries are open year-round; the museum is open seasonally. For more information, call 540-365-4416 or visit www.blueridgeinstitute.org.*

To reach Woolwine from Ferrum, travel southwest along Route 40 through Endicott and the community of Charity, where the trail passes Charity Primitive Baptist Church, organized in 1778.

STOP #3 WOOLWINE

Woolwine is about 30 miles from Ferrum through wooded areas and modest farms. Route 40 intersects Route 8 in Woolwine, where the trail turns south toward Stuart. The road into Woolwine crosses several streams with colorful names—Little and Big Widgeon and Joint Crack Creek, for starters. Woolwine retains remnants of its years as an early agricultural center. Visitors will enjoy the neat mill house near the town center and the small, utilitarian covered bridges on private property.

Bob White Covered Bridge

A small parking spot just off the road brings travelers to the entrance of the board-and-batten Bob White Covered Bridge. Built in 1922, the 80-foot oak-timbered structure is one of the longest operating covered bridges in the state. A walk through the bridge over the Smith River brings visitors to a pretty, shaded spot facing the entrance of the Smith River Church of the Brethren. The church's entryway points away from the modern-day paved road to recall earlier days when the bridge connected Elamsville Road residents with their house of worship. The bridge is maintained by the Patrick County Historical Society. *It is located a mile south of Woolwine. From Route 40, turn onto Elamsville Road; signs point to the bridge, which is accessible year-round.*

Fairy Stone State Park

This park is well known for both its 168-acre lake and its fairy stones. The brown staurolite fairy stones range in size from a quarter-inch to an

Bob White Covered Bridge, Woolwine
Photograph by Anna Fariello

inch in length. Geologists have explained that the crosslike formations occurred as a result of heat and pressure exerted during the formation of the Appalachian chain. When the first roads were cut in Patrick County, settlers were stunned to find these little crosses in the roadbeds. For many years, people held them in superstitious awe, firm in the belief that they protected wearers against witchcraft, sickness, accidents, and disaster. In addition to scouting fairy stones, park visitors can fish, swim, picnic, and hike the 11 wooded trails of varying lengths and degrees of difficulty. The visitor center has exhibits on area plant and animal life and fairy-stone folklore. *The park is located 10 miles from Woolwine; follow Route 8 South to Route 57 East to reach the entrance. Admission is charged. The park grounds are open year-round; the visitor center is open seasonally. For more information, call 276-930-2424.*

JACK'S CREEK COVERED BRIDGE

This oak-timbered bridge, constructed in 1914, runs 40 feet across the Smith River. Older than the nearby Bob White Covered Bridge, it is one of eight covered bridges still standing in Virginia. Like the Bob White Covered Bridge, it is maintained by the Patrick County Historical Society. Visitors may park along the road and walk through the Virginia Historic Landmark. *Located two miles south of Woolwine on Route 615 (Jack's Creek Road) off Route 8, it is accessible year-round. For more information, call 540-694-6012.*

MOUNTAIN ROSE INN

The Mountain Rose Inn was built by local entrepreneur Joseph DeHart in 1901 of wood cut and dried on the property and bricks fired in the property's kiln. The 100-acre homestead faces the original site of the famed Mountain Rose Distillery, one of the few legal distilleries operating in Virginia during Prohibition. Situated close to Rock Castle Creek, the distillery offered farmers a way to profit when grain prices dipped. Five large rooms are available at the inn, each with a working fireplace, a porch, and a private bath. Guests enjoy a three-course breakfast and afternoon tea or sherry in a parlor illuminated by oil lamps. They have access to walking trails, a swimming pool, and a trout-stocked creek. *Located on Route 40*

Smith River Church of the Brethren, Woolwine
PHOTOGRAPH BY ANNA FARIELLO

(1787 Charity Highway) about two miles outside Woolwine, the inn is open year-round. For more information, call 276-930-1057 or visit www.mountainrose-inn.com.

OLD SPRING FARM BED-AND-BREAKFAST

On the way up this farm's winding gravel drive is a small family cemetery tucked beneath mixed hardwoods. An 1885 marker is dedicated in memory of a "Darling Grandmother." The gravel road leads to an 1883 farmhouse bordered by fences, pastures, and an array of barns and outbuildings set amid a beautiful Blue Ridge landscape. Old Spring Farm, purchased 20 years ago by a Connecticut horse breeder, operates today in conjunction with a working farm. Guests can witness the rearing of Appaloosa saddle horses, meet foals, and, with luck, catch a timely glimpse of Canada geese, hawks, wild turkeys, and deer. The accommodations are in spacious rooms with skylights and Jacuzzis. *Located between Ferrum and Woolwine on Route 40 (7629 Charity Highway), the bed-and-breakfast is open year-round. For more information, call 276-930-3404 or visit www.oldspringfarm.com.*

1947 Star Theater, Stuart
Photograph by Anna Fariello

In Woolwine, the Eastern Lowland Trail picks up Route 8 South for about 10 miles to its intersection with U.S. 58. It then follows U.S. 58 East to Stuart before traveling on to Martinsville.

Stop #4 Stuart

In 1884, the Patrick County seat was moved to Stuart in honor of Confederate general Jeb Stuart, who was born in nearby Laurel Hill. Educated at West Point, Stuart rose through the ranks of the military to become a key player in the War Between the States. He and his famed horse, Cavalry, have gone down in history as Robert E. Lee's eyes and ears in northern Virginia. Dappled with old dairy barns, the gently winding Route 8 travels past the I. M. Akers General Merchandise Store and its service-station carport, constructed in the 1920s by a local businessman from the Buffalo Ridge community. Today's quiet community of Stuart was once a thriving commercial center dubbed "the Heart of the Blue Ridge." Its rail depot saw considerable activity shipping bushels of chestnuts and other agricultural products to Northern cities.

Blue Ridge Mission School Historic Marker

According to a historic marker along the east side of Route 8 outside Stuart, the Blue Ridge Mission School was established in 1916 under the supervision of Virginia Baptists. Such church-supported schools were often the only educational institutions in the mountains until the state assumed responsibility for education. Virginia's educational system developed slowly; the state was among the last to pass compulsory education laws. The mission school accommodated day and boarding students in the elementary and secondary grades. *The marker stands northwest of the school's original site at the intersection of Route 613 (Pilson Sawmill Road) and Route 8. It may be viewed from the road year-round.*

Historic District

Listed on the Virginia Landmarks Register, Stuart's historic district encompasses roughly six acres along Main and Blue Ridge streets. Among the buildings in the historic district are the Patrick County Courthouse and the 1938 cream-colored brick Stuart Drugstore on Main Street, the town's only surviving example of the commercial Art Deco style. Just down the hill in what seems like a separate town is Stuart's original industrial and commercial center. This lower section developed around the railroad depot. Today, a restoration effort is focused on refurbishing notable buildings like the 1947 Star Theater on Patrick Avenue. In its heyday, the venue boasted 300-plus seats in an air-conditioned environment. *The historic district runs along U.S. 58 and Route 8 through town.*

Patrick County Courthouse

Patrick County's second courthouse, built in 1822 in the Roman Revival style by Abram Staples, replaced a previous log building with plaster walls. In 1856, plans were made for a third, much larger official building. Designed by C. Y. Thomas and completed in 1859, the classic antebellum structure with a four-columned portico and stone steps is considered a local landmark. On the northwest corner of the grounds, a Confederate memorial pays homage to Jeb Stuart, the man for whom the town was named. *Located at 101 West Blue Ridge Street, the courthouse is open regular business days. For more information, call 276-694-7213.*

Patrick County Historical Society and Museum

Located at the edge of Stuart's historic district, the county historical society and museum share a space with the town library. Founded in 1974, the museum highlights over 200 years of mountain culture. Exhibits include the Fred Clifton Collection of Patrick County artifacts, a large assortment of Native American arrowheads and spear points artfully arranged in vertical glass cases, and a generous display of antique glass and china. Among the larger pieces are a weaving loom, apothecary props, a mini switchboard, and an interesting montage of academic artifacts including textbooks, quill pens, inkwells, photographs, and report cards. *Located at 116 West Blue Ridge Street in the public library building, the historical society and museum are open select days. For more information, call 276-694-2840.*

Stuart Post Office

The 1940 post office boasts an interior Works Progress Administration mural depicting an idyllic agricultural scene of a father reading a newspaper outdoors to his family while they sit around him. During the 1920s and 1930s, agricultural values merging love of land, respect for nature, and an ethic of hard work were national in scope. *Located at the corner of West Blue Ridge and North Main streets, the post office may be viewed during regular business hours. For more information, call 276-694-3332.*

Visitor Center

The Patrick County Visitor Center is staffed by friendly and knowledgeable folks who can answer questions about area events, activities, and landmarks. The center offers a wide selection of brochures, maps, and complimentary guides for travelers. Its offices are at the rear of the large display room. *Located at 212 Johnson Street, the center is open regular business days. For more information, call 276-694-6012 or visit www.patrickchamber.com.*

W&W Produce

Owned and operated by a husband-and-wife team, W&W Produce offers travelers gassing up a complimentary windshield wash, recalling the service tradition of a bygone era. Surrounding the entrance to the market are tiers of fresh produce. The outdoor bins segue into an awning-covered area filled with additional vegetable bins and buckets of seasonal potted flowers. W&W has one of the most complete selections of local produce on the trail. Inside, the restrooms are labeled "Bucks" and "Does." Chain-saw woodcarvings are perched throughout the retail space. A true community center, the market offers homemade barbecue on race days, courtesy of the conspicuous grill and smoker in the front parking lot. *Located on U.S. 58 (16112 Jeb Stuart Highway) on the outskirts of Stuart, it is open daily except Sunday. For more information, call 276-694-4602.*

WOOD BROTHERS RACE SHOP AND MUSEUM

At one time, cars were actually built at this shop, which now houses the Wood Brothers administrative center. Family owned and operated for two generations, Wood Brothers Racing is the oldest continuously running team in NASCAR history, as well as one of the most successful. The team is noted for being the first to make the pit stop a finely choreographed

Wood Brothers Race Shop and Museum, Stuart
PHOTOGRAPH BY ANNA FARIELLO

event. It was founded over 50 years ago by brothers Glen and Leonard Wood in partnership with the Ford and Motorcraft corporations. The business has been handed down to Glen's two sons, who continue the family legacy of success in stock-car racing. Guided tours are available, and visitors can pick up racing souvenirs at the gift shop. *The shop is located off U.S. 58 at the Route 1025 exit; just off the exit ramp, watch for signs for 21 Performance Drive. It is open regular business days and the Saturdays of the Martinsville races. For more information, call 276-694-2121.*

> The trail departs Stuart on U.S. 58 East for seven miles. At the intersection with Route 626, it turns north for two miles to the community of Critz.

STOP #5 CRITZ

Sites in Critz include those along U.S. 58 on the way to Martinsville.

FAIRY STONE MINE MUSEUM

This tiny building houses a unique museum devoted to thousands of examples of the area's fairy stones, a geological phenomenon. Staurolite crosses have been found in distinct shapes resembling three different crosses—the Roman, Maltese, and St. Andrews. Black, brown, white, and yellow fairy stones can be found loose in dirt or embedded in the surface of larger rocks. The museum showcases crosses from the Southwest, the Southeast, Russia, and Australia. *It is located 10 miles east of Critz on U.S. 58 East (17529 Philpott Highway); look for the signs. It is open most weekdays. Admission is charged. For more information, call 276-957-4873.*

REYNOLDS HOMESTEAD

Built as the Rock Springs Plantation in 1843, the authentically restored 717-acre homestead of Hardin and Nancy Reynolds has been designated a National Historic Landmark and a Virginia Historic Landmark. The grounds

Historic graveyard fencing, Reynolds Homestead, Critz
COURTESY OF
WILLIAM S. ROGERS METALS
AND REYNOLDS HOMESTEAD

include a brick three-floor kitchen and milk house, a log icehouse and granary, and a graveyard bounded by a recently restored decorative iron fence. A successful farmer, merchant, and tobacco manufacturer, Hardin Reynolds was the father of tobacco magnate R. J. Reynolds, who was born here. Family descendants have furnished the home with heirlooms such as a rosewood grand piano, an oil lamp, and a mahogany four-poster bed. Nearby, a modern building with 4,000 square feet of classroom, studio, and reading-room space offers concerts, courses in traditional handicrafts, and readings by local and national authors. Staffed by Virginia Tech personnel, the Homestead Research Center occasionally hosts field days. *The homestead is located about 10 miles out of Stuart on Adam Penn Highway (462 Homestead Lane). It is open for tours April through October. Admission is charged. Visitors may call ahead to arrange a guided tour and learn about scheduled events. For more information, call 276-694-7181 or visit www.reynoldshomestead.vt.edu.*

VIA'S ORCHARD

In August, Via's Orchard hosts the Virginia Peach Festival. From May to December, visitors can pick apples, peaches, strawberries, blueberries, and blackberries. During the summer, fresh vegetables are also available. *The orchard is located halfway between Stuart and Martinsville off U.S. 58; drive 1.5 miles on Route 697 to 2478 Via Orchard Road. It is open seven days a week in season. For more information, call 540-694-7286.*

Auto touring in southwestern Virginia, circa 1920
COURTESY OF ROBERT B. BASHAM COLLECTION

From Critz, the Eastern Lowland Trail returns to U.S. 58 and
continues east for about 20 miles into Martinsville,
the county seat of Henry County.

STOP #6 MARTINSVILLE

The drive into Martinsville from Critz on U.S. 58 crosses the Patrick
County-Henry County line and then the Mayo River, where drivers can
see a pretty falls. Martinsville was officially designated the Henry County
seat in 1793. The town was named for Brigadier General Joseph Martin, a
native son and longtime member of the Virginia General Assembly. Martin
is credited with preventing the Cherokee Nation from joining the British
during the Revolutionary War. Antebellum Martinsville, like much of Henry
County, was primarily agricultural. After the Danville-Wytheville Turnpike
arrived in 1851 and the Danville & Western Railway in 1883, the landscape

changed dramatically. The population boomed, and a busy tobacco processing and shipping center developed. Interest in automobiles exploded in the early 20th century. Henry Ford himself traveled through Martinsville in 1910 with fellow magnate Harvey Firestone.

CHURCH STREET

The 300 block of Church Street is included within the Martinsville Historic District, noted for its intact blocks of commercial and residential buildings, many dating to the early 19th century. This particular section of Church Street presents an eclectic mix of architectural styles, including Tudor, Colonial Revival, and Craftsman. The imposing Gothic Revival Christ Episcopal Church with its dramatically arched windows and crenelated bell tower dates to the 1840s. Its neighbor is the historic Scuffle Hill at 311 Church Street, which serves today as a parish house. Constructed in 1920 by Colonel Pannill Rucker, Scuffle Hill was lost to fire that same year. Rucker rebuilt it in 1928 on the original foundation. Known for its finely landscaped dooryard, imposing columned portico, and floor-to-ceiling windows, it is listed on the National Register of Historic Places and the Virginia Landmarks Register. On the opposite side of the street at 324 Church stands

Historic commercial storefront, southwestern Virginia
PHOTOGRAPH BY ANNA FARIELLO

the John Waddey Carter House, locally known as "the Grand Grey Lady." This restored Queen Anne and Victorian structure was built in 1896 by a former Martinsville mayor for his young bride. Its impressive exterior features include a steeply pitched roof, a graceful corner tower, and tall vertical windows. The Carter family occupied the home for 91 years following its construction. In 1987, the landmark was purchased by a local real-estate company interested in restoring it to its original stature. It is also listed on the National Register of Historic Places. *All buildings in the 300 block of Church Street may be viewed from the road year-round.*

Henry County Courthouse

When Henry County was divided from Patrick County in the late 18th century, a new judicial seat was established in Martinsville. The first courthouse, constructed in 1793, had its logs painted a patriotic red, white, and blue. To meet the needs of a growing population with increasingly sophisticated tastes, a second building was constructed in 1824. Designed by George Tucker, the courthouse marked an early retreat from classicism in southwestern Virginia. The front lawn of the Federal-style structure boasts a monument to the Confederacy. Its 1901 dedication drew over 8,000 people. The monument is flanked by two iron naval cannons, moved here from the earlier town center down the road. Curiously, the 1885 cannons were dragged by a pair of elephants in town for a circus. *Located at 3160 Kings Mountain Road, the courthouse is open regular business days. For more information, call 276-634-4880.*

Little Post Office

Listed on the National Register of Historic Places and the Virginia Landmarks Register, this post office was built in 1893 by United States Mail contractor John Anglin. The little building is accessed by way of a stone entryway off Starling Avenue. Set amid a landscape of shiny vinca and honeysuckle, the building features thick panes of amber- and plum-colored glass and its original mail slot. *Located in a green space on the corner of Starling Avenue and Mulberry Road, it may be viewed year-round.*

Martinsville Speedway

In 1906, a national car company cosponsored a cross-country automobile trip that began in New York City and ended in Jacksonville, Florida. The route took drivers through the center of Martinsville and Ridgeway, a historic trading center and the home of Henry County's first post office and paved street system. History has it that by 1911, Martinsville imposed a speed limit of 12 miles per hour within the city limits. The automobile exerted its greatest influence on the town when H. Clay Earles opened the gates to the Martinsville Speedway in 1947. His racetrack has since grown to such proportions that it now accounts for a major portion of the city's revenue and is famous throughout the professional racing circuit. In 1976, Earles shocked the racing establishment by offering a $100,000 purse to race winners. In a single decade, the speedway incorporated an additional 40,000 seats. *To reach the speedway, follow U.S. 58 East, then take U.S. 220 South from downtown Martinsville. Visitors should call ahead for an event schedule. For more information, call 276-956-1600 or visit www.martinsvillespeedway.com.*

Patrick Henry Monument

Henry County was established in 1776 from a large tract of land that included neighboring Pittsylvania. In 1780, local citizens elected Patrick Henry as their representative to the Virginia House of Delegates. It was in Richmond in 1775 that he uttered his famous line, "Give me liberty or give me death." Henry owned a 10,000-acre plantation in the Leatherwood area of Henry County. When he was criticized for allowing British forces to overrun Virginia, he retired there to farm and practice law. A boulder and plaque mark the site of the two-room brick house he built at Leatherwood. *Located east of Martinsville on U.S. 58, the site is accessible year-round.*

Piedmont Arts Association

In the early 1960s, the Virginia Museum of Fine Arts encouraged communities and artisans across the commonwealth to form local chapters. The Martinsville-Henry County Arts Association grew out of that grass-roots initiative. Now located in a restored historic home with classical features and roomy modern additions, the Piedmont Arts Association supports five galleries, a banquet facility, and a theater. Galleries in the restored Schottland House offer historically and culturally significant local, national, and international art exhibitions. The gifts for sale at the gallery shop include exhibit-related merchandise and local and regional arts and crafts. *Located at 215 Starling Avenue, the facility is open seven days a week. Admission is charged. For more information, call 276-632-3221 or visit www.piedmontarts.org.*

Virginia Museum of Natural History

This museum houses over 10 collections encompassing archaeology, earth science, and fossils. Permanent exhibits include the Age of Reptiles Hall, which features an animatronic replica of a triceratops; Nature Nook, which has hands-on activities for children; the Rock Hall of Fame, which exhibits many of Virginia's geologic treasures; and the Virginia Mammal Hall. The museum offers guided field trips to research sites including Carmel Church, a major archaeological excavation of ancient whale skeletons, and the Solite Quarry, which is emerging as an important paleontology site. Annual events include the Earth Day Festival in the spring and the Indian Heritage Festival and Powwow every fall. *Located at 1001 Douglas Avenue, the museum is open seven days a week. Admission is charged. For more information, call 276-666-8600 or visit www.vmnh.net.*

From Martinsville, a spur follows Route 57 northwest for about 10 miles into the community of Bassett. Fairy Stone State Park can be accessed from Route 57 east of Bassett. The Eastern Lowland Trail then reconnects with U.S. 220 North to head toward Rocky Mount.

Spur to Bassett

Bassett is located just south of where Henry, Patrick, and Franklin counties intersect. This region is sometimes called "the Land Between the Lakes," as it is situated between Philpott Lake and Smith Mountain Lake.

Fort Trial

In 1756, after Native American tribes clashed with European settlers moving west across Virginia, a trio of protective forts was built within the bounds of Henry County. The only true military fort of the three, Fort Trial was constructed on a hill overlooking the confluence of Beaver Creek and the Smith River. It consisted of a common frame house surrounded by a fence of split logs anchored four feet into the earth and extending 16 feet above it. George Washington visited Fort Trial during his 1776 inspection tour. *The historical marker commemorating the site is located along Route 57 (Appalachian Drive) six miles north of Martinsville. It is accessible year-round.*

The Great Road

Near Bassett, a section of road called "the Great Road" crosses Route 57 and cuts south in the heart of the Smith River Valley. In colonial America, the Great Road (or Great Wagon Road) was the main thoroughfare from Philadelphia into the Southern colonies. It followed the Valley of Virginia, taking a turn into the eastern lowlands through Rocky Mount and passing near what is now Martinsville on its way to North Carolina. *The Great Road (Route 683) is accessible from Route 57 Alternate (Riverside Drive) just south of Bassett.*

Philpott Lake

Located about 10 miles outside Martinsville on the way to Bassett, this 4,000-acre lake was created in 1948 to provide flood control and hydro-electric power. It also provides recreational opportunities. Philpott offers three campgrounds with electric and water hookups, swimming areas, and docks. Primitive camping is available on Deer Island. The lake is stocked annually with largemouth and smallmouth bass, walleye, bluegill, catfish, and trout. Walking paths encircle the lake and meander through the surrounding forest. Lucky hikers may catch a glimpse of local wildlife including beavers, muskrats, rabbits, deer, quail, grouse, and mallard, wood, and black ducks. *From Route 57, turn onto Route 822 (Goosepoint Road) and follow the signs. The lake is open daily year-round. Admission is charged. For more information, call 276-629-2703.*

Farmstead, southwestern Virgnia
PHOTOGRAPH BY ANNA FARIELLO

STONELEIGH

In the first quarter of the 20th century, America's residential architects and their affluent clients favored styles that mimicked the designs of England's Tudor and Stuart periods. Stoneleigh was commissioned in the 1920s for former Virginia governor Thomas Stanley and his family. The 28-room country house, finished in 1929, signified Stanley's arrival. A self-made man, he was born on a small Henry County tobacco farm and worked in a coal mine before heading north for a college education. Upon returning to Virginia, he established a highly successful furniture factory before entering state politics. He served as governor for four years. Stanley's home, listed on the National Register of Historic Places and the Virginia Landmarks Register, is privately owned. *Located off Route 57 on Oak Level Road, it may be viewed from the road year-round. For more information, call 703-365-2121.*

Horse barn, southwestern Virginia
PHOTOGRAPH BY ANNA FARIELLO

From Martinsville, follow U.S. 220 North toward Rocky Mount, where the trail picks up Route 122. Route 122 North winds in and out of tulip poplar stands bordered by agricultural scenes for seven miles to Burnt Chimney. Note that Rocky Mount sites are included at the start of the Eastern Lowland Trail.

Stop #7 Burnt Chimney

The travelers emigrating south along the Great Wagon Road were English, Scottish, Irish, and German. Some left the road in Franklin County, attracted to the rich alluvial pastureland and the rolling hills. One group that stayed was comprised mostly of German Baptists, who established the close-knit farming community of Burnt Chimney. Three-fourths of the land in Franklin County is level or rolling. Roughly a third of the county's privately owned land is used for agriculture, whether for producing beef cattle and dairy products or growing tobacco, fruits, and vegetables.

Boone's Country Store

At the heart of Burnt Chimney's German Baptist community is Boone's Country Store, which offers a variety of homemade baked goods including cakes, rolls, and its signature half-moon fried pies made with dried apples. Visitors can also browse the locally made soaps, pillows, baskets, and quilts. Boone's offers quilting classes and a wide selection of supplies to get started. *Located at 2699 Jubal Early Highway, it is open Tuesday through Saturday. For more information, call 540-721-2478.*

Hales Ford Academy

This classical and mathematical school was founded in 1888. The old schoolhouse was destroyed by fire but has been reconstructed according to its original specifications, complete with an oblong iron stove at the rear of the classroom and a teacher's "pulpit" at the front. Visitors can leaf through a copy of the original curriculum, which included Latin, Greek, mathematics, science, and history. Hales Ford was unique among Franklin County academies in that girls were encouraged to attend. Although there are many such one-room schoolhouses on the five heritage trails in this book, Hales Ford is special for the walk-in experience it provides. *From Route 122 North, turn onto Route 116 (Burnt Chimney Road), drive four miles, and turn south on Route 834 (7250 Brooks Mill Road). Visitors may call ahead, and the schoolhouse will be open when they arrive; call 540-721-2621.*

Homestead Creamery

Homestead Creamery is operated as a family business. In the recent past, it added equipment and workspace to produce finished products for the public, rather than shipping its milk to a central processing facility. Well known for its old-fashioned glass bottles filled with hormone-free milk from farm-raised Holsteins, Homestead wraps butter blocks in wax paper, recalling days gone by. Visitors may tour the complex, greet the four-footed ladies, and sample Homestead's yogurts, flavored milks, dairy dips, and ice cream. *Located on Route 122 (7254 Booker T. Washington Highway), it is open daily except Sunday. For more information, call 540-721-2045.*

Overhome Bed-and-Breakfast

Situated on 100 acres of rolling fields and meadows near the base of Lynnville Mountain, this 1857 Italianate-Greek Revival home offers a choice of three elegantly furnished rooms named for the owners' ancestors, who grew up in them. Guests may enjoy the front porch, the enclosed sun porch, and the walking trails. The inn serves a full country breakfast featuring family recipes. *Turn off Route 122 onto Route 116 North and travel four miles to 130 Lovelace Lane. Overhome is open year-round. For more information, call 540-721-5516.*

The trail continues north on Route 122 toward Bedford with a stop along the way at Booker T. Washington National Monument and the surrounding national park.

Stop #8 Booker T. Washington National Monument

The Federal Antiquities Act of 1906 was designed to protect precious archaeological and natural sites for future generations. President Theodore Roosevelt established the first national monuments; subsequently, several were converted to national parks. The first national monument to honor an African-American was George Washington Carver National Monument in Missouri, established in 1951. Just five years later, Booker T. Washington's birthplace was named a national monument.

Booker T. Washington National Monument

Famed orator Booker T. Washington was born into slavery on this 207-acre tobacco farm in 1856. He spent his earliest years living in a log cabin on the property with his mother, sister, and brother. Washington's emancipation, education, and many achievements, including the founding of

Booker T. Washington speaking on the campus of the Christiansburg Institute, 1909
COURTESY OF THE FRIENDS HISTORICAL LIBRARY AT SWARTHMORE COLLEGE AND THE CHRISTIANSBURG INSTITUTE

Alabama's Tuskegee Institute, led to his becoming one of the most important—and sometimes controversial—African-American leaders of his time. This national monument, one of 12 African-American sites administered by the National Park Service, preserves the archaeological footprint of Washington's childhood home, a 14-by-16-foot log cabin described in his autobiography, *Up from Slavery*. In addition to the historic site, the park features restored and reconstructed 19th-century agricultural buildings. Guided tours, educational programs, exhibits, and living-history demonstrations interpret Washington's early life and illustrate the workings of Virginia's plantation system. Modest hiking trails wind through the park. The Plantation Trail is a quarter-mile jaunt, while the Jack-o-Lantern Branch Trail is a more challenging 1.5-mile path through the Piedmont countryside. A walking-tour brochure points out the various flora and introduces the property's four-legged residents—horses, hogs, rabbits, and geese. The visitor center offers a selection of educational gift items. *Located about 11 miles north of Rocky Mount on Route 122 (12130 Booker T. Washington Highway), the national monument is open seven days a week but is closed major holidays. For more information, call 540-721-2094.*

The Eastern Lowland Trail continues north on Route 122 over the Roanoke River and into Moneta.

STOP #9 MONETA

In 1740, two European pioneers, brothers Gideon and Daniel Smith, were among the earliest settlers to build permanent homesteads in this region. Smith Mountain, rising 400 feet above lake level to the southeast, was named in honor of this early pair of pioneers. For nearly two centuries, the region was agricultural in character. A mid-20th-century dam project changed that, creating Smith Mountain Lake and initiating a burst of residential development.

ATKINS LAKESHORE GALLERY

This gallery specializes in the work of P. Buckley Moss, a local artist of national fame and an activist for adults and children with disabilities. Her whimsical prints, plates, tiles, and etchings embrace a variety of subjects, people, and settings. The gallery also features the work of local craftsmen. Objects include handmade furniture, baskets, and textiles. *Located at 13105 Booker T. Washington Highway, the gallery is open daily except Sunday. For more information, call 540-721-7267.*

CAMPERS PARADISE

This facility is located on tiny Paradise Creek. Visitors may arrive by boat or car. Famous for its hearty Southern breakfasts and country cooking, the restaurant at Campers Paradise offers griddlecakes, chicken and sausage gravy with biscuits, fresh pies, and much more. After lunch, guests can visit the rental center for a pontoon, paddle, or fishing boat or sign up for a guided fishing trip. *Located off Route 122 at 1336 Campers Paradise Lane, it is open seven days a week. For more information, call 540-297-6109.*

Diamond Hill General Store

This landmark opened in 1857. The store was staffed by James Debo (Moneta's first postmaster) and his family for nearly 135 years. Completely restored in 1992 and outfitted with a potbelly stove, the store is stocked with a variety of local and regional products, including folk art, Virginia wines, pottery, and freshly baked cookies, biscuits, and breads. *Located 4.5 miles west of Route 122 at 1017 Diamond Hill Road, it is open daily except Sunday. For more information, call 540-297-9309.*

Little Gallery on the Lake

This gallery features original watercolors, oils, and pastels by over 200 international, national, and local artists. It also offers contemporary crafts including stained and blown glass, woodwork, and a wide selection of handcrafted jewelry. Visitors may attend a new show almost every month and demonstrations during the winter. *Located just over the Franklin County line across a bridge in Bridgewater Plaza (16430 Booker T. Washington Highway), it is open seven days a week. For more information, call 540-721-1596 or visit www.thelittlegallerysml.com.*

White frame church, southwestern Virginia
PHOTOGRAPH BY ANNA FARIELLO

Smith Mountain Lake

Encompassing 22,000 acres of striking scenery and offering outstanding recreational opportunities, Smith Mountain Lake is being exposed to increasing traffic and rapid development. A number of small shops and art galleries have cropped up. Many of the galleries feature paintings and handcrafted objects by local and regional artists. Several restaurants around the lake are accessible by boat or car. The visitor center at Smith Mountain Lake State Park overlooks the lake's dam. The center is staffed to answer questions and provide information. Visual and audio exhibits tell the story of the dam's construction. A wall mural depicts Smith Mountain Gap before the filling of the lake. *From Route 122 in Moneta, head south along Route 608 to Route 626, then follow Route 626 for two miles to the entrance to the state park. The park is open daily year-round. Admission is charged. For more information, call 540-985-2587 or visit www.visitsmithmountainlake.com.*

From Moneta, the Eastern Lowland Trail continues along Route 122 North for about 20 miles to the historic town of Bedford.

Stop #10 Bedford

Bedford is the seat of Bedford County, formed in 1754 and named for John Russell, the duke of Bedford under King George II. Bedford County is one of the largest counties in the commonwealth, encompassing 764 square miles of Piedmont plateau in the west-central portion of Virginia. The terrain descends from elevations upwards of 4,000 feet along the crest of the Blue Ridge to a mere 800 feet in the lake basin. New London, in Bedford County's eastern section, was the original seat until the county's borders were altered and the more centrally located town of Bedford— originally called Liberty—was chosen. Bedford's Liberty Hotel was noted for hosting traveling theatrical groups and local musicians. By the mid-19th century, the bustling town had become a center for commerce, drawing tobacco and textile manufacturers, artisans, professionals, and politicians. Many of Bedford's existing structures date to the late 1880s and 1890s. The downtown is an interesting mix of architectural styles, including Victorian, Italianate, and Classical Revival. Bedford's downtown has been incorporated as a Virginia Main Street Community. The local historical society has affixed plaques to several commercial buildings noting the years of construction and the buildings' original functions.

BEDFORD CITY-COUNTY MUSEUM

This museum was organized by local Daughters of the American Revolution and United Daughters of the Confederacy chapters in 1932. After several moves, the 1895 Masonic Lodge Building became its permanent home. A prime example of Romanesque Revival architecture, the striking historic structure has handsome stone archways and terra-cotta ornamentation around its bay windows. Interior features include hand-carved windows and doorframes and original doors with glass panels bearing old office names. The museum exhibits illustrate Bedford's history from Native American days through the mid-20th century. Indian relics, pioneer tools, Revolutionary War and Civil War artifacts, handmade items, and historic photographs are on display. The museum shop stocks souvenirs, books, and other items of historical and genealogical interest. *Located at 201 East Main Street, the museum is open year-round except for major holidays. Admission is charged. For more information, call 540-586-4520 or visit www.bedfordvamuseum.org.*

BEDFORD COUNTY COURTHOUSE

The original Bedford County Courthouse was constructed in 1782 out of hewn logs on a lot near today's Main and Market streets. That early structure was replaced in the mid-1800s by a stone building in the Italianate style with overhanging eaves and a decorative corner entrance. A third courthouse was constructed in 1930 on the foundation of its stone predecessor. Designed in the Classical Revival style, the Flemish brick building is embellished with an ornate cupola, a clock tower, and a porch supported by Ionic columns. On the lawn are monuments honoring soldiers from Bedford who participated in the Revolutionary War, the Civil War, and both World

Wars. The courthouse maintains a large collection of historical records. *Located at 123 East Main Street, it is open regular business days. For more information, call 540-586-7632.*

Civil War Trails

Virginia led the Confederacy in both the production of essential mineral resources and the length of rail line within the state's boundaries. An interpretive marker details the arrival of Union troops in Bedford in the summer of 1864. Their mission was to destroy rail lines and supply depots. *Located at the intersection of Main and Bridge streets, the marker may be viewed year-round.*

D-Day Memorial

Dedicated in June 2001, this memorial boasts a dramatic bronze-and-granite monument honoring the courage of the American soldiers involved in the June 6, 1944, D-Day conflict. The monument portrays the storming of the Normandy beaches. Beneath an arc of international flags representing participating nations are a reflecting pool and a waterfall. An expansive horticultural garden was created to resemble the insignia worn by members of the Allied Expeditionary Force. Guided tours of the memorial are available, weather permitting. As there is no concession or restaurant on the premises, the D-Day Memorial Foundation suggests that guests picnic at nearby Liberty Park, a half-mile from the monument. The memorial store offers a selection of clothing and commemorative and gift items related to D-Day. *The memorial is located at the intersection of Route 460 and Route 122 (Overlord Circle); signs are posted. It is open year-round except for major holidays. For more information, call 540-586-8973 or visit www.ddaymemorial.info.*

Emerson Creek Pottery

This pottery was first located in a Massachusetts farmhouse belonging to descendants of Ralph Waldo Emerson. Emerson Creek relocated to Virginia in 1977. The two founding potters perpetuated their strong ties with the past by setting up shop in a historic 1825 log cabin built by local blacksmith Silas Wade. Visitors can tour the original log studio as well as the expanded modern facility and the gift shop, which offers first runs and specialties at reasonable prices. Emerson Creek's hand-painted nature-inspired pottery is sold in all 50 states. *The pottery is located eight miles south of Bedford at 1068 Pottery Lane. Follow Route 43 to Pecks Road (Route 725). Pottery Lane is two miles down Pecks Road. The pottery is open seven days a week. For more information, call 800-666-1977 or visit emersoncreekpottery.com.*

Farmers' Market

Thanks to the area's productive soil and temperate growing season, early settlers were able to plant a tremendous variety of crops, including corn, potatoes, tobacco, oats, and wheat. The farmers' market offers a variety of seasonal fruits and vegetables, freshly baked goods, Bedford-area honey, jams, and jellies. Local artisans set up booths to exhibit and sell their woodwork, quilts, and other handcrafted products. *Located at the intersection of Washington and Center streets in downtown Bedford, the market is open select days seasonally. For more information, call 540-586-2148.*

Main Street, Bedford
Courtesy of Norfolk & Western Historical Photograph Collection, Virginia Tech Special Collections

Hamilton's Books

This stately brick house on Main Street in downtown Bedford is home to an independent publishing company run by local author Peter Viemeister. Hamilton's specializes in regional and local history. A small retail showroom is stocked with these volumes as well as titles by Viemeister, who has published books on Bedford's mysterious Beale treasure. Thomas Jefferson Beale, a Bedford native, left behind a set of documents describing how he had buried a vast horde of silver, gold, and gemstones at various sites in the late 1700s. He also left a set of codes that, if broken, promised to lead the seeker to his wealth. The Beale treasure has never been found—which of course has encouraged visiting "detectives" to keep searching. Visitors may also browse a limited selection of rare books. *Located at 155 West Main Street, the shop is open regular business days. For more information, call 540-586-5592 or visit www.peterv.com.*

Historic Avenel

Avenel is the earliest documented residence in Bedford's historic district. The Federal-style mansion with Greek Revival characteristics was built in 1838. It boasts a large wraparound porch, intricate woodwork, and ornate crown moldings. The stately home of William Burwell and Frances Steptoe was the center of a 40-acre plantation that catered to eminent guests such as Robert E. Lee and Edgar Allan Poe. Eventually, the acreage surrounding the residence was subdivided and sold. The homes constructed on the new lots became Bedford's Old Avenel neighborhood, a residential complement to the commercial Centertown district near the courthouse and train tracks. Avenel's history includes tales of supernatural events. The home is listed on the National Register of Historic Places and is a Virginia Historic Landmark. *It is located at 413 Avenel Avenue. Tours are available by appointment. For more information, call 540-586-5978.*

Historic Centertown

Near the railroad tracks in Bedford are old industrial buildings that housed woolen mills and tobacco factories. Around the corner from the courthouse and its Court Street parking lot is the site of the town's first railroad depot, a hub of commercial activity at the turn of the 19th century. The historic Centertown community includes properties along Longwood Avenue and Peaks, Oak, Grove, and Washington streets. *To view the historic industrial center, follow Bedford Avenue, which runs along the north side of the Norfolk Southern rail bed. The area may be viewed from the road year-round.*

HISTORIC MEETING HOUSE

This meeting house, built in 1838 by local Methodists, was eventually outgrown by the expanding congregation. Bedford Episcopalians purchased the building in 1886 and renovated it to serve the religious and educational needs of recently emancipated African-Americans. Today, it is listed on the National Register of Historic Places. All the furnishings are original. Major architectural features like the brickwork, the pedimented roof, and the belfry with its original bell are still intact. *Located at 153 West Main Street, it is open on special occasions and by appointment. For more information, call 540-586-8188.*

INN ON AVENEL

Situated across the street from Historic Avenel, this 1915 Greek Revival home has high ceilings, brass fixtures, hardwood floors, and an ornate central staircase. The four guest rooms are decorated with period furniture and handmade quilts. Guests enjoy refreshments upon arrival and have access to all common areas, including the formal dining room, the living room, and the wraparound porch. *Located at 416 Avenel Avenue, the inn is open year-round. For more information, call 540-586-5978 or visit www.innonavenel.com.*

LIBERTY HOUSE INN

Situated in the heart of Bedford's historic district, this 1932 inn offers four guest rooms, each with a private sitting area and bath. Guests have access to all common areas on the first floor, including the dining room and the library, each decorated in vintage 1940s style. Amenities include a full breakfast, coffee served in the upstairs hallway to start the day, and dessert each evening. Visitors enjoy relaxing in the hammock and bird-watching from the chairs and benches. *Located at 602 Mountain Avenue, the inn is open year-round. For more information, call 540-587-0966 or visit www.libertyhouseinn.com.*

Liberty Presbyterian Church

This Greek Revival structure with ornate columns, pedimented portico, and square, louvered belfry was built in 1844 to serve the original town of Liberty. The giant sycamore on the front lawn is a local landmark. *The church is located at 105 West Main Street. Sunday services are open to the public. For more information, call 540-586-5284.*

Longwood Cemetery

This was the original public cemetery for the town then known as Liberty. Early markers dating back to 1826 are noteworthy for their elaborate artistry and hand-carved inscriptions. One point of special interest is the grave of John Goode, Jr., Virginia's representative in the Confederate Congress and at the Secession Convention. The Monument of Valor marks the final resting place of 192 Civil War veterans. Along the cemetery's borders are the remnants of hitching posts erected for the convenience of family members traveling to grave sites on horseback. *Located northeast of the town center on Longwood Avenue, the cemetery is accessible year-round during daylight hours. For more information, call 540-587-6061.*

Olde Liberty Station

Dining in this restored station decorated with train-related memorabilia and hand-painted murals is a trip back in time to the days of glamorous rail travel. The rooms have apt names like the Norfolk & Western Boardroom. Guests enjoy the salad and dessert bars, the char-grilled steak and chicken dishes, and the barbecue and seafood specials. *Located at 515 Bedford Avenue, the restaurant is open daily except Sunday. For more information, call 540-587-9377.*

Poplar Park

Since 1940, the American Foresters nonprofit organization has worked to document and preserve the largest known specimens of native and non-native tree species in the country. This Bedford park is home to the largest yellow poplar in the United States. Listed on the National Register of Big Trees and recognized by the Virginia Big Tree Program, the beautiful poplar rises 111 feet and measures 32 feet around. Visitors can roam the landscaped grounds or relax with a picnic lunch. *Located off Smith Street on Grande Arbor Drive, the park is accessible year-round. For more information, call 540-587-6061.*

Rainbow Tree Artisans Gallery

Co-owned and operated by Cindy Connor, a local glass artisan, Rainbow Tree features regional artists' work in mixed media. Craftsmen exhibit custom-made furniture, original art, photographs, and work in wood, glass, and metal. *Located at 117 South Bridge Street, the gallery is open select days and by appointment. For more information, call 540-586-6206.*

Visitor Center

The knowledgeable staff at Bedford's visitor center is ready to assist with directions and questions about local destinations. Housed in a glass-fronted building, the center looks out on the Peaks of Otter and the D-Day Memorial. Several racks and tables of brochures, maps, and newspapers regarding historic, cultural, and commercial sites in Bedford and outlying areas are situated throughout the center. *Located a half-mile south of the town center at the intersection of Route 460 and Route 122 (816 Burkes Hill Road), it is open throughout the year on regular business days and seasonally on weekends. For more information, call 540-587-5681.*

West Main Street Cottage

Bedford, originally known as Liberty, was established in 1782 on an early turnpike that linked Lynchburg with Salem. In a largely agrarian county, Liberty was cosmopolitan and urbane, attracting residents who were interested in culture and entertainment. Originally a gardener's cottage on the property of a stately home, this 1834 stone building is the oldest in Bedford.

Farmstead, southwestern Virginia
PHOTOGRAPH BY ANNA FARIELLO

In its second incarnation, it served as the Bedford Female Seminary, one of several private schools that opened in Bedford around 1900. Restored in 1987, the historic building currently houses commercial offices. *Located at 132 West Main Street, it may be viewed from the road year-round.*

WHARTON HOUSE AND GARDEN

Originally the home of an affluent Bedford couple, Charles and Louise Wharton, this brick Italianate house was built in 1883. To its rear is a memorial garden. Surrounded by perennial and shrub borders, it contains annual beds, a gazebo, brick walks and terraces, and a mature boxwood maze. The home currently serves as the headquarters of the Bedford Historical Society. The gardens are maintained by volunteers for the enjoyment of the community. *The home is located at 315 North Bridge Street. The gardens are accessible seven days a week.*

View of Liberty (now Bedford) and Peaks of Otter, Bedford County
MID-19TH-CENTURY PAINTING BY EDWARD BEYER,
COURTESY OF THE VIRGINIA HISTORICAL SOCIETY

Following the Warriors Path

Demographers estimate that when the first European explorers entered Virginia, approximately 20,000 Native Americans were living there. By the time the English arrived on the shores of Virginia in 1607, the Cherokees had emerged as a populous and powerful southeastern tribe. Most numerous in western North Carolina and eastern Tennessee, the Cherokees inhabited 40,000 square miles of Appalachian uplands and valleys as far west as the Ohio River. They traveled frequently through southwestern Virginia.[1]

In the 18th century, Native Americans met a series of devastating forces beginning with a smallpox epidemic in the 1730s and culminating in the bloody French and Indian War, which ended by treaty in 1763. The upheaval altered the balance of power among native groups. In contrast, the Revolutionary War consolidated the strength of the new nation and increased its need for expansion. New federal laws and treaties increasingly affected the Cherokees, who lived in small farming settlements and were governed by a national constitution. Settlers and speculators, wanting the rich bottom lands occupied by the Cherokees, supported a call to displace them from their traditional homelands. In 1838, the United States government, barely half a century old, decreed that all Cherokees move off their ancestral lands. More than 17,000 men, women, and children were forced to make the long trek to a reservation set aside for them in Oklahoma. By the end of the 1,000-mile journey, one-third had perished along what has become known as the Trail of Tears.

Long before that low point in American history, the Cherokees, Iroquois, and other native peoples had traveled through the Valley of Virginia. That lowland trace was the primary route for nomadic resettlement, hunting parties, and trading missions. By the 1720s, the valley route was being used by Europeans who wanted to explore the continent beyond its settlements along the Atlantic coast. In 1744, the Treaty of Lancaster gave title of the valley to the colonists in Philadelphia. With politically assured free passage along its length, the Appalachian valley pike became the most widely used road on the continent. While dry goods were usually carried by wagon, livestock was moved on the hoof. Men called drovers moved hundreds of hogs, sheep, and turkeys along the primitive roadway. Stray animals were kept from wandering away by groups of boys who followed with whoops and cries to keep the herds heading in the proper direction. Teams of drovers stopped to rest at small wayside inns located at intervals along the road. They most often paid for their stay with an animal or two, slaughtered to provide meals for the next round of travelers.

By 1775, tens of thousands of individuals of all ages had passed over the road's still-rough surface, moving animals and possessions and utilizing a variety of horse- and ox-drawn vehicles. Towns along the road prospered as places where the unending parade of travelers could trade goods and find accommodations. In Winchester, Staunton, and Rocky Mount, one could get a bed and a meal at a small inn called a public house. An ordinary, as its name implies, was a plainer boardinghouse in which guests ate serviceable fare such as eggs, bacon, and Indian hoecakes (cornbread) at the owner's table.

It has sometimes been stated that, in the early days, more vehicles traveled the Great Wagon Road than all other roads put together. Certainly, in the years around the birth of the nation, tens of thousands of travelers moved through the Valley of Virginia along the road. Improved to accommodate wagons and goods, it followed the traditional Native American pathway. From 1607—when the first settlement at Jamestown was established—until 1744, this route through the Valley of Virginia was called the Warriors Path.

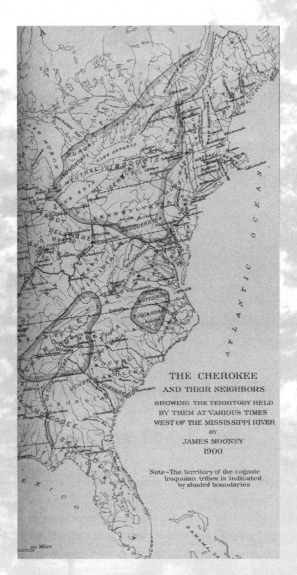

Map from James Mooney's Myths of the Cherokee, *1902*
COURTESY OF WESTERN CAROLINA UNIVERSITY SPECIAL COLLECTIONS

[1] **Chris Bolgiano,** *The Appalachian Forest: A Search for Roots and Renewal* **(Mechanicsburg, Pa.: Stackpole Books, 1995), 35-58; Ted Olson,** *Blue Ridge Folklife* **(Jackson: University Press of Mississippi, 1998), 2-3.**

View of Bedford and the Peaks of Otter, circa 1929
COURTESY OF NORFOLK & WESTERN HISTORICAL PHOTOGRAPH COLLECTION,
VIRGINIA TECH SPECIAL COLLECTIONS

From Bedford, take U.S. 221/Route 460 West for 21 miles to Milepost 105 of the Blue Ridge Parkway. Follow the parkway north. Exit the parkway at Milepost 86, following the signs for the Peaks of Otter. The Peaks of Otter can also be reached by following Route 43 North out of Bedford.

STOP #11 PEAKS OF OTTER

These three peaks—Sharp Top, Flat Top, and Harkening Hill—were first explored by Native Americans foraging for wild fruits and tracking big-game animals. The earliest permanent settlers were European immigrants who arrived in the mid-18th century. Some of the first accounts of the climb to Sharp Top were recorded by Thomas Jefferson and Robert E. Lee. The first inn was constructed in 1834. Bounded almost entirely by

Jefferson National Forest, the peaks are now a popular destination along the parkway.

Abbott Lake

This man-made triangular-shaped lake nestled in the valley at the foot of the Peaks of Otter is named for Stanley William Abbott, the parkway's first resident landscape planner and architect. Abbott Lake is a favorite site for fishing and picnicking. Visitors may follow a one-mile trail around the lake through wooded areas and open fields. If luck prevails, the soft lake sounds may be interrupted by a loon's song. On the northeastern shore, the park service has restored an old log cabin. Dubbed Polly Wood's Ordinary, it was originally a small roadside accommodation serving mid-19th-century travelers. *Located between Mileposts 86 and 85 of the Blue Ridge Parkway, the lake is accessible year-round, weather permitting. For more information, call 540-586-4357 or visit www.wp21.com/peaksofotter.*

Appalachian Trail Access

The Appalachian Trail intersects the Blue Ridge Parkway at a fire road from which a spur trail departs to the right. At the end of a quarter-mile

Jack-in-the-pulpit
PHOTOGRAPH BY ANNA FARIELLO

jog, hikers will reach the Cornelius Creek Shelter. *The trail intersects the parkway near Milepost 80, about five miles north of the Peaks of Otter. The trail is accessible year-round, weather permitting.*

Flat Top Mountain Trail

This loop trail begins and ends at the parkway. The 4.5-mile hiking path starts at an elevation of 2,500 feet and runs south to a picnic area below the Abbott Lake Dam. A steep ascent to the summit of Flat Top at 4,004 feet reveals a recognizable shift in forest ecology. The Fallingwater Cascades Mountain Trail is a 1.5-mile loop off Flat Top that follows the cascades of Fallingwater Creek through dense stands of rhododendron. *Located between Mileposts 86 and 83 of the Blue Ridge Parkway, Flat Top Mountain Trail is accessible year-round, weather permitting. For more information, call 540-586-1081.*

Johnson Farm Trail

The trailhead for this easy two-mile jaunt is just north of the Peaks of Otter Visitor Center parking area. Situated near the midpoint of the trail loop is the Johnson Family Farm, restored by the park service to depict an early-20th-century Blue Ridge farmstead. Living-history demonstrations are presented on a seasonal basis. From here, visitors may follow the path back to the visitor center or take a rather strenuous three-mile loop that climbs to an elevation of 3,372 feet on Harkening Hill. *Located between Mileposts 86 and 85 of the Blue Ridge Parkway, Johnson Farm Trail is accessible year-round, weather permitting. For more information, call 540-586-1081.*

Otter's Den Bed-and-Breakfast

This bed-and-breakfast is one of three original chestnut log structures built in the late 1700s as Blue Ridge homesteads. Totally restored and renovated, the Otter's Den has four rooms furnished with family antiques and heirloom pieces. Guests have access to hiking trails on the property, a picnic area, and an outdoor hot spa. The inn serves a full country breakfast. *Located at Milepost 86 of the Blue Ridge Parkway (8578 Peaks Road), it is open year-round. For more information, call 800-542-5927 or visit www.ottersden.net.*

Peaks of Otter Lodge

Tucked among three of Virginia's most famous peaks, this lodge, in operation since 1964, offers rooms with double or king-sized beds, private baths, and balconies overlooking Abbott Lake and Sharp Top Mountain. Amenities include access to the Sharp Top bus, which takes visitors to a desirable viewing spot; the Peaks Coffee Shop will prepare picnic lunches for the trip. The restaurant at the lodge serves three Southern-style meals daily featuring such traditional dishes as fried green tomatoes, barbecued pork, and homemade cobblers. The wine selection includes Peaks of Otter private labels and a selection of white and red Virginia wines. *Located at Milepost 86 of the Blue Ridge Parkway, the lodge is open year-round; the restaurant is open seven days a week. For more information, call 540-586-1081 or visit www.peaksofotter.com.*

Peaks of Otter Winery and Johnson Orchards

The Johnsons' Blue Ridge Mountain farm and orchards were established in 1919 at the foot of the Peaks of Otter. A family-run business, the orchard produces over 200 varieties of pick-your-own peaches, apples, plums, berries, and nectarines. The winery is a recent but successful venture established in 1996. Its wines, as diverse as the orchard's offerings, include such pleasant-sounding varieties as Sweet Concord Grape, Apple Elderberry, Spiced Honey, and Sweet Plum. Guided tours of the winery and vineyard are available, or guests may wander the nature trails and greet the farm animals on their own. *Take Route 460 West out of Bedford for one mile to Route 680, then follow the apple-shaped signs for five miles to the orchard at 2122 Sheep Creek Road. It is open seasonally. For more information, call 800-742-6877 or visit www.peaksofotterwinery.com.*

Ron Loque Gallery of Virginia Arts and Crafts

Situated at the foot of the Peaks of Otter, this log-cabin-style gallery features Ron Loque's realist paintings of Virginia landscapes and wildlife. It offers a variety of handcrafted products by local and regional artisans, including jewelry, woodcarvings, hand-loomed shawls, walking sticks, and leather crafts. Visitors also enjoy the edibles corner, stocked with Virginia

White-oak split basket, southwestern Virginia
PHOTOGRAPH BY ANNA FARIELLO

wines and ciders, local fruit butters and honey, and Virginia's famous peanut brittle. *Located at Milepost 86 of the Blue Ridge Parkway (7535 Peaks Road),
the gallery is open seasonally. For more information, call 540-586-5001.*

SERENITY'S EDGE

Set on 51 acres climbing the side of Taylor's Mountain, Serenity's Edge
offers guests a choice of cottage, bungalow, or bed-and-breakfast accommodations. The two-story cottage and the English country bungalow have
full kitchens and dining areas. All guests have access to the tropical so-
larium with exercise equipment, the hot tub and sauna, and the library
filled with books. The decks and walkways open onto paths that wind
through the wooded mountainside. Appointments for therapeutic massages
are available. *Located at 4404 Murray Hollow Road, Serenity's Edge is open year-
round. For more information, call 540-947-2468 or visit www.serenitysedge.com.*

SHARP TOP MOUNTAIN TRAIL

The most popular trail at the Peaks of Otter begins at the camp store across from the visitor center. Though only a modest two miles in length, it is a steep and strenuous climb. Bus service is available for those who would like to reach the summit but are concerned about the difficulty of the hike. The pinnacle offers a 360-degree view of the Peaks of Otter area, the Blue Ridge Mountains, and the Shenandoah Valley. Just shy of the summit, a moderate spur trail to Buzzard's Roost offers additional views. *Located at Milepost 80 of the Blue Ridge Parkway, the trail is accessible year-round. Bus service is not available in winter. For more information, call 540-586-1081.*

To return to the Eastern Lowland Trail's starting point in Rocky Mount, follow the Blue Ridge Parkway south to Roanoke, then take U.S. 220 South into Franklin County.

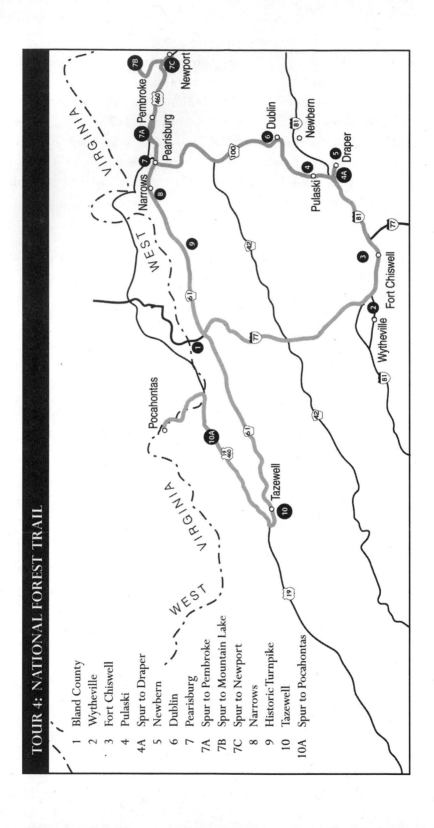

TOUR 4: NATIONAL FOREST TRAIL

1   Bland County
2   Wytheville
3   Fort Chiswell
4   Pulaski
4A Spur to Draper
5   Newbern
6   Dublin
7   Pearisburg
7A Spur to Pembroke
7B Spur to Mountain Lake
7C Spur to Newport
8   Narrows
9   Historic Turnpike
10 Tazewell
10A Spur to Pocahontas

Big Walker Lookout, Bland County. PHOTOGRAPH BY ANNA FARIELLO

Chapter 4

NATIONAL FOREST TRAIL

This trail loop begins at the welcome center near the south entrance of the East River Mountain Tunnel on I-77. The interstate enters the commonwealth through this mile-long tunnel, opened in 1974 to connect Virginia and West Virginia. The dividing line lies about midway through the four-year, $40 million structure. The trail heads south on I-77. Its first stops are in Bland County. Bastian, lying along U.S. 52, can be reached via Exit 58 or Exit 52 off I-77; the town of Bland is at Exit 52. The National Forest Trail is named for Jefferson and George Washington national forests, which encompass a combined 1.8 million acres. A 300-mile stretch of the Appalachian Trail passes through this rural landscape. The National Forest Trail follows I-81 North into Pulaski County before circling north on Route 100 into Giles County and west on Route 61 into Tazewell County to complete the loop. A spur leads visitors to the historic coal town of Pocahontas.

Stop #1 Bland County

Formed in 1861 from parts of Wytheville, Tazewell, and Giles counties, Bland County was named for Revolutionary War hero Richard Bland. Rocky Gap lies at the county's northern end and the county seat of Bland to the south. Both fall along I-77. Bastian, originally called Parkersburg, is located halfway between them. Bastian was once home to the Wolf Creek Railroad, established in 1914 to serve the logging industry. The train ran from Narrows to Rocky Gap and then on to Bastian. The establishment of the Virginia Hardwood Lumber Mill brought electricity to the area long before it was available elsewhere. A Civilian Conservation Corps camp in Bland County provided work for hundreds of young men during the Great Depression. Its legacy includes trails and bridges in Jefferson National Forest.

Appalachian Trail Access

Some of the most infrequently traveled segments of the Appalachian Trail wind through this region of southwestern Virginia. The AT traverses stands of mixed Appalachian hardwoods and conifers and crosses highland meadows as it winds its way for 300 miles through Jefferson National Forest. Marked posts lead hikers through the high country. Hikers may want to hop off the trail to visit Bastian's country store for refueling. *Route 282 is accessible from U.S. 52 about a mile south of Bastian; an AT access point is marked with signage. The trail is accessible year-round, weather permitting.*

Big Walker Lookout Tower

In the 1940s, a couple named Kime decided to invest in the dramatic view from the crest of Big Walker Mountain. They constructed a 100-foot lookout tower that provides panoramic views of several states. Near the base of the lookout, a mile-long hike leads uphill to Monster Rock, an immense outcrop that hovers above the trail. Adjacent to the foot of the tower is a small gift shop, interesting for its original chestnut cabinets and trim. Today, the couple's son and daughter-in-law look after the tower and operate the shop, which offers locally made products, arts, and crafts. *From I-77, take Exit 52 and travel west to Big Walker Lookout Tower. Admission is charged. The lookout is accessible year-round, weather permitting. For more information, call 276-228-4401.*

Big Walker Tunnel

Big Walker Tunnel's 4,229-foot length connects Bland and Wythe counties. The I-77 tunnel was built over a five-year period from 1967 to 1972. At the time of its construction, it was the single most expensive interstate undertaking in the state's history. The Big Walker Scenic Byway runs through the national forest and farmland for 16 miles, past wildflowers and historic markers. The byway begins to climb Big Walker Mountain at the fourth mile. *The tunnel is located at the intersection of U.S. 52 and Route 615. The byway entrance is about five miles north of Wytheville at the intersection of I-77 and Route 717. The tunnel and byway are accessible year-round, weather permitting. For more information, call 276-228-4401.*

Virginia City Gem Mine and Campground

This reinvigorated historic community on Big Walker Mountain offers travelers a unique cultural experience that includes a working gristmill, a sluice mining system, a gem shop, and a general store. Visitors may sign up for a guided tour of the mining village or rent a pan from the general store and set up along the stream. The 250-acre property also boasts a number of waterfalls, a picnic area, and plenty of rewarding hiking trails. *From I-77, take Exit 52 and travel west to the mine. It is open select days seasonally. Admission is charged. For more information, call 276-223-1873 or visit www.vacity.com.*

Wolf Creek Indian Village and Museum

More than eight centuries ago, Native Americans made their home in a valley tucked between two mountains located at what is now the town of Bastian. In the 1970s, state archaeologists uncovered evidence of an Indian village containing several domestic structures, fire and storage pits, and

Wolf Creek Indian Village and Museum, Bland County
PHOTOGRAPH BY ANNA FARIELLO

burial grounds. The Bland County Historical Society subsequently arranged to have the settlement reconstructed as a living-history museum. The palisaded site is located near the archaeological footprint of the early settlement. A dramatic bronze sculpture welcomes visitors to the museum. The reconstructed circular village is staffed by costumed guides who demonstrate day-to-day activities of the Eastern Woodland Indians. Walking trails weave through dense patches of rhododendron. Guided tours are available daily. The gift shop on the premises offers souvenirs, T-shirts, locally made crafts, and jewelry. *Depart I-77 at Exit 58 and head north on U.S. 52; the entrance is marked with brown signs. The village is open year-round. Admission is charged. For more information, call 276-688-3438 or visit www.indianvillage.org.*

The National Forest Trail continues south on I-77 to the historic crossroads community of Wytheville, located at the intersection of I-77 and I-81 and the older U.S. 52 and U.S. 11.

STOP #2   WYTHEVILLE

A small community called Evansham was founded in the 18th century at what would become an important regional crossroads. The village's location along the well-traveled Wilderness Road and Ingles Ferry Trail meant it was bound to become a center of culture. In fact, a portion of the Wilderness Road lies beneath the pavement of what is now Main Street. A cluster of commercial buildings along the north side of East Main Street, reported to be the oldest structures in town, served as boardinghouses for summer visitors. In 1839, the growing village was renamed Wytheville. During 1863 and 1864, the Wythe County seat suffered four Union raids. Federal forces targeted the nearby lead mines at Austinville, the salt flats at Saltville, and Wytheville itself, the rail hub of the region. When Northern army officials headquartered in Tazewell were ordered to destroy the local section of the Virginia-Tennessee railroad, a young girl named Molly Tynes rode her pony, Fashion, through the mountain pass to warn the citizens of Wytheville to protect their depot.

BEAGLE RIDGE HERB FARM

Beagle Ridge is an organic farm and education center situated on 160 acres. Its display gardens are filled with lush, colorful plants both native and exotic. The farm hosts sessions on herbs, flowers, vegetables, and the basics of organic gardening. Famous for its garlic fields, it sells heavy braids of the organic stuff in the gift shop on the premises, along with herbal lotions, potpourri, and potted plants in season. Another bonus is the five miles of wooded nature trails that wind their way up to Buzzard's Roost and down to Hemlock Cove. *Follow U.S. 21 South out of Wytheville for 10*

Main Street signage, Wytheville
PHOTOGRAPH BY ANNA FARIELLO

miles. Turn east on Route 690 to reach 1934 Matney Flats Road. The farm is open on weekends seasonally. For more information, call 276-621-4511 or visit www.beagleridgeherbfarm.com.

BETHEL A.M.E. CHURCH

The town's original Methodist church was located on Tazewell Street next door to the home of a prominent local businessman. The services were so jubilant—and noisy—that the businessman made an offer to the congregation; he arranged for the church to move to a large piece of property on Main Street. The present church, constructed in 1892, is one of two remaining 19th-century frame churches in Wytheville. *It is located at 600 East Main Street. Sunday services are open to the public.*

COMMERCIAL SIGNAGE

Wytheville's Main Street is lined with commercial buildings in an array of colors and architectural styles. Vintage neon commercial signs and interesting three-dimensional advertising art add to the eclectic mix. A 31-foot metal pencil created by Wytheville shop owner John Findlay in the 1950s is suspended above the sidewalk on West Main Street. *The many interesting signs along Main Street can be viewed year-round.*

EDITH BOLLING WILSON BIRTHPLACE

Born in an upper-floor apartment in this historic building in 1872, Edith Bolling was educated at local schools and attended college in Abingdon. The daughter of Judge William Holcombe Bolling, she married President Woodrow Wilson in 1915 and is famous for the leadership position she assumed after his physical collapse. An interesting architectural note about this block of commercial buildings is that, while it appears to be three stories high, the third floor is actually a false front, its always-shuttered windows installed over a solid-brick façade. *Located at 115 Main Street, the birthplace may be viewed from the road year-round.*

LOG HOUSE RESTAURANT

Situated on the edge of historic downtown Wytheville, the Log House

Restaurant is believed to incorporate an original log cabin dating to the 18th century. Local historians have traced the building's existence to 1784. Restored by the current owner, the cedar-and-oak structure serves Wytheville as a full-service family-style restaurant. The lunch and dinner menus include such dishes as oven-fried chicken, apple-glazed turnips, and freshly baked pies. A walk from the restaurant to Wytheville's town center reveals the eclectic, well-preserved façades of an early residential district. *Located at 520 East Main Street, the restaurant is open seven days a week. For more information, call 276-228-4139.*

MILLWALD THEATER

Named for original owners Morris Miller and Rolfe Ewald, the brick Millwald Theater opened on a 1928 August evening with the black-and-white silent film *Beau Broadway*. According to local history, the theater's basement was designated a bomb shelter and stocked with emergency rations during the 1950s. Today, the theater shows first-run films and is being renovated to preserve its early-20th-century façade and vintage marquee. The Art Deco-inspired Millwald has been recognized as the state's oldest continuously operating movie house. *It is located at 205 West Main Street. Visitors should call ahead for a schedule. Call 276-228-5031 or visit www.millwald.com.*

REED CREEK MILL

This gristmill is perched above Reed Creek just beyond the town's corporate limits. An excellent example of the evolution of a traditional mountain industry, the weatherboard-sided mill still grinds local corn into meal and flour and produces animal feed sold in mom-and-pop grocery stores. The Reed Creek Mill is one of the last operating in the region. *For a view of the mill, follow Sixth Street from Wytheville down the hill to where it becomes Clay Street and then Church Street before crossing Reed Creek.*

ROCK HOUSE MUSEUM

Constructed in 1823, the Rock House was the home of Wytheville's first resident physician, Dr. John Haller. The Haller-Gibbony home was used as a hospital and school during the Civil War and as a boardinghouse in bustling postwar Wytheville. Now a museum, the preserved homeplace re-creates a vision of genteel family life during the 19th and early 20th centuries. Its rooms are filled with family heirlooms like an antique wedding gown, a silver-plated tea set, and a mahogany poster bed with a red velvet canopy. The outdoor garden is filled with common and unusual varieties of herbs and flowering annuals. *Located at 205 East Tazewell Street, the museum is open select days year-round. Admission is charged. For more information, call 276-223-3330.*

Skeeter's

Skeeter's is located in the historic E. N. Umberger Store, which sits on the corner of East Main Street across from the 1927 George Wythe Hotel, a Classical Revival building constructed by a Roanoke architectural firm. Skeeter's vintage commercial building has a retro hand-painted advertise-ment on its street side boasting of its "World-Famous Hot Dogs," served to local residents since 1920. The restaurant estimates the total sold to be near 7 million. *Located at 165 East Main Street, Skeeter's is open daily except Sunday. For more information, call 276-228-2611.*

St. John Lutheran Church and the Flohr House

A Lutheran congregation was organized in Wythe County in 1799. Its original church was built in 1800. This site features the restored 1854 church, the congregation's second. After George Flohr, a German school-master, arrived with a minister's certificate to serve as pastor, Wytheville was positioned at the center of Lutheranism in the area throughout the 19th century. Flohr's hewn-log home, originally located a mile north of the church, has been moved to the church grounds. Adjacent to the church and home is a cemetery, God's Acre. Its markers date to 1804. Some have detailed inscriptions, while others are hand-carved in a style reflective of German folk art. *Located northwest of Wytheville at the intersection of I-81 and U.S. 21/U.S. 52 (Forest Street), the church is accessible year-round. Sunday services are open to the public.*

St. John's Episcopal Church

Dedicated in 1858, this church was designed in a cruciform pattern after London's famous St. Martin in the Fields. Wytheville native Edith Wilson, referred to locally as "the First Lady *Extraordinaire*," donated a stained-glass window in honor of her late mother and father, prominent local citizens. *The church is located at 275 East Main Street. Sunday services are open to the public. For more information, call 276-228-2562.*

St. Mary's Catholic Church

Constructed in 1845 on nearby Pepper's Ferry Road, this church was nicknamed "the Cathedral in the Wilderness" for being the first formal place for Catholic worship in the 200 miles between Lynchburg and Bristol. The single-story brick building that bears the name St. Mary's today was constructed in the 1930s and dedicated in 1937. *It is located at 370 East Main Street. Sunday services are open to the public.*

Stowe Studio

Woodcrafter Tommy Stowe has been making art out of wood since he was eight years old. He's fashioned a career carving wildlife figures and teaching at the John C. Campbell Folk School in western North Carolina. At his workshop, Stowe carves heirloom-quality artwork from linden and oak. He specializes in public, religious, and commissioned pieces. Visitors can stop by his studio in historic downtown Wytheville to view, purchase, or commission their own. *Located at 160 Tazewell Street, the studio is open select weekdays. For more information, call 276-228-1172.*

Thomas J. Boyd Museum

Named for Thomas Jefferson Boyd, the designer of Wytheville's early downtown street plan, this museum showcases the personal histories of the town's early settlers. Among the items on exhibit in the 1924 building are Native American artifacts, mannequins in Civil War-era garb, and Wytheville's first fire wagon. The museum's discovery center provides hands-on educational experiences for children. It offers a child-sized general store and weaving and combing demonstrations. The gift shop has a wide selection of souvenirs, reproductions, local art, and publications on Wytheville people and places. *Located at 295 East Tazewell Street, the museum is open select days year-round. Admission is charged. For more information, call 276-223-3330.*

VISITOR CENTER

On a hill overlooking downtown Wytheville, a pair of yellow-and-green frame buildings houses the town's visitor center, where a large collection of artifacts from local history is on display. *Located at 975 Tazewell Street, it is open regular business days. For more information, call 877-347-8307.*

WILLIAMS ORCHARD

This orchard and pick-your-own pumpkin patch hosts a harvest weekend in October. Families with children can enjoy a bumpy hayride, a complicated corn maze, and apple-butter-making demonstrations. Quarts of fresh apple cider and glass jars filled with local honey, jams, and preserves are available for purchase. *Located eight miles west of Wytheville on U.S. 11 (5175 Lee Highway), the orchard is open seasonally. For more information, call 276-686-4851.*

WYTHE COUNTY COURTHOUSE

Wytheville's first government center was a two-story frame building erected in the 1790s. That structure was replaced in 1818 by a three-story brick courthouse famed for its fish-shaped weathervane. Locals called upon their adversaries to settle their disputes "under the fish." The third and present official building was designed in the classical style with Corinthian columns by Frank Milburn, who was working simultaneously on the South Carolina Statehouse. As a consequence, the two buildings share certain architectural features, such as their elaborate bell towers and domed roofs. The 1902 Wythe County Courthouse still has its original pressed-tin ceilings. *Located at 225 South Fourth Street, it is open regular business days. For more information, call 276-223-6050.*

Wytheville Baptist Church

The Wytheville Baptist congregation formed in 1889 and originally worshiped in a small frame building. In 1916, it arranged for a Charlotte, North Carolina, architect to design a Classical Revival brick church to be located on the site of Big Spring, a mineral fountain noted for its restorative qualities. *The church is located at 200 Church Street. Sunday services are open to the public. For more information, call 276-228-3712.*

Wytheville Heritage Preservation Center

This center has brochure racks stocked with information on area events and attractions. Local maps and newspapers are also available. For a modest fee, visitors can rent a cassette tape, a player, and a headset for a Wytheville walking tour narrated by a local historian. The center's gift shop offers old-time toys, brass ornaments in the image of Wytheville's most notable historic structures, and publications on local history. *Located at 115 West Spiller Street, the center is open seven days a week. For more information, call 800-446-9670 or visit www.museums.wytheville.org.*

Wytheville Training School

After the Civil War, Virginia's law prohibiting education for African-Americans was overturned. In 1876, educator Richard Henry Scott was hired to teach at a school housed in a frame building on East Franklin Street. Six years later, a new school was built for 125 children enrolled in grades one through 11. That educational facility was the only one to serve Wytheville's African-American students for much of the 20th century. At the rear of the property is a small frame building known as the Rock Dale School House, relocated to the site in 1944 to accommodate elementary classes. In the 1960s, the local school board sold the buildings to a private owner. The green-and-white board-and-batten Wytheville Training School has been renovated to commemorate Wytheville's African-American heritage. The Training School Cultural Center sponsors events and hosts tours of the historic grounds. *Located at 410 East Franklin Street at the intersection with Fifth Street, the site is open most weekdays. For more information, call 276-625-0042.*

Wagon transport, Montgomery County, circa 1900
COURTESY OF SOUTHWEST VIRGINIA IMAGES COLLECTION, VIRGINIA TECH SPECIAL COLLECTIONS

Blazing the Wilderness Road

Because so many roads branched out into unexplored sections of wilderness along the length of the valley floor, there were many roads that carried the local name Wilderness Road. These led off the main thoroughfare through natural gaps in upland ridges lining both sides of the Valley of Virginia. Traveling through these gaps rather than over the mountains minimized the danger of sliding off a steep path and possibly losing one's load—or one's life. Park Rouse, in his classic text *The Great Wagon Road*, described the danger in vivid detail: "The path, scarcely two feet wide, and traveled by horses in single file, roamed over hill and dale, through mountain defile, over craggy steeps, beneath impending rocks, and around points of dizzy heights, where one false step might hurl horse and rider into the abyss below."[1]

The northern end of the great Appalachian road emerged from the cultured city of Philadelphia. The road's ultimate destination was the Cumberland Gap, one of only a few natural cuts through some of the most rugged peaks of the Appalachians. One of the earliest recorded attempts to pass through the gap came in 1750 by Dr. Thomas Walker, a physician turned land speculator.

Walker kept a journal that provides a record of his early exploration deep into the Appalachians and gives insight into what the experience may have been like. For example, he wrote, "We killed in the Journey 13 Buffaloes, 8 Elks, 53 Bears, 20 Deer, 4 wild Geese, about 150 Turkeys, besides small Game. We might have killed three times as much meat, if we had wanted it."[2]

Thomas Walker brought along two important traveling companions—Joshua Fry, an Oxford-educated surveyor, and Peter Jefferson, a fellow land speculator and father of future president Thomas Jefferson. Fry and Jefferson made the first map that identified the route through the Valley of Virginia. Marking the route as the Great Wagon Road, the cartographers defined its span as "from the Yadkin River [in North Carolina] through Virginia to Philadelphia distant 435 miles." The Great Wagon Road led south through the valley corridor to what is now Roanoke, where it forked. An eastern prong traveled through Rocky Mount along the Staunton River Valley into North Carolina's Yadkin River Valley. The western prong continued into the New River Valley toward the Cumberland Gap.

In Virginia, there were two main ferries across the New River—Peppers Ferry and Ingles Ferry. People and wagons were loaded on a flat boat that was poled across to the other side. Emerging from the New River, the Wilderness Road continued in a southerly direction. Travelers sought rest and refuge at Fort Chiswell, constructed in 1758 to protect the nearby lead mines of James Chiswell. The fort served as the Montgomery County seat immediately after the Revolutionary War. Today, a road marker stands over the archaeological site of the fort. The Wilderness Road continued along the valley floor, roughly following the path of what is now I-81 through Wytheville, Marion, and Abingdon. Departing the valley, explorers, speculators, traders, and pioneer settlers then traveled the Wilderness Road into unsettled territory.

Woodsman Daniel Boone earned a reputation as a competent guide, leading hunting forays and exploratory ventures into the wilderness. In the 1760s and 1770s, Boone traveled into Kentucky through the Cumberland Gap. On one of his trips, he wrote, "We found everywhere abundance of wild beasts of all sorts, through

Home of Mary Draper Ingles on the New River, 1947
COURTESY OF NORFOLK & WESTERN HISTORICAL PHOTOGRAPH COLLECTION,
VIRGINIA TECH SPECIAL COLLECTION

this vast forest. The buffaloes were more frequent than I had seen cattle in the settlements, browsing on the leaves of the cane, or cropping the herbage on those extensive plains, fearless, because ignorant, of the violence of man. Sometimes we saw hundreds in a drove, and the numbers about the salt spring were amazing."[3] In 1773, Boone brought his family with him to establish a settlement near the gap. His encampment subsequently came under attack. Several of his party, including his teenage son, were tortured and killed. Not one to be turned back, Boone returned two years later with a crew of 30 woodsmen, who wielded their axes to fell trees and blaze a trail along a 200-mile stretch of roadbed that came to be known as Boone's Trace.

In the last years of the 18th century, the road through Virginia's southwestern corner, finally wide enough to accommodate wagons, received the official title of Wilderness Road. A flood of westward settlers passed through the Cumberland Gap to open the West, the grandparents and parents of future president Abraham Lincoln among them. The migrants included many pioneer families hoping for a better life in Kentucky. Others, including many African-Americans, went unwillingly. At the time of Boone's trailblazing, Kentucky's population was 12,000. A hundred years later, by 1880, it had increased to 220,000.[4]

In 1843, this westward migration was recalled in vivid detail, as recorded in *The Wilderness Road* by Thomas Speed:

> Thousands of men, women, and children came in successive caravans, forming continuous streams of human beings, horses, cattle, and other domestic animals, all moving onward along a lonely and houseless path to a wild and cheerless land. Cast your eyes back on that long procession of missionaries in the cause of civilization; behold the men on foot with their trusty guns on their shoulders, driving stock and leading pack horses; and the women, some walking with pails on their heads, others riding with children in their laps, and other children swung in baskets on horses, fastened to the tails of others going before; see them encamped at night expecting to be massacred by Indians; behold them in the month of December, in that ever memorable season of unprecedented cold called the "hard winter," traveling two or three miles a day, frequently in danger of being frozen or killed by the falling of horses on the icy and almost impassable trace, and subsisting on stinted allowances of stale bread and meat; but now lastly look at them at the destined fort, perhaps on the eve of merry Christmas, when met by the hearty welcome of friends who had come before, and cheered by the fresh buffalo meat and parched corn, they rejoice at their deliverance.[5]

[1] Park Rouse, *The Great Wagon Road from Philadelphia to the South* (New York: McGraw-Hill, 1973), 168.

[2] Robert L. Kincaid, *The Wilderness Road* (Indianapolis, Ind.: Bobbs-Merrill, 1947), 52.

[3] Rouse, *The Great Wagon Road*, 108.

[4] Thomas Speed, *The Wilderness Road: A Description of the Routes of Travel by Which the Pioneers and Early Settlers First Came to Kentucky* (Louisville, Ky.: J. P. Morton & Company, 1886), 42.

[5] Speed, *The Wilderness Road*, 41.

Fort Chiswell Mansion, Fort Chiswell, circa 1929
COURTESY OF NORFOLK & WESTERN HISTORICAL PHOTOGRAPH COLLECTION,
VIRGINIA TECH SPECIAL COLLECTIONS

From Wytheville, the National Forest Trail follows I-81 North
for eight miles to Fort Chiswell. Depart the interstate at Exit 80.

STOP #3 FORT CHISWELL

Constructed in the mid-18th century, Fort Chiswell was a stopping
point for westward-traveling settlers along the Wilderness Road. This section of interstate shared by I-81 and I-77 is curious. While the road actually
travels west and east, it is marked I-81 North and I-77 South.

FORT CHISWELL MANSION

Colonel John Chiswell discovered lead in the area as early as 1756.
Local mines centered at nearby Austinville were instrumental in supplying
ammunition for Patriots during the Revolutionary War. In 1779, a town
was laid out, and Fort Chiswell was named the first official seat of Montgomery County. This five-story brick antebellum home, built by the
McGavock brothers in the Greek Revival style, sits on a tract first sur-

Headstone carved by Laurence Krone,
McGavock family cemetery, Fort Chiswell,
circa 1830
PHOTOGRAPH BY ANNA FARIELLO

veyed in 1747. The historic mansion, located on the south side of the service road
running parallel to I-81 near Exit 80, may be viewed from the road year-round.

HISTORIC FORT CHISWELL

This fort, constructed in 1758 under the direction of Colonel William Byrd, served as a supply house for exploratory expeditions into the surrounding territories. Fort Chiswell remained a military outpost until 1776, guarding against attacks by neighboring Cherokees. The fort was later significant in the Confederate defense of the nearby lead mines. Though little if anything of the original structure remains, the site of the historic fort is marked by a stone pyramid. A historical marker points out the essential facts of the fort's history. *Located along the service road a half-mile north of I-81 at Exit 80, the site may be viewed from the road year-round.*

From Fort Chiswell, take I-81 North for 12 miles to Exit 92.
The National Forest Trail follows U.S. 11 North into Pulaski.

STOP #4 PULASKI

Pulaski County was formed from Montgomery and Wythe counties in 1839. Situated in the New River Valley, the little community was originally

Vintage signage over Peak Creek, Pulaski
PHOTOGRAPH BY ANNA FARIELLO

known as Martin's Tank for local businessman Robert Martin, whose Mountain View plantation encompassed most of what is now downtown Pulaski. In 1854, the Virginia-Tennessee Railroad ran tracks through the new county seat. The railroad connected the town to the state line at Bristol by 1856. Martin's Tank was renamed Pulaski in honor of Polish émigré and Revolutionary War hero Casimir Pulaski. It was incorporated in 1886. In its early days, the town supported the county's only opera house and newspaper and was home to the Maple Shade Inn, a long, rambling resort built across from the train station. The town exported locally mined zinc, coal, and iron. A turn-of-the-20th-century boom town, Pulaski still boasts streets lined with historic bungalows and stately Victorian residential structures. Its vintage commercial brick storefronts provide a rare view of a 20th-century American small town. Peak Creek runs through the picturesque downtown.

BUSHONG

Photographer and artist David Cloyd Kent lived almost all his life in Pulaski. Although he studied in New York and traveled extensively throughout the South, Kent remained attached to his hometown. Famous locally for his portraiture, Kent operated out of a modest studio in downtown Pulaski, where he was commissioned to cover public and private events.

He was also nationally recognized as the principal photographer for the construction of the Radford Arsenal and Claytor Lake Dam. In 1950, after years of planning and sketching, David and Sally Kent built the modernistic home they called Bushong. The triangular white-brick design was influenced by an exhibition on solar-powered homes Kent had viewed during a visit to New York City. Taking inspiration from the work of architect Frank Lloyd Wright, he created Pulaski's first contemporary masterpiece. The home is now occupied by Kent's niece, who preserves his sculptures and paintings and Bushong's original furniture. She opens the house to the public on occasion. *Located at 44 Seventh Street NW, Bushong may be viewed from the road year-round.*

CALFEE PARK

Calfee Park was constructed in 1935 as part of Franklin D. Roosevelt's Depression-era Works Progress Administration and dedicated to Ernest Calfee, then the mayor of Pulaski. The Civilian Conservation Corps employed jobless men to make improvements to public parks and parkways.

Calfee Park, Pulaski
PHOTOGRAPH BY ANNA FARIELLO

The medieval-themed entry gate with arched entrances was designed by local engineer Edgar Millirons. The original grandstand and dugout of the community ballpark still stand intact, as do the residential neighborhoods surrounding the park. The facility, renovated in 1999, is listed on the National Register of Historic Places. It is currently home to the Pulaski Blue Jays, the Appalachian League affiliate of Toronto's major-league baseball team. *Located on U.S. 11 west of town, the park is open year-round. For more information, call 540-994-8624.*

Count Pulaski Bed-and-Breakfast

This turn-of-the-20th-century four-story inn offers guests a choice of three elegant rooms with private baths, each inspired by the proprietor's travels in Europe and Asia. The common areas are furnished with family antiques and ethnic treasures. Guests enjoy the fireplaces, the comfortable nooks stocked with literature and light reading, the full gourmet breakfast served each morning in the formal dining room, and the landscaped grounds and gardens. Dinner is served upon request. *Located at 821 North Jefferson Avenue, the inn is open year-round. For more information, call 800-980-1163 or 540-980-1163.*

Draper Mountain Overlook

Situated 3,330 feet above sea level, this overlook was constructed by the Civilian Conservation Corps—or Roosevelt's "Tree Army," as it was called during the Great Depression. Walking trails on either side of the road lead to vistas of Draper Valley to the south and Pulaski to the north. The park has picnic tables, restrooms, and walking paths that circle the mountaintop. *Located about two miles southwest of Pulaski on U.S. 11, it is accessible year-round during daylight hours. For more information, call 540-980-7705.*

Fine Arts Center for the New River Valley

An excellent example of Victorian commercial architecture, this two-story brick building dates to 1898. The fine-arts center showcases the work of New River Valley artists in various media and hosts traveling art exhibits, poetry and literature readings, and musical performances. Its gift shop features locally produced arts and crafts and a selection of regional literature. *Located at 21 West Main Street, the center is open daily except Sunday. For more information, call 540-980-7363 or visit www.fineartscenternrv.org.*

Gatewood Park and Recreation Center

Situated in northern Pulaski County, this 400-acre park includes a primitive campsite and a 162-acre lake stocked with big bluegill and redear sunfish. For day travelers, Gatewood offers miles of nature trails and a picnic area with tables and grills. Educational programs are regularly held in the park's amphitheater. *Follow West Main Street out of downtown Pulaski onto Magazine Street. Take Route 710 West (Mount Olivet Road) and watch for the signs. The park is open seasonally. For more information, call 540-980-2561.*

Historic Pulaski County Courthouse

In the late 1800s, a fire destroyed the courthouse at Newbern. Pulaski, a cultural center boasting the county's only opera house and town newspaper, vied for the right to rebuild the official structure. The general assembly granted that wish, swayed by the town's promise that residents would aid in the construction of a new courthouse. Completed in 1911, the sandstone courthouse features Romanesque and Queen Anne architectural details, an impressive clock tower, and a belfry. Historians cite the Pulaski building as an example of Victorian thinking; its elegance represents the town's prospects for growth and progress. The courthouse has historical exhibits on the area's geology, African-American history, and local civil-rights activist Chauncey Harmon. *Located at 52 West Main Street, it is open regular business hours. Visitors may call ahead to schedule a guided tour; the number is 540-980-7750.*

Historic Pulaski Railway Station and Museum

Pulaski was once a major stop along Norfolk & Western's popular passenger route. Its historic rail station was constructed in 1886. Built from locally quarried stone and embellished with ornate gables and heavy arched doors, the building is striking for both its length and its appearance. It is now home to the Pulaski Chamber of Commerce and the Raymond Ratcliff Memorial Museum. The museum's exhibits include a collection of railroad models and a number of photographs and artifacts depicting Pulaski since 1800. Behind the museum, a quarter-mile walking trail winds along the train track, shaded by black willows, white pines, and red maples. *Located at 20 South Washington Street, the station is open seven days a week. For more information, call 540-994-4200.*

JACKSON PARK

The grounds of this gently landscaped park were originally part of a parcel belonging to the majestic Maple Shade Inn, torn down in 1963. The existing stretch of green space runs along a section of the Norfolk & Western train track. Jackson Park's Victorian-style gazebo is a perfect place to take a relaxing break while exploring. The park is home to a historical marker and several military monuments, including a bronze Confederate soldier at the park's First Street end. The soldier is flanked by a dedication to World War I veterans and a pair of cannons dating to the mid-19th and early 20th centuries. *Located at the intersection of First Street NW and Washington Avenue, the park is accessible year-round.*

VETERANS MEMORIAL BRIDGE

The Veterans Memorial Bridge spans Peak Creek at the town center. The creek rushes through the heart of Pulaski for three miles, neatly contained most of the way by beautiful hand-set stone embankments. At some locations, the waterway reaches 100 feet in width. It is known to overflow during heavy rains. Like many smaller area waterways, Peak Creek flows into the New River. *A viewing platform is located on Washington Avenue across from the post office. It is accessible year-round.*

Claytor Lake ferry manned by Duncan and Graham, circa 1930
COURTESY OF SOUTHWEST VIRGINIA IMAGES COLLECTION,
VIRGINIA TECH SPECIAL COLLECTIONS

The National Forest Trail departs I-81
North at Exit 92 and follows Route 76 into the small community
of Draper. The trail then returns to the interstate.

SPUR TO DRAPER

On the way into town on Route 76, two distinctly different churches
are situated between Draper's elementary school and the community's commercial district. The immense, brick Draper United Methodist Church sits
across from the diminutive, white frame Draper Christian Church with its
tin-roofed bell tower. The latter church was established in 1896. Just past
the Methodist church, a concentration of whitewashed frame commercial
buildings, several with interesting false fronts, comprises the mercantile

center. Country roads departing from this junction are lined with old farm-houses and apple orchards.

CLAYTOR LAKE HOMESTEAD INN

This two-story Federal-style inn on well-groomed grounds offers five airy rooms and one suite. A complete breakfast is served in the dining room, which offers views of Claytor Lake. The property runs along 550 feet of private lakefront—thus the beach cabana and the shed with small boats. Guests have access to a small library and a telescope room. *Depart I-81 at Exit 92 and follow Route 76 to Route 651, on the left. The inn is located at 2652 Brown Road. It is open year-round. For more information, call 800-767-LAKE or 540-980-6777 or visit www.homesteadinnonclaytorlakebandb.com.*

NEW RIVER TRAIL ACCESS

When Norfolk Southern stopped using this portion of its southwestern Virginia rail line, the company donated the tract to the state so that the bed could be converted to a mixed-use recreational path for hikers, bikers, and horseback riders. Among the 15 access points along the trail's 57-mile length, Draper is located just about in the middle. Almost two-thirds of the trail runs along the New River. *A trail access is located on Route 658 as you drive east through Draper. It is accessible year-round, weather permitting.*

Private ferry on the New River, Kentland, Montgomery County
COURTESY OF SOUTHWEST VIRGINIA IMAGES COLLECTION, VIRGINIA TECH SPECIAL
COLLECTIONS

Ferrying across the New

Save for a few explorers' journals, little was written about the New River before 1762, when William Ingles petitioned the state for permission to establish a ferry across the river. The New has its headwaters in North Carolina. It is unique in that it is the only Virginia river to flow westward into the Kanawha and eventually into the Gulf of Mexico. Virginia's other rivers—the James, the Roanoke, and the Dan—flow eastward into the Atlantic. Throughout the 18th century, colonists pushed southwest along a road that roughly traveled the path of what is now I-81 up the steep Christiansburg Mountain and onto the Blue Ridge plateau. Descending into the New River Valley, the road stopped at the edge of the calm, broad New.

Sometimes, settlers traveled with a particular destination in mind—with a plan to join family or pursue an opportunity. Just as often, the site of one's homestead was a matter of circumstance—a wagon broke down, illness curtailed travel, or an abundance of good water presented itself. For travelers coming down the road through the Valley of Virginia, the New River was a barrier that marked the end of many a journey.

Those who continued had to pay William Ingles for a ride across the river. A local history by Lula Porterfield Givens describes the scene: "Pioneers crossed in covered wagons, on horses, and on foot. Droves of hogs and beeves were ferried over. Many times thirty-six wagons waited to be set across the river."[1] The area continues to inspire visitors like author Noah Adams: "At sunset on the New River at Radford the gold light flickers through the trees and gleams off the water. The settlers' accounts, from this region, speak of the 'pale green light' in the land they called the Great Forest."[2]

The emergence of the road on the far side of the river marked the edge of the wilderness, where travelers faced the unknown in a wild tangle of forest and underbrush. From there, the rutted road that had been wide enough for a wagon above the river narrowed to barely a path through the forest beyond its crossing. On the immediate far side of the New lay the community of Newbern, where one could find a meal and a bed. Today, Newbern's historic district preserves many original log structures along both sides of a two-lane country road. On a peaceful overlook on the south side of the road is the Wilderness Road Museum, a place that holds some of the region's stories. One of the most memorable is a tale of bravery and miraculous escape that for many years was reenacted annually on the river's edge in nearby Radford.

A small community of families had settled in Draper's Meadow, near what is now Blacksburg in Montgomery County. In 1750, Mary Draper married William Ingles, and the two set up household in Draper's Meadow. As more settlements crowded Native American lands along the frontier, tensions resulted in increasingly violent confrontations. The French and Indian War had begun. Roving bands of Native Americans continually fought settlers over land. In the summer of 1755, settlers suffered a deadly encounter when their cabins were set upon by raiders in an attack known locally as "the Draper's Meadow Massacre." Many were killed, including Colonel

Historic homesite, possibly that of the Ingles family, on the New River, Pulaski County
PHOTOGRAPH BY ANNA FARIELLO

James Patton, who had stopped briefly to visit family.

Mary Draper Ingles was carried off to Ohio by a band of Shawnees. In a daring escape, she fled her captors and followed the New River upstream through thickly forested and mountainous terrain. According to an account later penned by her son, she traveled "exposed to the Inclemancy of the weather & verosity of wild beasts Hunger & starvation for forty two days and a half in an unknown willderness."[3] Living on berries and leaves, she made it as far as Giles County, where she found help.

In the 1760s, Mary and William Ingles settled on a large tract of land spanning the New River, where they set up a ferry. There, for almost 200 years, the Ingles family ferried people, animals, and goods across the river using a long pole to push against the rocky river bottom.

[1] Lula Porterfield Givens, *Christiansburg, Montgomery County, Virginia: In the Heart of the Alleghenies* (Christiansburg, Va.: 1981), 21.

[2] Noah Adams, *Far Appalachia: Following the New River North* (New York: Dell Publishing, 2001), 90.

[3] John Ingles, *Escape from Indian Captivity* (privately published by Roberta Ingles Steele and Andrew Lewis Ingles, 1969), 16.

STOP #5   NEWBERN

In 1810, Adam Hance set out 28 lots along the Wilderness Road. His pioneer zoning restrictions required that a family purchasing a lot had to construct a hewn-log home with paned windows, a shingled roof, and a stone chimney. Today, Newbern retains the look of a 19th-century turnpike town. Among its 19 historical properties are a mercantile and post office, an early-1800s log cabin, and a frame antebellum church. The town's landmarks, both publicly and privately owned, are marked with small plaques delineating their original functions. Known locally for its seasonal arts-and-crafts and heritage festivals, the entire community of Newbern is listed on the National Register of Historic Places.

CLAYTOR LAKE STATE PARK

In 1939, the Appalachian Power Company constructed a 130-foot dam across the New River. The dam widened the river behind it, flooding the early Pulaski County settlement of Dunkard's Bottom and creating Claytor Lake. Pioneer William Christian's home was close enough to the early village that when the area was flooded, only the stone chimney was visible. The home has since been rescued from its watery hold and reconstructed next door to the state park's visitor center, located in the historic Howe House. The visitor center has static and hands-on exhibits about lake ecology, wildlife, geology, and forestry. It also hosts talks by professionals in the natural sciences. Visitors are invited to sign up for guided hikes through mature oak and hickory forests. The park offers campsites, picnic shelters, a full-service marina, and boat rentals. Visitors may fish the 21-mile lake for catfish, walleye, and striped bass. *From Newbern, follow Route 611 East to*

Route 660 South (4440 State Park Road). The park is open year-round; the visitor center is open seasonally. Admission is charged. For more information, call 540-643-2500.

HISTORIC NEWBERN JAIL

Dating to 1842, the brick Newbern jailhouse was the first in Pulaski County. Local history tells of two men hanged from the gallows, one for stealing foodstuffs from the Hance farm outbuildings across the way. The old jail is a Virginia Historic Landmark. A marker in the open lot between Wilderness Road and the tin-roofed structure commemorates the site of the first Newbern courthouse, Pulaski County's earliest seat. *Although the old jail is not open to the public, visitors can view it year-round from the Wilderness Road (Route 611) or the historic Cross Street extension.*

HISTORIC STONEHENGE

Now a private residence, this striking antebellum home is one of the first historic sites to come into view on the drive into Newbern. Located on the north side of the road, the two-story structure is distinguished by its heavy porch and stone columns. It was these oversized rock columns that prompted one of the building's early residents to name it after the famous prehistoric assemblage of stones in southern England. Confederate general James Walker was among the many notable residents of this historic home. *Located on Route 611 (Wilderness Road), it may be viewed from the road year-round.*

HISTORIC WILDERNESS INN

Built in the 1830s, the Haney Hotel served as a stagecoach stop for travelers along the Wilderness Road. In its second incarnation, the structure was called the Valley Pike Inn. Its double exterior porches enabled those upstairs to take in the evening air. According to local lore, Andrew Jackson stayed here when traveling through the region. *Located at 5266 Wilderness Road, the inn may be viewed from the road year-round. For more information, call 540-674-6800.*

Kathy's Kottage

Realist painter Kathy Sledd has renovated this example of an early starter home. A simple two-room frame structure like this would have suited a newly married couple until they could afford a larger and more comfortable house. Dating to the early 1800s, the property still has its original corncrib, utility shed, and chicken coop. Sledd has added a studio and increased the interior space to showcase her pastel and watercolor renderings of rural community life. The artist also creates prints, note cards, and calendars from canvas-captured images. *Located on Route 611 (5232 Wilderness Road), Kathy's Kottage is open select days. For more information, call 540-674-5241 or visit www.kathyskottage.com.*

Newbern Christian Church

This 1860 Greek Revival church with an open belfry is one of the few religious structures in the area to survive the Civil War. The church was designed with two entrances—one for men and one for women—and a balcony for African-American worshipers. When the interior was modified in the 1930s, the church was no longer segregated. The open gallery along the side of the sanctuary was divided to make six Sunday-school rooms. The original potbelly stoves have been replaced with gas heat. *The church is located on the north side of Route 611 (Wilderness Road). Sunday services are open to the public. For more information, call 540-980-2843.*

Historic 1870 waterworks, Newbern
Photograph by Anna Fariello

Waterworks

Newbern was ahead of its time in developing a community water system. Dating to 1870, the original brick reservoir has a section of original pipeline still in use today. Adjacent to the reservoir is a hydraulic ram that pumped water some 2,000 feet. Next door to the Church of God's fellowship hall is a dainty cherry-red hydrant that served all of Main Street. *Located along the north side of Route 611 (Wilderness Road), the waterworks may be viewed from the road year-round.*

Wilderness Road Regional Museum

This museum's main building was Newbern founder Adam Hance's original home. It is comprised of two structures dating to 1810 and 1816. The eastern portion was one of Hance's prescribed hewn-timber cabins, built on one of the core 28 lots. The weatherboard west wing, constructed six years later, was joined to the cabin in 1851. Also intact on the property are slave quarters, an 1818 barn, a granary, and a log loom house. Operated by the New River Historical Society, the Wilderness Road Regional Museum is filled with exhibits, vintage furnishings, and artifacts spanning the period from 1810 to 1865. The gift shop has biographies of area notables, regional cookbooks, and books on such subjects as local Civil War

Log outbuilding at the Wilderness Road Regional Museum, Newbern
PHOTOGRAPH BY ANNA FARIELLO

history. Maps, note cards, and calendars are also available. *Located on Route 611 (5240 Wilderness Road), the museum is open seven days a week. Admission is charged. For more information, call 540-674-4835 or visit www.rootsweb.com/ ~vanrhs/wrrm.*

From historic Newbern, the National Forest Trail follows the Wilderness Road (Route 611) to its intersection with Route 100 North. It takes Route 100 North into Dublin, then meanders another 20 miles, leaving Pulaski County for Giles County.

STOP #6 DUBLIN

In 1854, a Virginia-Tennessee Railroad depot with a roundhouse, a woodhouse, and a well was constructed in Dublin. On July 5 of that year, the citizens of nearby Pulaski hosted a grand outdoor dinner. Invitations appeared in newspapers as far east as Petersburg. When the railroad offered excursion passes for the celebration, 8,000 people traveled through Dublin. The next time the depot held so many visitors was in April 1861, when the Pulaski Guard departed for Richmond. The depot became a center for the shipment of Confederate military supplies. War reports and casualty lists were posted at the telegraph office. Today, the sleepy little town gears up every August for the New River Valley Fair, a regional celebration that includes the American Dairy Goat Show, a horse pull, musical entertainment, and big-top circus performers.

CIVIL WAR TRAILS

Union soldiers arriving at Cloyd's Mountain on May 9, 1864, took just two days to sever the Virginia-Tennessee Railroad at Dublin and inflict severe casualties on Southern defenses. Nearly a quarter of the Confederate soldiers who fought here were killed, making the Battle of Cloyd's Farm one of the most devastating in southwestern Virginia. The Union victory prevented the flow of supplies to Richmond for a year. When the entire depot, the telegraph office, and many homes were set aflame, the blaze could be seen from as far away as what is now Radford. *A historical marker is located on Route 100 five miles north of Dublin. It is accessible year-round.*

DUBLIN TOWN HALL HISTORIC EXHIBIT

On St. Patrick's Day 2001, in honor of the Irish city for which their town is named, the citizens of Dublin were invited to attend a town-hall celebration commemorating local heritage. Residents brought family photographs and albums, which were scanned and arranged together as a collage of images revealing the social and architectural history of the village. *The collage is on display at the Dublin Town Hall, located at 143 Third Street. The town hall is open regular business days. For more information, call 540-674-4798.*

HISTORIC DUBLIN INSTITUTE

A coeducational institute and boarding school founded in the early 20th century, the Dublin Institute offered a variety of college preparatory courses. The building underwent several transitions during the century, serving as both a high school and grade school. The imposing front entrance, marked

Train wreck, Dublin, circa 1897
COURTESY OF SOUTHWEST VIRGINIA IMAGES COLLECTION, VIRGINIA TECH SPECIAL COLLECTIONS

by four massive columns, leads to an open indoor atrium. The main classroom building is flanked by smaller support structures at the edge of a lot that opens to fields populated with majestic white oaks. Today, the building functions as a special-use facility for the local board of education. A small exhibit on the institute's history is on display at the visitor center south of town. *The old Dublin Institute is located north of the town center across from Dublin Elementary School on Dunlap Road. It may be viewed from the road year-round. For more information, call 540-643-0200.*

Wysor Observatory and Museum

Located behind Dublin Elementary School, this observatory is equipped with a 16-inch Meade telescope that is open once a week for stargazing. Images from the telescope are projected to a first-floor viewing screen for visitors who don't want to climb the spiral stairs to the observatory dome. During regular business hours, visitors may also view the museum's geological collections. *Located north of the town center at 600 Dunlap Road, the observatory is open select hours, weather permitting. Call ahead for an appointment; the number is 540-674-2724.*

From Dublin, follow Route 100 North for 20 miles to Pearisburg. This north-south connector through the rural countryside was first paved in the 1930s.

Stop #7 Pearisburg

Established as the Giles County seat in 1808 and originally called Giles Court House, Pearisburg was incorporated under its current name in 1854. The town, situated on a plateau overlooking the New River, was historically at the junction of two primary roads—the Newbern-Lewisburg Turnpike (now Route 100) and River Crossing Road (now Route 61). Pearisburg is one of two towns that shares its main street with the Appalachian Trail. Residents greet hikers while running errands or having a meal downtown. About 1,000 hikers stop over annually. A brochure outlining a walking tour of the town's historic district is available at the Giles County Historical Society Museum.

Andrew Johnston House

Constructed in 1829 from handmade bricks, this Colonial Georgian home has been restored to its original status. Among the home's interesting features are its pine floors, 10-foot ceilings, original stone chimney, and gabled roof. Also on the property is an 1850 outbuilding where Dr. Johnston ran his medical practice. The little building is significant for the four days in 1862 when it served as headquarters for Union leaders William McKinley and Rutherford Hayes. The home is listed on the National Register of Historic Places. *Located adjacent to the Giles County Historical Society Museum at 208 North Main Street, it is open select days. Admission is charged. For more information, call 540-921-1050 or visit www.personal.picusnet.com/gileschs.*

Appalachian Trail and Angel's Rest Overlook

Pearisburg is a major refueling point for Appalachian Trail hikers needing supplies and overnight accommodations. A local church operates a hikers' hostel with beds and laundry facilities. This section of the trail runs along the Allegheny plateau through open meadows and stands of mixed hardwoods. A favorite spot along the trail is Angel's Rest Overlook at 3,633 feet. The outlook provides an excellent view from atop Pearis Mountain that extends to the Blue Ridge. From the overlook, it's a steep two-mile descent to town via switchbacks on a trail lined with flowering azaleas and rhododendrons in season. *In Pearisburg, follow Johnston Avenue to Morris Avenue (Route 634). The AT crosses Morris Avenue less than a mile from the intersection; there are signs for roadside parking. The AT is accessible year-round, weather permitting. For more information, call 540-552-4641.*

Chamber of Commerce

An active community organization since 1937, the Giles County Chamber of Commerce has offices in the Western Hotel, the oldest building in Pearisburg's historic Olde Town section. The two-and-a-half-story brick edifice dates to 1827. It evolved from a private residence into an inn with a bar and ballroom that lit up evenings in Pearisburg from 1860 through the turn of the 20th century. Staffed during regular business hours, the chamber stocks a generous supply of brochures, local and regional maps, and publications on Giles County history. *Located at 101 South Main Street at the intersection with Wenonah Avenue, it is open regular business days. For more information, call 540-921-5000.*

First National Bank Building

Established in 1889, the Bank of Giles was reorganized as a national bank in 1906 with two vice presidents and one cashier. The dramatic Romanesque structure with a rock façade and a pair of stone turrets at the front is undergoing a total restoration by private owners. *Located across from the Giles County Courthouse at the intersection of Main Street and Wenonah Avenue, it may be viewed from the road year-round.*

Giles County Courthouse

Designed and built in 1836 by architect Thomas Mercer and listed on the National Register of Historic Places, the Giles County Courthouse is one of the oldest judicial buildings in southwestern Virginia. The Federal-style complex consists of a central structure flanked by opposing wings and embellished with a four-column portico and an octagonal cupola. Atop the hip roof is a fish-and-ball weathervane. On the lawn surrounding the courthouse are a marker detailing the general history of Pearisburg, a Confederate monument consisting of a single bronze soldier, and "McClaugherty's Millstone," the original bed stone from Giles County's first gristmill, which dated to 1794. Next door to the courthouse are the original Colonial Revival sheriff's office and jailhouse. The rooflines help distinguish the two buildings—a gabled roof is over the administrative fa-

Giles County Courthouse, Pearisburg
PHOTOGRAPH BY ANNA FARIELLO

cility, while a flat roof extends over the cellblock. *Located at 501 Wenonah Avenue, the courthouse is open daily except Sunday. For more information, call 540-921-2525.*

GILES COUNTY HISTORICAL SOCIETY MUSEUM

This museum maintains two floors full of interpretive exhibits and artifacts. Items on view include heirloom linens and furniture, Civil War memorabilia, antique automobiles and buggies, and an extensive collection of letters, photographs, and documents. The gift shop stocks locally made soaps, candles, walking sticks, and artwork. *Located adjacent to the Andrew Johnston House at 208 North Main Street, the museum is open select days. Admission is charged. For more information, call 540-921-1050 or visit www.personal.picusnet.com/gileschs.*

INN AT RIVER BEND

Dramatically situated on 14 acres overlooking the New River Valley, this inn welcomes travelers for a stay in one of seven guest rooms. Each room has splendid views, a stocked refrigerator, and a private bath. Guests enjoy a three-course breakfast, wine and hors d'oeuvres in the evening, and access to the surrounding orchards and grounds. Available upon request are massage therapy, dinner for two, cut flowers, and champagne service. *From downtown Pearisburg, follow Virginia Heights Drive to 125 River Ridge Drive. The inn is open year-round. For more information, call 540-921-5211 or visit www.innatriverbend.com.*

NEW RIVER OUTFITTERS

Three of Giles County's towns lie along the New River, an anomaly to many. The New, unlike most rivers in western Virginia, flows into West Virginia, rather than east into the Atlantic. Taking advantage of its clear pools and Class II rapids are the many outfitters who will provide everything needed for a fun-filled and safe float down the New. *Outfitters are located throughout the county; watch for their signs. They are open seasonally.*

From Pearisburg, the National Forest Trail follows U.S. 460 East for about six miles across the New River. There, it departs the highway for spurs to three popular Giles County stops—Pembroke, Mountain Lake, and historic Newport.

SPUR TO PEMBROKE

This community's first settler is recorded to have been a Pennsylvania Dutch pioneer by the name of Phillip Lyebrook, who arrived in the mid-1700s. Local history has it that the first post office was opened in 1845 by a Lyebrook descendant. This postman is said to have discovered the name Pembroke in a book he was reading and painted the name on a wooden sign he hung above the office door. The name stuck. Incorporated as Pembroke in 1940, this typical small town has a downtown with several churches, a barbershop, and a five-and-dime. Pembroke is home to Cascades Recreation Area and White Rocks Recreation Area, located off Big Stony Creek Road (Route 635) in Jefferson National Forest.

Cascades Falls

A pair of hiking trails begin at a picnic area where restrooms, tables, and barbecue pits are situated beneath the shade of pear and apple trees. The hikes are routed along Little Stony Creek, a trout stream approved for single-lure fishing. The lower trail winds through dense stands of rhododendron, past native tree species like yellow birch and hemlock, and over rocks and roots near the creek. The upper trail is wider, more gradual, and easier to follow, though hikers miss the chance to wade in the streambed. Constructed by the Civilian Conservation Corps in the 1930s, the trails culminate after two miles at the base of a 66-foot waterfall. Hikers wanting to continue may pick up the Nature Conservancy Trail and follow its

Brown's Ferry crossing the New River, McCoy, 1939
COURTESY OF SOUTHWEST VIRGINIA IMAGES COLLECTION, VIRGINIA TECH SPECIAL COLLECTIONS

ascent to a fire tower on Butt Mountain. Situated at an elevation of 4,108 feet, the overlook provides an excellent view of the New River Valley. *The trailhead is located north of Pembroke off U.S. 460 on Route 623 (Cascades Road). The road is marked with a sign for Cascades Recreation Area. The trails are accessible year-round, weather permitting.*

CASTLE ROCK

The carbonate rocks such as limestone and dolomite underlying much of the New River Valley have resulted in a karst terrain—a dramatic landscape of caves, sinkholes, and springs. Castle Rock, a cliff of exposed Paleozoic carbonate rock, is an example of the dramatic geological formations of karst topography. The imposing bluff overlooking a slow bend in the New River is aptly named for its tiered immensity. *To view the bluff, turn south off U.S. 460 West onto Snidow Road. Bear left on River Road toward the access. Castle Rock may be viewed year-round, weather permitting.*

HISTORIC PEMBROKE HIGH SCHOOL

The old Pembroke High School is an Art Deco-inspired building dating to 1938. Among its touches of stylistic geometry are the brick-and-limestone patterns across the façade and the alternating long, rectangular glass panes and smaller square pieces. The ziggurat above the door is embellished with a graphic proclaiming the school to be a "Torch of Learning." The former high school has been converted into private apartments. *Located along the south side of U.S. 460 a mile from the town center, it may be viewed from the road year-round.*

NEW RIVER ACCESS

Officially discovered in the mid-17th century, the New is one of the oldest rivers on the North American continent. Surface rock exposed in some areas dates back over 300 million years. The river runs northward from its source in North Carolina through the commonwealth and into neighboring West Virginia, where it joins the Kanawha en route to the mighty Mississippi. The New varies as it travels. Some sections are wide and meandering, suitable for a family canoe outing. Other segments—like that through the New River Gorge—offer moderate whitewater rapids and spectacular scenery. Pioneer Christian Snidow established a ferry over this portion of the New in 1786 and built a residence nearby. In the late 1800s, a wooden railroad bridge was constructed to span the New above the ferry. Today, Route 623 crosses the river on a bridge that replaced an old iron span. The view of immense Castle Rock, the 125-foot bluff jutting over the river bend, adds atmosphere to a summer trip to this prime river access, known locally as the Pembroke Pool. *Turn south off U.S. 460 West onto Snidow Road. Bear left on River Road toward the access. The river is accessible year-round, weather permitting.*

Pat West Studio and Gardens

Artist Pat West invites visitors to make an appointment to visit her hillside studio, handcrafted home, and gardens. Ms. West's home is surrounded by terraced gardens and walking trails that serve as an inspiring backdrop for her bold, vibrant, and often humorous paintings. The artist displays her work in an old barn loft that's been converted to gallery space. *The studio is located off U.S. 460 at the end of Route 617 (741 Croft Road). For more information, call 540-626-7647.*

Pembroke Library

This historic 1880 building is one of the oldest—and smallest—libraries in use in the commonwealth. Originally a carriage stop and pony-express checkpoint, the building housed Pembroke's first post office and was the site of several local elections in the early 20th century. Relocated from a nearby site in 1999, the library is run by the Pembroke Women's Group. The neat little building has its original door and mail slot. *Located off U.S. 460 at 107 Cascade Drive, it is open regular business days. For more information, call 540-726-3466.*

From Pembroke, the National Forest Trail continues along U.S. 460 East for about six miles to Route 700 (Mountain Lake Road). The intersection is well marked. A seven-mile climb leads to a historic hotel and several natural features. From Mountain Lake, return to U.S. 460 the same way.

SPUR TO MOUNTAIN LAKE

The seven-mile access winds up Salt Pond Mountain, offering views of the valley and occasional glimpses of wildlife. This area is home to a rare freshwater lake, a nature conservancy, an old-growth forest, and a historic hotel.

APPALACHIAN TRAIL ACCESS

A well-worn portion of the Appalachian Trail traverses the top of Potts Mountain at an elevation of 4,100 feet. Close to the summit, a series of rock outcrops leads to a heady cliff called Wind Rock. This scenic overlook offers panoramic views of Jefferson National Forest and Giles County. On a clear day, the Stone Creek Valley and Fork and Peters mountains are distinct landmarks. *The access is located off Mountain Lake Road (Route 700). Take Route 613 around the lake to the trail parking area. From the War Spur Trail parking lot, continue north on Route 613 to where the AT crosses the road. The trail is accessible year-round, weather permitting. For more information, call 540-552-4641.*

BRADLEY COVERED BRIDGE

This is one of eight covered bridges still standing in Virginia. Such bridges were often built as revenue sources by property owners, who charged neighbors a modest toll for crossing with wagons, horses, and early automobiles. While contributing to the community transportation system, these early bridges were also the sites of many a moonlight stroll and summer fishing trip. *Though the Bradley Covered Bridge is on private property, it may*

be viewed year-round from a pull-off on the road. It is located 0.2 mile off U.S. 460
on Mountain Lake Road (Route 700).

MOUNTAIN LAKE HOTEL

Mountain Lake is one of two naturally occurring freshwater lakes in the state. Along its shore lies a hotel whose history dates to the 1860s. In the early 1900s, this summer destination offered an incentive plan to guests, who were invited to build and furnish their own cottages in exchange for a generous discount on meals and maid service. Long after many of the cottages became the property of the hotel, they still carry the names of their builders. In the 1930s, a new owner tore down the frame inn and put up a dramatic structure in native stone. The iconic hotel was chosen in 1986 as the location for *Dirty Dancing*, and Hollywood crews moved in to film the box-office smash. Today, visitors can choose from a suite in the main house

Lake outing, circa 1920
COURTESY OF ROBERT B. BASHAM FAMILY COLLECTION

or a cottage on the property. Reservations come with breakfast and dinner. On-site activities include boating, fishing, gaming, and horseback recreation. The gift shop and gallery on the premises are accessible to the public. *The hotel is located off U.S. 460 on Route 700 (115 Hotel Circle); follow Route 700 seven miles north to Mountain Lake. The hotel is open seasonally. For more information, call 800-346-3334 or 540-626-7121 or visit www.mtnlakehotel.com.*

War Spur Trail and Chestnut Trail

Two miles north of Mountain Lake, a parking lot along the side of the road is the access point for a pair of trails that form a three-mile hiking loop through a rare old-growth forest. A stand of hemlocks, spruces, and firs makes a canopy that shades fields of ferns and flowering plants. An overlook on Salt Pond Mountain halfway through the hike offers dramatic views of the valley below. Between the overlook and the parking lot on the War Spur Trail side, a connecting path departs for the Appalachian Trail. *The trails are located off Mountain Lake Road (Route 700). Take Route 613 around the lake to the trail parking area. The trails are accessible year-round, weather permitting. For more information, call 540-552-4641.*

The National Forest Trail descends from Mountain Lake back to U.S. 460 and continues east. To reach Newport, follow U.S. 460 East a few miles to Route 42. Turn onto Route 42 East to reach Newport's historic center. After your visit, return to U.S. 460.

Spur to Newport

Although this area was settled in the late 18th century, the first post office did not open until 1842, when the mountain settlement was known as New Port, an important transportation junction. Also known as Chapman's Mill, it was a regular stagecoach stop along the well-traveled

Flour mill on Sinking Creek, Newport, 1937
COURTESY OF SOUTHWEST VIRGINIA IMAGES COLLECTION,
VIRGINIA TECH SPECIAL COLLECTIONS

Fincastle-Cumberland Gap Turnpike where it crossed the Salt Sulphur Turnpike, which linked Christiansburg with West Virginia. In 1872, the community was incorporated as Newport. The establishment of a smelting furnace brought commerce. The tight little valley with steep walls and flowing water was well suited for water-powered mountain industry. The community became a regional processing center for agricultural products. In the early years, a tannery, a flaxseed mill, several gristmills, and the Newport Woolen Mill thrived. In 1902, a devastating fire, rumored to have been sparked in response to a local prohibition law, destroyed many homes and businesses near the town center.

CLOVER HOLLOW BRIDGE

Built in 1916, this red-painted covered bridge is on Clover Hollow Road across from the 1840 Zell House. The frame bridge, constructed according to an 1840 design patent held by William Howe, spans 70 feet of Sinking Creek. It features Howe's combination of iron uprights and wooden supports. The restored bridge is accessible by foot. Clover Hollow is the site of a celebration each September that includes live mountain music and vendors displaying local crafts including needlework and baskets. A wide array of country-style sweets and eats is available. *Located north of Newport on Route 601, the bridge is accessible year-round.*

Historic Newport Center

Newport boasts several historic structures, including seven pre-Civil War homes and two of the three covered bridges in the county. Near the town center, the Beaux-Arts Sinking Creek Valley Bank, built around 1927, sits opposite the historic Newport Inn. A collection of stylistically diverse residential structures and the remains of an old mill are located on a short street across from the entrance to Route 42. Founded in 1872, the Johns Mountain Iron Company produced pig iron that was transported by wagon along what are now Route 42 and U.S. 460, from where it was carried to the railroad at Cambria, 20 miles away. The town of Newport has been designated a National Rural Historic District. *The town center is located along Route 42 a few miles from its intersection with U.S. 460. All sites may be viewed from the road year-round.*

Newport-Mount Olivet U.M.E Church

This Methodist-Episcopal church sits on the bank of Sinking Creek just off Route 42. Constructed in the 1850s, it was remodeled in 1906 in the Gothic Revival style by a local cabinetmaker, who added stained-glass windows, pointed-arch doors, and decorative siding. Other interesting architectural features include the pressed-tin roof and the bell hanging in the gingerbread-trimmed tower. *The church is located on the north side of Route 42 just outside the town center.*

From Newport, the National Forest Trail retraces its route 20 miles west along U.S. 460, back through Pearisburg to the border town of Narrows. The trail then leaves Narrows via a historic turnpike that winds along Wolf Creek.

Stop #8 Narrows

Settled in 1778, Narrows was named for the cut the New River makes through the Appalachians between Peters Mountain and East River Mountain. Like most of the mountain villages on the trails in this book, Narrows grew up around a local gristmill. A mill on Wolf Creek operated under various terms of ownership from the mid-1800s until 1954. The pace of life of this quiet frontier town changed abruptly when the railroad arrived in the late 1800s. Within a quarter-century, new industries developed to take advantage of Narrows' dual access to rail and river. The town's early commercial operations included the S. L. Johnston Steam Laundry and the Narrows Bottling Company, which packaged local spring water and advertised it for its healthful qualities. The downtown fell victim to floods in 1916, 1933, and 1940, among other years. Today, the community has embarked on a full-scale revitalization program to showcase its history. As part of the plan, the milldam has been restored and Main Street restored. The town hosts arts-and-crafts events during the summer, the Fall Fest in October, and the Snowflake Festival in December.

MacArthur Inn

This historic, recently restored brick building features an ornate columned portico. Guests have a choice of single or double rooms, some with full kitchens and all with private baths. The New River winds along the back edge of the property, affording excellent scenery. During migratory season, large flocks of Canada geese fly overhead. *Located on Route 61 East*

Bend in the New River near Narrows
COURTESY OF NORFOLK & WESTERN HISTORICAL PHOTOGRAPH COLLECTION, VIRGINIA TECH SPECIAL COLLECTIONS

at 17 MacArthur Lane, the inn is open year-round. For more information, call 540-599-7439 or 540-552-4773.

Narrows Art Gallery

The Narrows Art Gallery features work by local and regional artists including Robert Tuckwiller, Jack Scott, and Elva Davis. Works in a variety of media are on display. Watercolor and acrylic paintings hang next to black-and-white photographs and pen-and-ink sketches. Appalachian mountain crafts are also for sale. *The gallery is located at 302 Main Street. Hours vary, as it is staffed by volunteers. Visitors may want to call ahead; the number is 540-726-3022.*

New River Access

This section of the New River is channeled through a narrow gap in the Allegheny Mountains between Peters Mountain to the northeast and East River Mountain to the southwest. It flows through the last of the thrust-fault folds of what is known as Virginia's "Valley and Ridge geologic province," creating a beautiful water gap in the sandstone. *This river access, located in a fairly dense sycamore grove, is just shy of where Wolf Creek empties into the New east of town.*

The trail departs Narrows on Route 61 West. The two-lane country turnpike runs about 20 miles, passing from Giles County into Bland County and on to Rocky Gap, where it crosses the interstate; this point can be accessed via Exit 64 off I-77. The National Forest Trail then continues along Route 61 West for another 30 miles toward Tazewell.

Stop #9 Historic Turnpike

Route 61 West runs alongside Wolf Creek through a winding valley framed by mountain ridges that roll away north and south, the road switching back and forth along a rushing stream with frequent, modest cascades. At Rocky Gap, the landscape opens up into a wide valley with gently sloping sides. A natural migratory pathway, the route was used in prehistoric times by creatures seeking the brine springs and ponds near what is now Saltville. Later, a human footprint was left by Native Americans passing through the region's game-abundant, heavily forested, mountainous landscape. Europeans followed the increasingly worn byway in the spirit of westward expansion, establishing communities such as Burke's Garden and Pisgah near what is now Tazewell.

Appalachian Trail Access

The Appalachian Trail is accessible at Walkers Gap, which lies along the Tennessee Valley divide across Chestnut Ridge. From that point, it's a 1.3-mile hike to Chestnut Knob, one of the major ascents along Virginia's stretch of the Appalachian Trail. The bald mountaintop offers panoramic views from an elevation of 4,407 feet. At the summit, a stone shelter with tables and bunks is shared by hikers and day-trippers. *From Route 61, take Route 623 South into Burke's Garden. From the Burke's Garden post office, drive southwest on Route 727 for three miles to where it crosses the AT. The trail is accessible year-round, weather permitting.*

Burke's Garden

This area stands out from the air as a geological indentation encircled by mountain peaks. Native American tribes referred to it as "the Great Swamp." The high-elevation valley is also known as "God's Thumbprint." It was discovered by Europeans on a surveying expedition in 1748. Explorer James Burke, leaving the group's charted course to track an elk, came upon lush meadows filled with wildlife. The surveying party set up camp and remained in the area until an early winter surprised them. Departing hastily, they buried their refuse, including potato peels, to avoid being tracked themselves. The next spring when they returned, a vast potato patch had grown, giving the settlement the name of Burke's Garden. For visitors who don't want to follow the eight-mile road into the valley, a historical marker on Route 623 gives a brief history of the area considered

Buggy, Burke's Garden, Tazewell County
PHOTOGRAPH BY ANNA FARIELLO

one of Virginia's largest rural historical districts. *From Narrows, follow Route 61 West for about 40 miles. Exit onto Route 623, the only paved road into the valley. Travel south on Route 623, following the handmade signs to Burke's Garden.*

GARDEN MOUNTAIN FARM

An authentic working farm, Garden Mountain specializes in free-range poultry and hormone- and antibiotic-free lamb, pork, and beef. It also sells Appalachian and Amish handicrafts made by Burke's Garden natives and other Virginia artisans. Tours of the facilities can be arranged. Visitors are invited to chat with the staff as they prepare and package meats to order. Farm Day in May celebrates the arrival of newborn chicks, foals, calves, and piglets; it includes a tour and a barbecue lunch. Garden Mountain also participates in the valley-wide Fall Fest, which features homemade kettle corn, hayrides for kids of all ages, and demonstrations of blacksmithing, basket weaving, and apple-butter making. *Follow Route 61 West to Route 623* and drive nine miles into Burke's Garden. Located off Route 623 on Route 625 (Banks Ridge Road), the farm is open seasonally. For more information, call 276-472-2511 or visit www.gardenmountainfarm.com.

Garden Mountain Farmhouse Bed-and-Breakfast

This farmhouse dates to the early 1900s. Its original interior features include a dramatic central staircase with newel posts and hand-turned spindles. The newly refurbished two-room suite has an upstairs bedroom and private bath and a downstairs living area with south-facing views and a stone fireplace. Guests enjoy a full country breakfast with farm-fresh eggs and afternoon tea and cakes. Dinner can be arranged upon request. *From downtown Tazewell, take Route 61 East, then follow Route 623 for nine miles. Located off Route 623 on Route 625 (Banks Ridge Road), the inn is open seasonally. For more information, call 276-472-2511.*

Historic Chapels

The East Chapel Community Church, situated above a small waterway, is an interesting architectural interpretation of a country church. The sanctuary's rudimentary window and door details stand out against its Mission-style façade. Just next door, the Hale's Chapel Methodist Church, built from local river stones, cuts a more traditional figure with its stained-glass windows and small stone chimney. *The churches are located about 12 miles west of Rocky Gap near the intersection of Old Wolf Creek Road and Route 61. They may be viewed from the road year-round.*

Rocky Gap

Rocky Gap is nearly the halfway point between Narrows and Tazewell along the historic turnpike that is now Route 61. The once-thriving community is situated at a natural cut-through between Wolf Creek Mountain and Rich Mountain. Mail was once delivered to a post office that switched locations based on the political party of the United States president. When the president was a Democrat, the post office was located above the Conley Store. When a Republican was in office, it operated from the Honaker Store. *Follow Route 61 West from Narrows for about 20 miles into Rocky Gap.*

Ostrich farm, Tazewell County
PHOTOGRAPH BY ANNA FARIELLO

SANDY HEAD OSTRICH FARM

Ostriches and emus are two of the several ratite species, a late-19th-century scientific term that refers to birds having small or rudimentary wings. Sue Carr's hormone-free birds are allowed to roam the farm's grounds. Visitors can sign up for a tour to view the ostriches, llamas, emus, and chickens as they sleep and play; the tour illustrates the breeding and incubation processes and educates onlookers about flightless birds. Pick-your-own flowers and vegetables are weighed at the gift shop, which stocks a number of ostrich-related items, from leather goods to soap. Packaged meats are available for purchase. In October, Sandy Head hosts the Ostrich Festival, which includes music, crafts, and plenty of good eats. *From Narrows, travel Route 61 West for about 40 miles. The farm, located six miles east of downtown Tazewell on the north side of the road, is open seven days a week. For more information, call 276-988-9090.*

Stop #10 Tazewell

The town of Tazewell, settled in 1799 in a narrow valley at the foot of Rich Mountain, was incorporated almost 100 years later. First called Jeffersonville, after Thomas Jefferson, the county seat was a thriving 19th-century community with industry, culture, access to transportation, and two academies. Visitors can envision the town's past as they walk the tree-lined streets and observe the well-maintained Victorian residences and historic commercial buildings. When the railroad arrived in 1888, a commercial center developed in its wake. A streetcar line connected Main Street to the rail depot in North Tazewell. The portion of the commercial and residential districts listed on the National Register of Historic Places includes some 112 buildings. Today, Tazewell hosts an annual festival featuring old-fashioned carriage rides down Main Street, an antique show, and traditional treats like barbecue and fresh funnel cakes dappled with sugar.

Chamber of Commerce

Locally staffed, the chamber is all function and no fuss. Its selection of material on local and regional sites includes maps, interpretive brochures, and commercial advertisements. *Located in the Tazewell Mall at the intersection of U.S. 19 and U.S. 460, it is open regular business hours. For more information, call 276-988-5091.*

Depot Area

The Norfolk & Western line arrived in the Clinch Valley in the 1880s, encouraging a flurry of residential and commercial development. The rail connection provided an outlet for Tazewell County fruits, vegetables, and

Rail depot, Tazewell
PHOTOGRAPH BY A. M. BLACK, COURTESY OF SOUTHWEST VIRGINIA IMAGES COLLECTION, VIRGINIA TECH SPECIAL COLLECTIONS

livestock. It also allowed residents access to manufactured goods produced in Northern cities. After the turn of the 20th century, increased automobile travel brought the closure of the North Tazewell passenger station, leaving today's depot a dense cluster of abandoned warehouses and other industrial buildings. *From the town center, follow Tazewell Avenue north to Riverside Drive and Railroad Avenue. The site may be viewed from the road year-round.*

GILLESPIE HOUSE

This home is representative of the many late-19th-century residences that grace Tazewell's streets. The Queen Anne-style Gillespie House sits on a large piece of property near the elongated public square that is Main Street. The residence has a single-story porch, a gabled roof, and a corner tower. The Gillespie estate is interesting for its largely intact collection of original outbuildings, including a barn, a springhouse with a stone foundation, and a root cellar. *Located at 200 West Pine Street, the house may be viewed from the road year-round.*

Historic Crab Orchard Museum

Archaeological studies performed in the vicinity of this museum have documented the presence of an Indian village as early as 1500 A.D. The property contains evidence of a walled Woodland settlement comprised of domestic structures, burial sites, and storage pits. Artifacts excavated during digs are on display at the museum, which has exhibits on early exploration, regional geology and ecosystems, and early pioneer life. Heirlooms include an extensive collection of regional antique coverlets. Among the buildings reconstructed on the museum grounds are a farmstead, a barn, and a log cabin. Crab Orchard offers living-history demonstrations by costumed interpreters who tend gardens and fields and perform the everyday duties of a pioneer family. The bookshop stocks a selection of works by local authors and books on local subjects. *Located four miles from Tazewell at the junction of U.S. 19 and U.S. 460 (Crab Orchard Road), the museum is open weekdays year-round and Saturday and Sunday in season. Admission is charged. For more information, call 276-988-6755 or visit www.craborchardmuseum.com.*

Historic Main Street

The preserved commercial buildings on the north and south sides of East Main Street recall the gradual growth of Tazewell during Reconstruction and

Historic Crab Orchard Museum, Tazewell
PHOTOGRAPH BY ANNA FARIELLO

the early 20th century. They include the modest 1878 *Clinch Valley News* Building and, across the street, the 1914 Greever Commercial Building at 209 East Main. Two doors down from the Tazewell County Courthouse is the Romanesque-style Bank of the Clinch Valley, built at the turn of the 20th century. Main Street was also populated by a number of professional offices. At one point in its history, it was referred to locally as "Lawyer's Row." *All structures may be viewed from the road year-round.*

PISGAH UNITED METHODIST CHURCH

Tazewell County records show that many local churches were constructed in the countryside before they were put up in the county seat. The Pisgah congregation first met in 1793 in a frame building, choosing the name of the biblical Pisgah peak, the point from which Moses first viewed the Promised Land. According to a nearby road marker, that early structure was the first church of any denomination in the county. Pisgah United Methodist Church was relocated to its present site in 1889 to accommodate the Clinch Valley Railroad. *Located across from the Historic Crab Orchard Museum and Pioneer Park, it may be viewed from the road year-round.*

TAZEWELL COUNTY COURTHOUSE

When Tazewell County was formed from Russell and Wythe counties in 1799, townsfolk gathered with tools to fell trees, hew logs, and put up walls and windows. The first judicial building, finished in a single day, served the county until it burned in the 1830s. The brick courthouse constructed atop the original footprint was eventually sold at auction. A new courthouse, built across the street in 1874 in the Second Empire style, was amended in 1913 by a Louisville, Kentucky, contractor. Today's beige-brick Classical Revival building has a pedimented portico, a pressed-metal ceiling, a clock tower, and a landscaped lawn. *Located at 101 East Main Street, it is open regular business days. For more information, call 276-988-7541.*

TAZEWELL COUNTY HISTORICAL SOCIETY

Like many single-story frame buildings constructed for professionals and merchants after the Civil War, this structure once accommodated both a residence and an office—that of local physician C. W. Greever. Boasting a petite post-and-spindle porch running the length of its façade, the historic Greever House, built around 1870, currently serves as the headquarters of the county historical society. The office stocks publications on local history and genealogy and displays historic photographs of Tazewell. The volunteer staff can answer questions about local sites and arrange for a historic tour of downtown. *Located at 100 Church Street, the historical society is open Wednesday and Friday. For more information, call 276-988-4069.*

Tazewell Post Office

Prior to 1935, the Tazewell post office was housed in rented commercial space, most likely along Main Street. The post office that stands today, built in 1936, is similar to other federally commissioned public buildings constructed throughout the region during the period, drawing from the Beaux-Arts style, used to convey the formal dignity of official government buildings. A two-part Depression-era mural depicts the shift from an agricultural to an industrial economy. The former is represented by a mother and child with sheep. The artist, William Calfee of Maryland, depicted industrial life in less flattering terms with a smaller mural around the corner from the main entrance. *Located at 200 West Main Street, the post office is open regular business hours. For more information, call 276-472-2922.*

Pocahontas is located in the northernmost corner of Tazewell County. Follow U.S. 460 East to Bluefield, then take Route 102 North and Route 644 West to Pocahontas.

Spur to Pocahontas

In 1750, Dr. Thomas Walker became the first person to record a visit to this settlement, originally called Powell's Bottom. Over a century later, coal was discovered here. A local landowner by the name of Nelson sold coal for a penny a bushel from a hole in the hill behind his blacksmith shop. That hole was the initial cut into the famous #3 seam at Pocahontas. The Norfolk & Western Railway added a leg to its line from Radford for the exportation of the valuable resource. Pocahontas grew quickly into a bustling town with an opera house and a company store, both of which still stand today. The town was so cosmopolitan that by the late 1920s, a dry-cleaning service opened down the street from the theater. Each September, Pocahontas hosts a Labor Day celebration that features a parade down Main Street and a candlelit service in the local cemetery to honor miners who lost their lives in the course of their duties.

HISTORIC POCAHONTAS

A typical company town, Pocahontas is fortunate to have several intact buildings constructed by the mining company. The 1895 opera house once hosted comedian W. C. Fields and other notable celebrities, as well as many first-run Broadway shows of the early 20th century. Other historic structures include the 1883 Masonic Lodge, the 1896 St. Andrews Catholic Church, and a synagogue dating to the early 1900s. *Visitors may inquire at the Pocahontas Exhibition Coal Mine and Museum about guided tours of the historic district. All structures may be viewed from the road year-round.*

LAUREL INN BED-AND-BREAKFAST

Located in the center of town within walking distance of the Pocahontas Exhibition Coal Mine, the Laurel Inn offers guests their choice of two bedrooms, a suite, and a cottage annex. The two Colonial-style rooms in the main house have private baths. The suite includes a kitchenette. The annex's five bedrooms and two and a half baths make it suitable for extended family getaways. The landscaped lawn and gardens surround an in-ground pool and pool house. *Located at 186 West Water Street, the inn is open year-round. For more information, call 800-341-3611.*

POCAHONTAS EXHIBITION COAL MINE AND MUSEUM

The famed coalfield named for legendary Indian princess Pocahontas began operations in 1882. By the early 20th century, the coal produced by

Pocahontas Exhibition Coal Mine, Pocahontas, circa 1950
PHOTOGRAPH BY EARL PALMER, COURTESY OF EARL PALMER COLLECTION,
VIRGINIA TECH SPECIAL COLLECTIONS

Pocahontas, unparalleled in quality, was the fuel of choice for the United States Navy. As the mine grew more productive, it drew Irish, Welsh, Polish, and Italian workers and families from afar. Today, trips into the mine are narrated by guides who explain the development of mining techniques from hand-loading to mechanization and offer anecdotal insights into the mine's history. In this hands-on fashion, visitors experience the underground environment that was home to hundreds of Appalachian workers in the late 19th and early 20th centuries. They may also arrange for a walk through the historic village. *Located off Route 644 at Exhibition Mine Road, the mine is open seasonally. Admission is charged. For more information, call 276-945-2134.*

From Pocahontas, follow the signs to Bluefield and take U.S. 460 East to its intersection with I-77 to complete the loop trail. From that point, I-77 leads north toward West Virginia and south into the heart of the Blue Ridge, where it connects with I-81 to North Carolina.

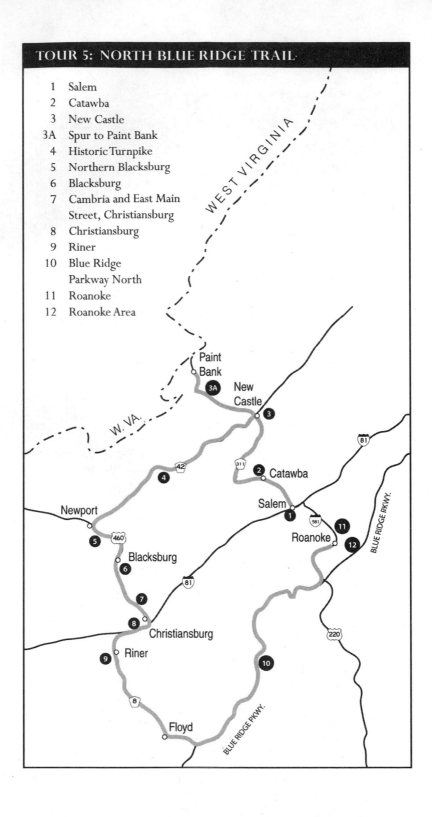

TOUR 5: NORTH BLUE RIDGE TRAIL

Roanoke City Market, Roanoke
COURTESY OF NORFOLK & WESTERN HISTORICAL PHOTOGRAPH COLLECTION,
VIRGINIA TECH SPECIAL COLLECTIONS

Chapter 5

NORTH BLUE RIDGE TRAIL

The first stop along the North Blue Ridge Trail is the town of Salem, located about 15 miles southwest of Roanoke. Salem is accessible from I-81 at Exit 140. The North Blue Ridge Trail winds along major and minor routes through the Roanoke and New River valleys. Heading north on Route 311, the trail travels through Craig County to Catawba, New Castle, and Paint Bank before tracing the path of a historic roadway along Route 42 West. In Newport, the trail intersects U.S. 460 East to head into Montgomery County and the towns of Blacksburg, Christiansburg, and Riner, then loops south along Route 8 to pick up the Blue Ridge Parkway on the far side of Floyd. Turning north, the trail covers a 40-mile section of the parkway, visiting sites in Floyd, Franklin, Montgomery, and Roanoke counties. It culminates in Roanoke.

Street scene in front of the county courthouse, Salem, circa 1896
COURTESY OF EARL PALMER COLLETION, VIRGINIA TECH SPECIAL COLLECTIONS

STOP #1 SALEM

The town of Salem is one of the oldest European settlements in the Valley of Virginia. Archaeological evidence indicates that its Native American history extends back over 10,000 years. Revolutionary War hero Andrew Lewis, responsible for ousting Virginia's last British governor, owned an expansive estate that included what is now Salem. In 1800, Lewis's son sold 31 acres to a gentleman, who in turn subdivided the land, offering individual lots for sale. These transactions brought about the formation of a town, officially founded as Salem two years later. Best known for its summer arts-and-crafts festival, Olde Salem Days, the town offers visitors much to explore. The historic downtown's main streets are lined with original storefronts and antique outlets. A walking map of the district is available at the visitor center and the local historical society.

BROOKS-BYRD PHARMACY

Visitors step back in time as they cross the threshold of this old-fashioned drugstore. The most distinctive feature of the Brooks-Byrd Pharmacy is the vintage soda counter, which serves freshly squeezed orangeade, lemonade, and limeade fountain-style. During the afternoon, it is not uncommon to find school kids gathered in conversation around a table near the store's entrance. *Located at 2 East Main Street, the pharmacy is open daily except Sunday. For more information, call 540-389-8111.*

DIXIE CAVERNS

These caverns, located five miles west of Salem, were discovered in 1920. Two local boys exploring one summer day noticed their dog had disappeared into an opening in a hillside. The pup's curiosity revealed a series of underground spaces that housed artifacts and the remains of ancient indigenous tribes. The items found inside indicated that the caves were used for shelter and food storage. In 1923, the caves were opened to the public. Today, a tour guide leads visitors into the underbelly of Fort Lewis Mountain via man-made pathways that weave among stalactites with descriptive names like "the Turkey Wing" and "the Wedding Bell." The gift shop is filled with geological specimens of all shapes and sizes. *Located at 5753 West Main Street, the caverns are open seven days a week. For more information, call 540-380-2085 or visit www.dixiecaverns.com.*

EAST HILL CEMETERY

Established in 1869 to accommodate a growing population, this 10-acre parcel overlooks Salem. Many graves of Revolutionary War and Confederate soldiers are located within its bounds. That of Revolutionary War general Andrew Lewis, one-time owner of an estate whose acreage encompassed most of what is now Salem, is distinguished by an interesting monument. *Located along East Main Street, the cemetery is accessible year-round during daylight hours.*

EAST HILL CEMETERY NORTH

Established in 1871 at Longwood Park, this two-acre lot was purchased for $82 and converted to cemetery grounds for Salem's African-American families. Many prominent figures are buried here, including the Reverend B. F. Fox of the First Baptist and Shiloh Baptist churches. *Located off East*

Main Street behind the Salem Historical Society Museum, the cemetery is accessible year-round during daylight hours.

FARMERS' MARKET

The 25 sheltered stalls at the farmers' market overflow with locally grown produce, potted and bulk herbs, cut flowers, honey harvested in the area, jams, preserves, and freshly baked goods. The market hosts several seasonal festivals. Christmas in July features a watermelon-eating contest and hayrides in place of sleigh rides. *Located at the intersection of Broad and East Main streets, the market is open seasonally during daylight hours. For more information, call 540-375-4098.*

FIRST BAPTIST CHURCH

In pre-emancipation days, members of the First Baptist Church's original congregation met "underground" in private homes and secret gathering places. At the close of the Civil War, residents of Salem's historic Broad Street constructed a church that became a spiritual center for newly freed people. Today, this 1867 Baptist church maintains an important position in Salem's African-American history. *Located at 226 South Broad Street, it is accessible year-round. Sunday services are open to the public. For more information, call 540-389-9648.*

HAMBLIN DULCIMER STUDIO

Craftsman Ken Hamblin creates hand-carved teardrop and hourglass dulcimers. His instruments are distinguished by their carefully selected combinations of wood grains and natural colors; Hamblin uses native hardwoods like butternut, walnut, and cherry. Visitors can stop by to purchase an instrument or request a commissioned piece. *Take East Main Street from downtown Salem, then turn onto Peck Street NW and follow it for a half-mile to 5033 Morwanda Street NW. The studio is open by appointment. For more information, call 540-986-1044.*

HISTORIC ROANOKE COUNTY COURTHOUSE

Roanoke County's first courthouse served as a meeting house and hospital during the Civil War. A second courthouse was built on its exact location in 1910 by Roanoke architect H. H. Huggins. Said to be Huggins's most ambitious plan, the brick building with a central section flanked by left and right wings was designed with Neoclassical and Victorian flair. Special features include a tiled cupola and a clock tower topped with a sculpted eagle with wings spread. The Confederate monument on the lawn was dedicated by the Daughters of the American Revolution in the year of the building's construction. When a new county courthouse was constructed in 1985, the former courthouse was purchased by Roanoke College. *Located at the intersection of Main Street and College Avenue, it is open regular business days. For more information, call 540-853-2473.*

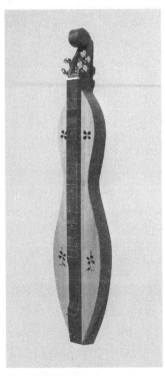

Dulcimer by Ken Hamblin, handcrafted in walnut and spruce with dogwood-flower sound holes
Courtesy of the Artist

Inn at Burwell Place

A Southern mansion dating to the early 1900s, the historic Inn at Burwell Place has been restored to its original splendor. Its four guest rooms are furnished with cherry and walnut antiques and have private baths with vintage tubs and showers, four-poster beds, and hardwood floors. Guests enjoy the 77-foot wraparound porch lined with white-washed rockers. A light breakfast of fruit and baked goods is served daily. *Located at 601 West Main Street, the inn is open year-round. For more information, call 800-891-0250 or 540-387-0250 or visit www.burwellplace.com.*

Mac & Bob's

A legendary hangout in downtown Salem, Mac & Bob's was founded in 1980 by graduates of nearby Roanoke College. The two partners, native New Yorkers, took a chance and opened a city-style pub-and-grub eatery. Today, Mac & Bob's caters to more sophisticated culinary tastes. The kitchen prepares dishes like the "Charleston Salad"—baby greens topped with yellowfin tuna and strips of London broil. The menu also features heaping plates of Southern-style ribs, a throwback to the eatery's original identity. The restaurant's logo features two lacrosse sticks, a tribute to the owners' days on their college team. *Located at 316 East Main Street, Mac & Bob's is open seven days a week. For more information, call 540-389-5999 or visit www.macandbobs.com.*

Olin Hall Gallery

This gallery on the Roanoke College campus features a large exhibition area that hosts changing events throughout the year. The exhibitions feature nationally renowned and regional artists working in assorted media, including watercolors, metal, and ink. The Corridor Gallery annex displays the college's rotating permanent collection. Student work is also on display. *Located off Main Street at 221 College Lane, the gallery is open seven days a week. For more information, call 540-375-2332 or visit www.roanoke.edu/finearts/Olin.*

Roanoke College

The Virginia Collegiate Institute was established by Dr. David Bittle in Augusta County's Mount Tabor community in 1842. When the school was incorporated three years later, management was assumed by a regional Lutheran organization. In 1847, the institute was relocated to Salem and renamed Roanoke College. Students from across the valley boarded for $10 a month and studied either primary subjects for $30 or a collegiate course in Latin, Greek, French, and German for an additional fee. Today, the prospering liberal-arts institution, the country's second-oldest Lutheran-affiliated college, adds culture and diversity to community life. The 150-acre campus is home to several structures listed on the National Register of Historic Places and the Virginia Landmarks Register. One noteworthy building is Bittle Hall, named for the school's Augusta County founder. A campus map is available at the visitor center. *The main campus, located at 221 College Lane, is accessible year-round. For more information, call 540-375-2500 or visit www.roanoke.edu.*

Salem Historical Society Museum

This two-story brick home, once a post office and general store, dates to 1845. The store was frequented by travelers along a stagecoach route that followed the path of the Great Wagon Road. Now listed on the National Register of Historic Places, the building is home to the Salem Historical Society Museum. Exhibits are devoted to Native American and pioneer cultures, Civil War memorabilia, 19th-century Roanoke County resorts, and the works of travel photographer A. H. Pecker. The museum shop is stocked with such gift items as vintage postcards and books on local and regional history. *Located at 801 East Main Street, the museum is open select days. Admission is charged. For more information, call 540-389-6760 or visit www.salemmuseum.org.*

Salem Presbyterian Church

Salem's Presbyterian congregation outgrew its original home on Academy Street in the early 19th century. In 1851, this Greek Revival structure was constructed of bricks hand-fired on the premises. It is thought that Roanoke's Deyerly family designed the building, as they did many other Greek Revival structures in the valley. *Located at the intersection of Main and Market streets, the church is accessible year-round. Sunday services are open to the public. For more information, call 540-389-3881.*

Visitor Center

This information headquarters, located in the lobby of the Salem Civic Center, is staffed to answer questions about the area. To learn about local sites and attractions, visitors may browse the extensive selection of pamphlets and brochures, including one that outlines a walking tour of historic Salem. *Located at 1001 Roanoke Boulevard, the center is open seven days a week. For more information, call 540-375-4047.*

STOP #2 CATAWBA

One of the oldest settlements in Roanoke County, this community was named for the Native Americans who settled along the rushing creek, according to local lore. Europeans arrived in the early 1700s. For a century after that, a period of quiet development unfolded. The village was recognized in the 1850s for its restorative mineral springs and fresh mountain air. The North Blue Ridge Trail makes an adventurous climb through the saddle between Fort Lewis and Brushy Mountain and descends Catawba Mountain into Jefferson National Forest.

APPALACHIAN TRAIL ACCESS

The Appalachian Trail crosses Route 311 at the ridge of Catawba Mountain. Access to the footpath is provided by the Catawba Valley Trail, which runs 2.5 miles along the ridge at elevations above 2,500 feet and crosses two creek branches. The last bit of trail climbs Tinker Mountain to Scorched Earth Gap. *From Salem, take Route 311 North to Catawba, turn right on Route 779 (Catawba Creek Road), and drive 10 miles to the Botetourt trailhead. The AT is accessible year-round, weather permitting.*

BLACKACRE ESTATE BED-AND-BREAKFAST

The 77-acre Blackacre Estate offers a choice of five rooms, some with private baths and Jacuzzis. Guests have access to the cathedral-ceilinged great room, the game room, numerous reading nooks and alcoves, and 4,700 square feet of deck space. The estate has open fields, a stocked pond, and an observation tower fitted with a telescope. Amenities include a full country breakfast of eggs and meats prepared to order, seasonal fresh fruit, and baked goods. The kitchen will pack box lunches for afternoon jaunts. *Located at 6694 Blacksburg Road, the inn is open year-round. For more information, call 540-384-6941.*

Catawba Valley General Store

Historically known as the Catawba Mercantile, this store, once the home of the Catawba post office, dates to the early 20th century. The wooden floors and clapboard walls recall days gone by. The present owners serve more than 400 hikers per year, providing a wide selection of foods and necessities. Visitors can have a deli sandwich made to order while they shop for postcards, locally made gift items, and hiking supplies. *Located on Route 311 (4905 Catawba Valley Drive), the store is open seven days a week. For more information, call 540-384-7455.*

Dragon's Tooth Trail

Dragon's Tooth is an Appalachian Trail access route that leads hikers up a 2.5-mile incline to the summit of Cove Mountain. The steep, rugged slopes offer interesting rock outcrops and views of nearby peaks. The trail's high

Dragon's Tooth, Catawba
Photograph by Anna Fariello

point is a mountain bald with a unique formation of Tuscarora quartzite that resembles a row of jagged teeth; the tallest "tooth" rises 35 feet from its base. *The trailhead is located on Route 311 north of Catawba. The parking area, just past the Catawba grocery on the west side of the road, is marked with signs. The trail is accessible year-round, weather permitting.*

Historic Roanoke Red Sulphur Springs

In 1857, a group of businessmen from Salem opened a mineral spa in the mountains. Their 700-acre resort operated for 52 years, closing in 1909. A single iron pavilion remains standing on the site today. The marble fountain at its center bears inscriptions written by past patients and visitors. Eventually, the resort reopened as the Catawba Sanatorium, the first tuberculosis care center in the commonwealth. Today, it carries on its healing tradition as a medical practice affiliated with the University of Virginia School of Medicine. Over the course of two centuries, this pristine location in the Catawba countryside has housed patients looking to recuperate in a gentle landscape of cold springs and thick greenery. *Located off Route 311 at 5525 Catawba Hospital Drive, the facility is accessible year-round. For more information, call 540-375-4200.*

Homeplace Restaurant

This restaurant is located in a historic farmhouse that has been expanded over the years to accommodate large crowds. Popular with families out for Sunday dinner and hikers fresh off the trail, the Homeplace serves down-home cooking like Grandma used to make. Guests come for the authentic fried chicken, country ham, pinto beans, coleslaw, fried apples, and desserts made fresh daily. Menu items are prepared from scratch and served at large tables family-style. After a hearty Southern meal, guests may walk the grounds or relax on the porch. *Located at 4986 Catawba Valley Road, the Homeplace is open select days. For more information, call 540-384-7252.*

Stop #3 New Castle

Situated at a three-road junction, New Castle has several residential and commercial structures dating to the late 19th century. In many of Virginia's county seats, it was not uncommon for a tavern to be quickly constructed on the courthouse square for the comfort of citizens having traveled on horseback or by wagon to reach the government center. New Castle's handsome Main Street is lined with historic buildings with colorful pressed tin along the upper-story façades. Travelers with children may want to stop in the C&M Grocery for a unique experience. Mounted behind the counter is a stuffed black bear emerging from the wall at its waist.

Big Pine Trout Farm

A getaway for amateur and serious fishermen alike, Big Pine offers guests their choice of two gingerbread-trimmed cottages within feet of the gurgling Meadow Creek. Each has a full kitchen and bath and a great room with a gas-log fireplace. For groups, the owners will arrange a fishing excursion and picnic fish fry. Day-trippers will enjoy time spent along a creek stocked daily with healthy rainbow and golden trout. The farm also offers organically grown pick-your-own blackberries in July and August. *It is located a mile south of Route 42 off Meadow Avenue; cross Meadow Creek and follow the signs. The farm is open seasonally. For more information, call 540-864-5555 or visit www.swva.net/troutfishing.*

Craig County Courthouse

Like its neighboring counties to the west and south, Craig County was rich in resources valuable to the Confederacy. New Castle, the county seat, was an obvious target for Union troops. It is said that upon close examination of the courthouse stairs, slash marks made by a Federal soldier's ax are still visible. The brick Greek Revival courthouse, built in 1852, has a columned portico and an octagonal cupola. The courthouse bell came all the way from Philadelphia, cast at the same foundry that takes credit for the Liberty Bell. New Castle's original community core consisted of the courthouse, a hotel, and the sheriff's office. Construction began on all three buildings in 1851, when the county was formed from neighboring Botetourt County and New Castle was named the seat. *Located at the corner of Court and Main streets, the courthouse is open regular business days. For more information, call 540-864-6141.*

CRAIG COUNTY HISTORICAL SOCIETY MUSEUM

Built in the 1840s, the Old Brick Hotel is one of the most prominent landmarks in downtown New Castle. Situated across the street from the courthouse, the three-story historic building currently houses the Craig County Historical Society Museum. Several rooms have been re-created as they were in the hotel's glory days; the kitchen appears as it did around 1910. Visitors may ask for a guided tour and browse the genealogical library. On Court Street adjacent to the museum is the refurbished Hawkins-Brizendine Log Cabin. *Located on Main Street across from the courthouse, the museum is open seasonally. For more information, call 540-864-7023.*

FENWICK MINES WETLANDS TRAIL

The Fenwick mining complex began operations in 1900. Carpenters erected company houses, a market, a hospital, and a school to accommodate the families of workers. Loads of high-grade iron ore were shipped daily from the mines on the C&O rail line for nearly a quarter-century. When the mines closed in 1924, commercial activity here came to a screeching halt. Today, the reclaimed mine site is popular among hikers and history buffs alike. The several small dams constructed along Mill Creek to support the mining operation created a marsh and wetland ecosystem rare to the Appalachians. Wheelchair-accessible boardwalks have been built through the marshes; tree species are identified by markers. Two moderate hiking trails begin at the site of the mining community. Hikers enjoy seeing long-defunct mine openings and remnants of old commercial and residential structures among the stands of hardwoods and pines. *The entrance, marked by forest-service signs, is located six miles east of New Castle off Route 615. The trail is accessible year-round, weather permitting. For more information, call 540-864-5195.*

FOREST INFORMATION CENTER

The Jefferson National Forest Ranger's Office is stocked with trail maps. Visitors may choose a historic route or one that features regional flora and fauna. The staff can answer questions about recreational opportunities in Craig County and the surrounding counties. *Located two miles north of New Castle on Route 615, the center is open regular business days. For more information, call 540-864-5195.*

Street scene in front of the Craig County Courthouse, New Castle
PHOTOGRAPH BY ANNA FARIELLO

Hoop Hole and Roaring Run Trails

The Hoop Hole Trail is an interesting blend of two hiking loops that traverse hill and valley, cross a rock-slide area, and wind through a mixed hardwood forest. The Roaring Run Trail passes along a small stream with cascades and a waterfall at its terminus; it is also accessible from the Fenwick Mines. Both trails are marked with forest-service signage. *To access the Hoop Hole Trail from New Castle, drive north on Route 615 for 16 miles to a marked pull-off. To access the Roaring Run Trail, take Route 621 rather than Route 615 and continue one mile to the parking area.*

Paint Bank is accessible via Route 311 North from New Castle. The 17-mile trip cuts over Potts Mountain, where travelers have majestic views of the Roanoke Valley. The route passes overlooks like Potts Mountain Wayside before descending into a farm-friendly valley.

Spur to Paint Bank

This tiny town, population 100, is served by an old-time general store, a post office, two modest country churches, and a firehouse. The name came from an antiquated method of dye production in which extracted mineral pigments were used to color paint and stain cloth. Settled in the late 18th century as a quiet agricultural and timbering community, Paint Bank saw its modest pace of life interrupted after the discovery of nearby mineral deposits. As mining companies extracted these deposits, the town grew, the railroad came, and dust and dollars dangled in the air. Once the resources were tapped out, the mining company moved on and Paint Bank returned to its quiet traditions. Today, the community offers a glimpse of agricultural life in an Allegheny valley where industry is exemplified by a single water-powered gristmill.

Depot Lodge

This historic rail depot dates to 1909, when Paint Bank was the terminal point of Norfolk & Western's Potts Valley Branch. In the 1930s, Route 311 replaced the branch route, and the station was closed. Today, it faces a quiet track. Restored and renamed the Depot Lodge, it offers five rooms, each with a private bath and a gas-log fireplace. Guests have access to decks overlooking the creek. For fun, a Norfolk & Western rail car has been renovated to accommodate a single bed and bath. The rail building retains its first-floor overhang and bay window, where travelers once purchased tickets and residents waited for passengers. *Located on Route 311 at its intersection with Route 600, the lodge is open year-round. For more information, call 800-970-DEPOT or 540-897-6000 or visit www.thedepotlodge.com.*

HOLLOW HILL FARM

Originally a series of sheep farms, Hollow Hill was converted to a bison ranch in 1989 and is now home to one of the largest herds on the East Coast. The bison, called "buffalo" by early explorers after the water buffalo of India, are raised on hormone-free diets and receive up-to-the-minute physical care. A ranch foreman conducts guided tours so visitors can view the shy, gentle giants. In autumn, the farm hosts an auction, the Intertribal Pow-Wow, and an old-time music competition. *Located off Route 311 North on Route 600 less than a mile from the village, it is open seven days a week. For more information, call 540-897-5786.*

MAPLE GROVE CHRISTIAN CHURCH

The 19th-century Maple Grove Christian Church, constructed in a style typical of local churches, has a delicate façade embellished with plum-and-amber stained-glass windows. Maple Grove is situated on the bank of a narrow, gurgling creek recommended by the *Virginia Birding and Wildlife Trail Guide* as a place to see a variety of butterflies, including the silver-spotted skipper and the tiger swallowtail, the official insect of Virginia. *The church is located across from the fish hatchery a mile south of town; follow Route 311 to Route 603. It is accessible year-round.*

Paint Bank Fish Hatchery

Operated by the Virginia Department of Game and Inland Fisheries, the Paint Bank hatchery features an early-20th-century brick building with decorative glass blocks; the building is situated above several tiers of raceways. At any given point, the concrete tanks are home to over a million fish in different stages of development. Paint Bank's cold-water facility raises three species of trout for stocking waterways in Giles, Roanoke, and Henry counties. *Located a mile south of town on Route 311 at its intersection with Route 603, it is open year-round. For more information, call 540-897-5401.*

Paint Bank General Store

Travelers will want to visit this Paint Bank institution for its old-time feel. Local customers are greeted by name at the village's only market, which offers a wide selection of regional jams and jellies and provides the makings for a picnic lunch. A cold case is stocked with packaged cuts of

Paint Bank General Store, Paint Bank
PHOTOGRAPH BY ANNA FARIELLO

Hollow Hill bison. Hot-lunch service is available at the rear of the retail space near a circle of rocking chairs. Decorative antiques in the store include a vintage Esso tank, tin signs, and historic photographs. The newly refurbished front porch has a six-foot carved wooden bear that greets visitors on the way in and a picnic table for enjoying homemade sweets on the way out. *Located on Route 311 in Paint Bank, the store is open seven days a week. For more information, call 540-897-5000.*

TINGLER'S MILL

Constructed in 1783, this historic water-powered gristmill ground corn and grain for nearly two centuries. Its 22-foot overshot wheel brought electricity to Paint Bank long before a line ever reached the county seat. During the Civil War, miller Henry Tingler, rumored to be a Union sympathizer, begged out of military service so he could continue to feed his neighbors. Located close to the Virginia-West Virginia border, the mill saw its address change five different times over the years, as boundary disputes placed it alternately in one state and then the other. At the close of the Civil War, its address was fixed at Paint Bank, Virginia. In 1897, Tingler's son-in-law reconstructed the mill to accommodate increased production. By that time, the Potts Creek establishment was one of the longest continuously operating mills in the region. *Located at the intersection of Route 311 and Route 600, the mill may be viewed from the road year-round.*

Tingler's Mill
PHOTOGRAPH BY ANNA FARIELLO

Photograph showing the need for "good roads."
ILLUSTRATION FROM ALBERT BRIGHAM'S *1903 GEOGRAPHIC INFLUENCES IN AMERICAN HISTORY*, COURTESY OF WESTERN CAROLINA UNIVERSITY SPECIAL COLLECTIONS

Building a Nation's Roads

By the time Thomas Jefferson took office as president in 1801, the country had left the wilderness behind for the era of the turnpike. Americans demanded roads with public access and some measure of maintenance. In the days before federal income taxation, there were no central government funds available for roads. Instead, money to build roads and bridges was raised through private investment and recouped via the collection of tolls. As a result, road building and road funding were sporadic and random. While passable roads continued to increase in number, the lack of a systematic program of construction meant that the nation's roadways were a confusing patchwork. To make matters worse, roads did not necessarily connect to others, many simply leading to a single destination.

The "good roads" movement advocated paving roads.
ILLUSTRATION FROM ALBERT BRIGHAM'S *1903 GEOGRAPHIC INFLUENCES IN AMERICAN HISTORY*, COURTESY OF WESTERN CAROLINA UNIVERSITY SPECIAL COLLECTIONS

In the 19th century, one road innovation was the turnpike, a road that led from one specific market to another. In 1808, the Warrenton Turnpike connected Washington, D.C., to Warrenton, Virginia. The Fincastle-Cumberland Pike linked Fincastle with Narrows and Tazewell on its way to the Cumberland Gap, roughly following what are now Route 42 and Route 61. The Fincastle-Cumberland Pike crossed the Salt Sulfur Pike, which ran from Christiansburg into West Virginia, roughly following what is now U.S. 460.

As the 19th century progressed, turnpikes covered greater distances and sometimes crossed state boundaries. The Buncombe Turnpike linked Tennessee to North and South Carolina as early as 1827. Turnpikes increasingly provided roadbeds in better condition than most other routes. A 92-mile stretch of the Great Wagon Road between Winchester and Staunton was paved in 1840. It became known as the Shenandoah Valley Turnpike.

One important purpose of having roads that connected was to allow for delivery of the mail. The newly formed Post Office Department purchased a number of stagecoaches for mail transport as early as 1800. The roads along which they traveled became known as post roads. Because of their official function, post roads were often in better condition than other routes, but they were also dangerous, providing a tempting target for thieves. While much of the earliest mail was carried by wagon, a faster system evolved in 1860. Using relay stations and fresh horses every five to 20 miles, horsemen riding for the pony express carried mail at the astounding rate of 10 miles per hour. Riders' routes averaged 100 miles. Delivering for the pony express was difficult and sometimes dangerous work that required a certain type of person. An ad in one newspaper read, "Wanted. Young, skinny, wiry fellows not over 18. Must be expert riders willing to risk death daily. Orphans preferred."

Since the original cost of mailing a letter was five dollars, mail was obviously limited to important messages. The fee was later reduced to a dollar per half-ounce, still making today's postal rates a bargain. When the pony express carried President Abraham Lincoln's First Inaugural Address across the country, it set a coast-to-coast travel record of seven days and 17 hours. But the pony express was a short-lived venture. Lasting only a year and a half, it was bought up by Wells Fargo in 1861.[1]

The first federally funded road in United States history was authorized in 1806. President Thomas Jefferson signed a congressional act to begin construction of the National Road. Linking Cumberland, Maryland, to the Ohio River, the National Road served the advance of settlers to the frontier. An authentic town-to-town highway, the National Road connected so many small communities along its path that its roadbed remains as Main Street in many American towns along what is now U.S. 40.[2]

An early-19th-century national concern focused on the barrier posed by the Appalachian range, which separated the

East Coast from the rest of the country. An analysis of Virginia's developing road system warned that the United States possessed but "half a continent divided by a spine of nearly impassable mountains into eastern and western areas with indefensibl[e] frontiers." Unless remedied, it was feared that the country might "split into two republics."[3] Ironically, the fear was that the nation would be divided east from west, not that it would become a house divided north and south along the Mason-Dixon line, as it was a half-century later. In addition to the National Road's obvious function as a physical connector, President Jefferson believed that a road spanning the formidable Appalachians was a necessity for the symbolic unification of the young country.

[1] Rickie Longfellow, "Transportation in America's Postal System," *U.S. Department of Transportation Federal Highway Administration*, http://www.fhwa.dot.gov/infrastructure/back0304.htm (accessed on June 1, 2005).

[2] Rickie Longfellow, "The National Road," *U.S. Department of Transportation Federal Highway Administration*, http://www.fhwa.dot.gov/infrastructure/back0103.htm (accessed on June 1, 2005).

[3] Nathaniel Mason Pawlett, *Historic Roads of Virginia: A Brief History of the Roads of Virginia, 1607-1840* (Charlottesville: Virginia Highway and Transportation Research Council, 1977), 13.

Stop #4   Historic Turnpike

Route 42 loosely follows the old bed of the Cumberland Gap Turnpike, which connected the Fincastle County seat with the Giles County seat at Pearisburg before continuing west to the gap that led to Kentucky. Along the 30-mile stretch of Route 42 between New Castle and Newport, the historic roadway bears remnants of once-thriving communities. A historical marker cites the homeplace and walking path of Virginia Tech's first student, Addison Caldwell, who trekked 26 miles to the Blacksburg campus on foot.

Eastern Continental Divide

A historical marker at an elevation of 2,704 feet signifies where Route 42 crosses the Eastern Continental Divide. Near this site, the waters of Sinking Creek flow westward in the direction of the mighty Mississippi, while Meadow Creek is diverted to the northeast and the Atlantic Ocean by way of the James River. *Located about eight driving miles from New Castle on Route 42, the marker is accessible year-round.*

Looney

Just a few miles outside New Castle, a green-and-white highway sign marks the community of Looney, where a 1898 one-room schoolhouse stands on the north side of the road. The historic building has an original bell and an iron water pump in the dooryard. Farther west toward Maywood, the Sinking Creek General Store is located on the south side of the road at the site of an 1867 mercantile. The market offers an eclectic mix of coun-

Looney Schoolhouse, Craig County
Photograph by Anna Fariello

try goods including overalls, canned foodstuffs, and galvanized washtubs. It is decorated with antique commercial objects and a handsome vintage iron safe. *Looney is located five miles west of New Castle on Route 42. Its sites may be viewed from the road year-round. The Sinking Creek General Store is open regular business hours.*

Maywood

Maywood's center is marked by a contemporary rock-and-flower garden maintained by the Maywood Garden Club. Just above the garden on a hill is the historic Maywood High School building, no longer in use. *The community of Maywood is located about 15 miles west of New Castle on Route 42. Its sites may be viewed from the road year-round.*

Silver Lining Farm

Eric Day and Nancy Gray operate a small Blue Ridge farmstead in the Newport area. Visitors can pick their own berries and asparagus and stock up on homemade honey and jam and fresh eggs. *The farm is located about 20 miles west of New Castle on Route 42 near the community of Huffman. Watch for the barn with the green roof, or call ahead for directions. It is open seasonally. For more information, call 540-544-7791.*

SIMMONSVILLE

A short, steep gravel drive bears south off Route 42 toward the Gravel Hill Christian Church. The church's wonderful architectural details include a gingerbread-trimmed bell tower and a tin roof. Across from the church and overlooking the historic village is the Kent family cemetery, surrounded by a vintage iron fence. Several empty buildings marking the community's defunct commercial core stand where Route 663 forks off the historic turnpike. *The highway sign for Simmonsville is located about 18 miles from New Castle at the intersection of Route 42 and Route 663. The community's sites may be viewed from the road year-round.*

The historic turnpike, Route 42, terminates at the small town of Newport, which is covered in chapter 4. The North Blue Ridge Trail follows Route 42 West to U.S. 460, then takes U.S. 460 East into Montgomery County. Entries in this section include the Virginia Tech campus and sites north of Blacksburg proper.

Stop #5   Northern Blacksburg

In the early days, the land that is now Montgomery County was a wild place of big-game animals and old-growth forests. The site of a few permanent Native American settlements, the area was valued for its rich alluvial soil, temperate valley climate, and fertile hunting. The first Europeans arrived from the Tidewater region, having traveled westward across the Blue Ridge Mountains and northward to settle the New River Valley.

Hahn Horticultural Garden

Established as the state's land-grant college, Virginia Tech was created with the mission of advancing agricultural practices as well as offering classroom education. Its campus includes experimental stations that study animal products, forestry, and plant propagation. The Hahn Horticultural Garden overflows with both exotic and domestic plants and shrubs. A tour of the garden can be arranged in advance. *The garden is located on Washington Street at its intersection with Duck Pond Drive on the Virginia Tech campus. During regular business hours, the visitor center, located off U.S. 460 on Southgate Drive, can provide campus maps and parking passes for garden viewing. For more information, call 540-231-5783.*

HISTORIC DRAPER'S MEADOW

Draper's Meadow was established in the mid-18th century as a frontier settlement. The 7,500-acre tract was made up of fertile land drained by Stroubles Creek. Famous among the community's historical figures is Mary Draper Ingles, who was captured and taken as far as what is now Ohio in a 1755 Shawnee raid. Her daring escape from Indian captivity is one of many events that color the area's pioneer history. *A historical marker telling the story of her capture and noting the site of the early settlement is located on the Virginia Tech campus.*

PANDAPAS POND

The man-made Pandapas Pond, located along the Eastern Continental Divide, is surrounded by the Appalachian hardwoods and pines of Jefferson National Forest. The pond sits in the bottom of a 500-acre bowl of woods, rhododendron groves, and clear mountain streams. Well-groomed trails for hiking, biking, and horseback riding depart from the pond, loop along Poverty Creek, and climb the north side of Brush Mountain. The pond offers glimpses of local wildlife and waterfowl. Beaver-established wetlands are located at the northeast end of the property and along the creek. *The pond is located three miles west of Blacksburg on U.S. 460; signs are posted. It is accessible year-round. For more information, call 540-552-4641.*

SMITHFIELD PLANTATION

This Georgian-style plantation was built in 1773 by Revolutionary War hero William Preston and his wife, the former Susanna Smith. The estate originally encompassed 1,900 acres. The Prestons designed their frame house in the style of Tidewater plantations along the James River. Among its distinct features are its Chippendale railings and glazed windows. One of the earliest and largest estates west of the Blue Ridge, Smithfield became known as a center of culture and politics in the area. The home was the birthplace of two Virginia governors, James Patton Preston and John Floyd, who advocated the abolition of slavery while he was in office during the 1850s. The Smithfield property, converted into a living-history museum, is managed today by Preservation Virginia. Examples of traditional fencing, including picket and split rail, are on the grounds. Architectural footprints mark the locations of the home's original outbuildings. Visitors can sign up for a guided tour with a costumed interpreter. *The plantation is located off U.S. 460 at the Southgate exit; the address is 1000 Smithfield Plantation Road. It is open seasonally. Admission is charged. For more information, call 540-231-3947 or visit www.civic.bev.net/smithfield.*

SOLITUDE

A rudimentary log house was constructed on this property in 1801. The cabin and tract were occupied off and on by the Preston family of nearby Smithfield. Robert and Mary Hart Preston enlarged Solitude in 1851, restructuring it in the Greek Revival style; it faced a road that led from Blacksburg to Smithfield. Twenty years later, a third-generation Preston sold the modest 19th-century home to serve as a college farm, part of the new land-grant university. Today, the home and a roadside historical marker are located in a picturesque section of campus at the edge of the Duck Pond, a popular spot for walking and relaxing. *Exit U.S. 460 at Southgate Drive and stop at the visitor center for a parking pass and a campus map. Solitude is located off West Campus Drive. The grounds are accessible year-round, weather permitting. The building is open on certain public occasions. Visitors should call ahead; the number is 540-231-6000.*

VIRGINIA POLYTECHNIC INSTITUTE AND STATE UNIVERSITY

The three-story brick Olin and Preston Institute, located on a five-acre site, was dedicated in 1854. A preparatory school designed primarily for students in technical fields, it operated for 18 years. In 1872, a critical meeting of the board at nearby Montgomery White Sulphur Springs marked the start of the Virginia Agricultural and Mechanical College, which incorporated Olin and Preston. Virginia Tech, as it is known today, was founded as a land-grant college to serve agricultural needs statewide. Now a leading engineering school, it has a 2,600-acre campus with over 100 buildings, most constructed of locally mined limestone. The university provides extensive outreach services in a number of fields, including economic development, continuing education, workforce development, and technology. It also operates a dozen agricultural experiment stations and six 4-H centers throughout the state. *During regular business hours, the visitor center, located off U.S. 460 on Southgate Drive, provides campus maps and parking passes for visits. For more information, call 540-231-6000 or visit www.vt.edu.*

VIRGINIA TECH FOOTBALL HALL OF FAME AND MUSEUM

Virginia Tech's football team has launched the school into a new realm of collegiate fame. The walls of the foyer in the athletic complex are decorated with memorabilia from Tech's sporting history. An atrium is lined with cases full of trophies and life-sized cutouts of Tech record holders

Virginia Tech War Memorial, Blacksburg
PHOTOGRAPH BY ANNA FARIELLO

and alumni who went on to play in the NFL. A freestanding podium at the rear is empty, waiting for an NCAA championship trophy. Floor-to-ceiling windows afford a great view of the stadium and practice fields. *From U.S. 460, exit at Southgate Drive. The facility is located off Washington Road next to Cassell Coliseum. During regular business hours, stop by the visitor center, located off U.S. 460 on Southgate Drive, for a campus map and parking pass. For more information, call 540-231-6000.*

Virginia Tech Museum of Geological Science

This on-campus museum houses a large collection of minerals native to Virginia. Among the interesting displays are a gemstone and fossil collection, a working seismograph, and a full-scale 22-foot model of a dinosaur called an allosaur. The small selection of items for sale includes rocks, minerals, and fossils. *The museum is located at 2062 Derring Hall on West Campus Drive. During regular business hours, stop by the visitor center, located off U.S. 460 on Southgate Drive, for a campus map and parking pass. For more information, call 540-231-3001.*

The North Blue Ridge Trail departs U.S. 460 Bypass to pick up U.S. 460 Business East, Blacksburg's Main Street. It follows Main Street into the college town to visit its mix of unique and interesting shops, restaurants, and bars. Draper Road runs parallel to Main Street in the downtown area. Sites in this section are in downtown Blacksburg and south of the town center.

Stop #6 Blacksburg

In the mid-18th century, a farming community grew around the headwaters of Stroubles Creek. It was incorporated in 1776. The Ingles family of the Draper's Meadow settlement is credited with the sale of 650 acres to Samuel Black, whose two sons, John and William, inherited the land. William's 1797 contribution of 38 acres, divided into 16 squares, constituted the original 16-block grid that makes up Blacksburg's downtown. Commercial and residential buildings within the grid date from 1839 to 1906. In 1872, Blacksburg was selected as a candidate for a land-grant college. Today, it is still largely defined by its relationship with Virginia Tech.

ALEXANDER BLACK HOUSE MUSEUM

Alexander Black was a fourth-generation descendant of the family patriarch, Samuel Black. Alexander's original home was a standard two-story frame structure with a hip roof and a porch. When the house was lost to fire, Black decided to rebuild in more ornate fashion, constructing a Queen Anne-style home on the same site. Rivaled by few in the county, it was an example of opulence and elegance. Today, the historic residence is being restored to its original splendor to function as a town museum. Architectural details of note include the steep gabled roof, the original vertical windows, and the ornate trim. *The home is located on Draper Road between Wall Street and Washington Street. Visitors should call ahead to learn the museum's status and schedule. Call 540-961-1199 or visit www.blacksburg.gov/museum.*

College Avenue, Blacksburg
COURTESY OF HARRY TEMPLE COLLECTION, VIRGINIA TECH SPECIAL COLLECTION

Armory Art Gallery

This Art Deco structure dates to 1934, when it served Blacksburg as an armory building. As in many other small towns across the nation, when the armory was no longer needed, the space was given a new purpose. In the 1980s, it was leased by Virginia Tech and converted to house the Department of Art and Art History's offices and a new gallery. The linear, open exhibition space showcases work by Virginia Tech students and prominent regional and national printmakers, painters, photographers, and sculptors. *Located at 201 Draper Road, it is open Tuesday through Saturday. For more information, call 540-231-5447 or visit www.sota.vt.edu.*

Art Pannonia Gallery

Partners of the Art Pannonia Gallery include local sculptor J. Gail Geer. Visitors may see her soapstone and marble carvings on display alongside work by other area artisans. The gallery walls are enlivened by oil, watercolor, and acrylic paintings by New River Valley artists. *Located at 114 North Main Street, the gallery is open daily except Monday. For more information, call 540-552-0336.*

Capone's Jewelry

In her downtown store across from the Art Deco central office of the National Bank of Blacksburg, artisan Faith Capone designs and creates custom jewelry using a variety of metals and semiprecious and precious stones. Examples of her work are displayed in the glass cases lining the walls of the architecturally distinct shop. *Located at 101 North Main Street, the store is open regular business days. For more information, call 540-953-1000.*

Church Street

As its name suggests, Church Street is lined with houses of worship. Beginning on its northern end at Jackson Street, visitors can stroll past three historic sanctuaries. Christ Episcopal Church, designed by New York architect Emlen Little, is a Gothic structure dating to 1875. Across Roanoke Street are the First Church of God and its parsonage, built in 1904 to serve the local Presbyterian parish; the church is distinguished by five stained-glass windows made by the famed Tiffany studios. The Whisner Memorial Methodist Church, dating to 1906, was named for the president of the Olin and Preston Institute, an early educational facility incorporated into what is now Virginia Tech. *Church Street runs parallel to South Main Street between Jackson and Washington streets. All buildings may be viewed from the road year-round.*

CRANE CERAMICS STUDIO

David Crane, professor of art and art history at Virginia Tech, operates a ceramics studio in verdant Ellett Valley on the outskirts of Blacksburg, where he displays and sells his salt- and wood-fired functional pottery. *Located at 1449 Lusters Gate Road, the studio is open by appointment. For more information, call 540-961-2484 or visit www.davidcraneceramics.com.*

FARMERS' MARKET

Each year from May through November, Blacksburg-area farmers bring their products to the downtown farmers' market. Vendors offer fresh fruits and vegetables, homemade jams, baked goods, and farm products including honey and plant seedlings. Operations like Blacksburg's Greenstar Farm offer organic and indigenous produce, while folks from the Ladybug Micro

Horse-and-buggy transport, Blacksburg, circa 1910
COURTESY OF JOHN KLINE COLLECTION, VIRGINIA TECH SPECIAL COLLECTION

Creamery in Willis travel here to sell their all-natural cheeses. *Located at Roanoke Street and Draper Road, the market is open select days seasonally. For more information, call 540-961-1130.*

GILLIE'S

Gillie's was an iconic Blacksburg ice-cream parlor that opened in 1974. Now touted as the first vegetarian restaurant in town, it made the hop from ice cream to a menu of whole-food selections at reasonable prices. It also offers microbrews, fresh juices, and specials posted on an old chalkboard mounted to the wall. The restaurant's weekend brunch is a local favorite. An interesting arrangement of local art covers the earthy red walls. *Located at 153 College Avenue, Gillie's is open seven days a week. For more information, call 540-961-2703.*

HUCKLEBERRY TRAIL

In 1902, the Virginia Anthracite Coal and Railway Company added a spur connecting Blacksburg with a reliable coal supply. In 1911, the spur was purchased by Norfolk & Western, which began to accommodate traveling cadets. The cadets mocked the slow train, hopping off to snack on wild berries growing along the rail bed and nicknaming the engine "Huckleberry." The track gradually fell out of use as roads and automobiles improved. Today, as part of a national rails-to-trails initiative, the town of Blacksburg has converted the old track to a six-mile multiuse recreational path that crosses the southwestern portion of the Virginia Tech campus and stretches to Christiansburg and its terminus at the New River Valley Mall. The trail winds through wooded areas, where lucky pedestrians might see nesting hawks in spring. *The trailhead is located at the corner of Draper and Clay streets across from the public library. The trail is accessible year-round during daylight hours.*

LYRIC THEATRE

This historic 1930s theater was designed by Roanoke architect Louis Smithey in the Art Deco style, common to public and community buildings of the period. Listed on the National Register of Historic Places, the Lyric is a center for cultural and civic activities. It hosts stage events and shows first-run films. Visitors are treated to free popcorn during Monday-evening performances. *The theater is located at 135 College Avenue. Phone ahead for the schedule; call 540-951-4771 or visit www.thelyric.com.*

MATRIX GALLERY

This eclectic gallery features contemporary American crafts by artisans from Virginia and states up and down the East Coast. *Objets d'art* include pottery, glass items, jewelry, woodwork, and handmade leather creations. *Located at 115 North Main Street, Matrix is open seven days a week. For more information, call 540-951-3566.*

NIEWALD PAINTING STUDIO

Virginia Tech art professor Janet Niewald paints in a private studio outside Blacksburg in Ellett Valley, where she exhibits and sells her nature-inspired oil and watercolor paintings in a workspace adjacent to her country home. *Located at 1449 Lusters Gate Road, the studio is open by appointment. For more information, call 540-961-2484.*

PRICE HOUSE AND NATURE CENTER

The Price House is one of a handful of historic structures situated on the periphery of Blacksburg's original 16-block grid. Now home to a nature center, the white frame building dates to 1853. Among its interior features are original two-panel doors and elaborate decorative details. Renovated to educate the community about local ecosystems, the Price House has nature-related exhibits, mounted and stuffed local game and waterfowl, interactive exhibits for children and adults, and live-animal stations. It is surrounded by an iris garden showing off more than 200 varieties. *Turn east off Main Street onto Lee Street to reach the center at 107 Wharton Street. It is open select days. For more information, call 540-961-1133.*

Visitor Center

The visitor center offers brochures about Blacksburg's historic district, the Huckleberry Trail, and nearby attractions. *Located at 1995 South Main Street, it is open regular business days. For more information, call 540-552-4061.*

> The trail heads east on U.S. 460 Business or U.S. 460 Bypass to Christiansburg. It exits onto Route 111 (Cambria Street), which winds through a quiet residential section of the once-bustling rail hub to its intersection with East Main Street. Turning west onto East Main, the trail continues from historic Cambria into Christiansburg proper.

Stop #7   Cambria and East Main Street, Christiansburg

In 1854, the Virginia-Tennessee Railroad laid tracks through the New River Valley. Citizens of the thriving Montgomery County seat of Christiansburg, adamant that a train not run directly through their cultivated community center, suggested a compromise whereby the rail depot would be built just over the hill and out of sight. In the wake of construction, a populous community developed around the Christiansburg rail stop. First known as Bangs and then as Cambria, it was incorporated as the latter in 1906. Montgomery County's third-largest town, the community built a reputation as the region's first major commercial crossroads. Cambria, formally annexed as part of Christiansburg in 1964, still retains a sense of community, historic storefronts clustered at its center. Cambria Street, its main street, passes over the rail tracks beside the old freight depot. Connecting Cambria's historic passenger depot with Christiansburg's courthouse square is East Main Street, which climbs up and over High Street. This section of well-traveled road is noted for its many examples of Queen Anne and Colonial Revival architecture. Sites included in this stop are in Cambria and along East Main Street.

Cambria Street

A ride down Cambria Street brings visitors a view of Cambria's first medical practice, the 1885 Palmer's Market Building, the Cambria Baptist Church, and an Art Deco school building. Sites of note near the historic depot include the Old Altamont Hospital and the Cambria Emporium, an antique shop occupying a three-story red structure dating to 1902. This end of Cambria Street was once lined with warehouses that fronted the tracks, where raw materials and finished goods transported by rail were stored. *From U.S. 460, exit onto Route 111 (Cambria Street) to reach the railroad crossing and the historic town center.*

Christiansburg Institute's Hill School

The historic Hill School was the third classroom building of the Christiansburg Institute. Opened as a Freedmen's Bureau school at the close of the Civil War, the Christiansburg Institute educated newly freed African-Americans. The emphasis was on a literary and religious curriculum. The two-story Hill School, completed in 1885, housed five classrooms. Today a community center, the building is also home to the administrative offices of the Christiansburg Institute, Inc. *Located off East Main Street on High Street, it is accessible year-round. Visitors may call ahead to sign up for a guided tour. For more information, call 540-394-5001 or visit www.christiansburginstitute.org.*

Evergreen Bell-Capozzi House

This rambling Victorian-style bed-and-breakfast offers five guest rooms, each with hardwood floors, a poster bed, and a private bath. The property includes a rose garden, a fish pond, a gazebo, an in-ground heated pool, and a concert grand piano. Guests may join in a variety of activities including bocce on the lawn and bridge in the parlor. Breakfast includes such Southern items as homemade biscuits, cheese grits, locally canned jams, country ham, and silver-dollar pancakes. *Located at 201 East Main Street, the inn is open year-round. For more information, call 800-905-7372 or 540-382-7372 or visit www.evergreen-bnb.com.*

Historic Norfolk & Western Freight and Passenger Stations

This Italianate frame station, constructed in 1854 to accommodate passengers and goods, was one of the few depots along the Norfolk & Western rail line to survive the Civil War. In 1910, an additional station was constructed for passengers. It remains relatively intact today, although road improvements have all but obscured it from view. *The freight depot and passenger station, both privately owned, may be viewed from the road year-round. The freight station is located at the intersection of Cambria and Depot streets. The passenger station is along the tracks at the junction of Depot and East Main.*

Historic Public School Building

The first public school erected by the Montgomery County Board of Education was a two-story brick building with six to eight classrooms. Constructed in 1908, it served the town until the mid-1920s, when a larger facility was built on Junkin Street. It is now privately owned. *Located on East Main Street just west of High Street on the north side of the road, it may be viewed year-round.*

Postcard of railroad crossing, Cambria, 1904
COURTESY OF EARL PALMER COLLECTION, VIRGINIA TECH SPECIAL COLLECTIONS

Oaks Bed-and-Breakfast

Listed on the National Register of Historic Places, this century-old Queen Anne and Victorian structure sits on a hill overlooking historic Christiansburg. It was built by a Confederate general for his bride in 1889. The inn's eight guest rooms have claw-foot tubs and fireplaces. Guests have access to the large common room, the wraparound porch lined with rockers, and walking paths through perennial gardens and old-growth oaks. A three-course Victorian breakfast is included with each night's stay. *Located at 311 East Main Street, the inn is open year-round. For more information, call 540-381-1500 or visit www.bbhost.com/theoaksinn.*

Schaeffer Memorial Baptist Church

This brick church atop Zion Hill was built by Charles Schaeffer, the Union captain who headed the Freedmen's Bureau in this region following emancipation. Originally from Pennsylvania, Schaeffer came to Christiansburg in 1866. His faith led him to construct a number of African-American churches in the county. *Located at 570 High Street, the church is accessible year-round. Sunday services are open to the public. For more information, call 540-382-0562.*

> From East Main Street in Cambria, head downhill to the center of Christiansburg. Franklin Street (U.S. 460 Business) crosses Main Street at the town square. Heading south out of town, Main Street becomes Route 8.

Stop #8 Christiansburg

The town of Christiansburg, situated near the edge of a plateau between the Allegheny and Blue Ridge mountains, was originally known as Hans Meadows. The rural settlement was incorporated as the Montgomery County seat in 1792 and renamed for Revolutionary War hero William

Christian. It witnessed incredible growth due to its location along the path of a westward-leading wagon road and, later, the paths of the Norfolk & Western Railway and the early-20th-century Lee Highway. On the north side of Christiansburg were the smaller industrial communities of Cambria, Merrimac, and Vicker. To the northeast were two popular mountain resorts, Yellow Sulphur Springs and Montgomery White Sulphur Springs. These outlying communities, nestled among several small upland ranges, created commercial opportunities and attracted entrepreneurs, travelers, and explorers to the region.

BLUE MOUNTAIN FRAMING AND GALLERY

Blue Mountain specializes in custom matting and framing but also stocks prints and originals by local and regional artists including Jennifer Phillips, Ralph Mitchell, and Robert Tuckwiller. Visitors can select from portraits and scenes of local theaters, historic homes, natural landscapes, and wildlife. *Located on U.S. 460 Business (325 North Franklin Street), the shop is open daily except Sunday. For more information, call 540-382-9540.*

CHRISTIANSBURG INSTITUTE'S FARM CAMPUS

Founded in 1866 on Zion Hill overlooking Cambria, Christiansburg Institute moved to a larger campus in 1900 after Booker T. Washington became its supervisor. Although Washington never taught at the school, he influenced the curriculum by hiring his own Tuskegee graduates to staff the new campus under his supervision. Over the next 20 years, the campus developed to include a farm, dormitories, an administration building, and a hospital. Supported by the Quakers for nearly a half-century, the school was deeded to Montgomery County in 1947. It served as a public high school for African-American students from Montgomery and Pulaski counties and the city of Radford until it closed in 1966. The original 185-acre campus lay along what is now U.S. 460, bordered by Crab Creek at its lower end and extending as far north as the Route 111 intersection. Today, the revitalized institute makes its home in the 1927 Edgar A. Long Building. Its story is told by an award-winning Web site. *The school site is located off U.S. 460 Business at 140 Scattergood Drive. Call ahead to sign up* for scheduled events. For more information, call 540-394-5001 or visit www.christiansburginstitute.org.

CHRISTIANSBURG POST OFFICE

Designed in 1935, this Colonial Revival building is home to a mural depicting migration along the Great Wagon Road. Painter Paul Detroot was employed by the Works Progress Administration, Franklin Roosevelt's New Deal program, to create artistic representations of American life during better times than the depressed 1930s. Detroot's *Great Road* is one of 24 federally commissioned post-office murals in Virginia. On the small plaza buffering the post office from the busy intersection stands Montgomery County's monument to the "Lost Cause," shaded by the famous Constitution Oak. *Located at the corner of East Main and Franklin streets across from the courthouse, the post office is open regular business days.*

CHRISTIANSBURG PRESBYTERIAN CHURCH

This Presbyterian church is listed on the National Register of Historic Places. History credits early Scots-Irish and English settlers, relocated from Pennsylvania to southwestern Virginia, with establishing the Presbyterian faith in the region. In 1827, the first local Presbyterian church was built at the corner of what were then South Cross Street and Long Alley. The growing congregation required additional space to worship. A quarter-century later, in 1853, a new building was erected on West Main Street down from the courthouse. The Greek Revival structure, redesigned in 1908, has a dramatic pipe organ at the rear of the pulpit. *The church is located at 107 West Main Street. Sunday services are open to the public. For more information, call 540-382-2802.*

HISTORIC CHRISTIANSBURG HIGH SCHOOL

This 1936 Art Deco building was constructed over the foundation of the ill-fated Montgomery Female Academy, a Presbyterian-founded school for girls. That handsome institution, situated on a seven-acre campus, was quickly recognized throughout the region as a prestigious finishing school for young Southern ladies. As the school developed, the academic focus shifted toward a collegiate rather than a preparatory curriculum. Two student literary societies grew, the Hypatian and the Clinonean. The school was a longtime site of gala events. However, its attendance diminished during the tenure of the Wardlow sisters, known by many as "the Black Sisters" because they always dressed in black. The tale of the gloomily clad women is kept alive through local legend. *Located at 208 College Street, the school may be viewed from the road year-round.*

HISTORIC MONTGOMERY COUNTY COURTHOUSE

Designed by Roanoke architect H. H. Huggins and built by Cambria contractor Marshall Moore, the original Montgomery County Courthouse was an impressive brick structure with an elegant entryway. The 1909 Greek Revival building was marked by a flying eagle that sat atop a clock tower and by an ornate columned portico that was removed in the 1920s to ac-

Historic Montgomery County Courthouse, Christiansburg
COURTESY OF SOUTHWEST VIRGINIA COLLECTION, VIRGINIA TECH SPECIAL COLLECTIONS

commodate construction of the Lee Highway. The structure was leveled in 1979. Only the eagle remains today, positioned atop a pedestal in the yard. Along the modern courthouse's first-floor hallway, a glass case displays historic photographs and objects related to local history. *Located at One East Main Street, the courthouse is open regular business days. For more information, call 540-382-5760.*

Inn at Hans Meadow

The Inn at Hans Meadow is situated on three richly landscaped acres originally included as part of James Craig's estate. Craig was the donor of the land that comprises most of what is now Christiansburg. The rooms at Hans Meadow have private baths and are furnished with hand-carved hardwood furniture. The three suites with oversized baths offer views of the English gardens. The grounds feature a century-old boxwood maze, an exotic fishpond, and carefully tended flower beds. The artist Lewis Miller is said to have boarded here in the mid-19th century. *Located at 1040 Roanoke Street at the corner of Depot Street, the inn is open year-round. For more information, call 540-382-2060 or visit www.theinnathansmeadow.com.*

Lewis-McHenry Monument

A tiny, well-manicured plaza at the intersection of U.S. 11 and U.S. 460 bears a marker noting the site of the last duel in Virginia. Two men, Deputy Sheriff John McHenry and Thomas Lewis, dueled to the death over a property claim at this historic intersection in May 1808. That incident marked the beginning of the end of the lawlessness of the frontier. The duel resulted in the passage of the Barbour Bill, which outlawed gunfights in the commonwealth. Adjacent to the historical marker is a plaque that commemorates the completion of the Lee Highway through Christiansburg. Parents may test their children's spelling skills in finding an error on the hand-carved stone. *Located across from the courthouse at the intersection of East Main and Franklin streets, the site is accessible year-round.*

Montgomery Museum and Lewis Miller Gallery

The Montgomery Museum is located in the historic Pepper House. Built in 1848 of hewn beams and bricks fired on the property, it was the residence of an esteemed local physician. The museum has exhibits and photographs depicting early Montgomery County residents and events. An upstairs gallery showcases contemporary regional art. The gallery is named for its collection of the work of folk artist Lewis Miller. Miller traveled to Christiansburg in the mid-19th century and chronicled his journey with drawings and watercolors of the places he saw. He became a permanent resident of Christiansburg in 1862 and lived here until his death 20 years later. The museum bookshop has an interesting selection of local and regional authors' work. *Located off Roanoke Street at 300 South Pepper Street, the museum is open daily except Sunday. Admission is charged. For more information, call 540-382-5644 or visit www.montgomerymuseum.org.*

> The North Blue Ridge Trail follows Route 8 as it departs West Main Street in Christiansburg and heads south to Riner.

STOP #9   RINER

At the southeastern edge of Montgomery County is the community of Riner, first known as Five Points for its location at an intersection of country roads. It was renamed Auburn in the 1850s for a prominent local politician. Auburn High School, a striking example of Art Deco public architecture, educates the young men and women of today's Riner. Route 8, which bypasses the historic community center, is an important scenic highway connecting Montgomery and Floyd counties.

BRUSH CREEK BUFFALO STORE AND FARM

This store stocks cookbooks, coffee mugs, and a wide selection of packaged steaks, buffalo jerky, and cured hides. Visitors are invited to tour the Brush Creek Farm and meet the bison, which range in age from newborns to adults and range in weight from 50 to 300 pounds. The animals, raised on all-natural hormone-free diets, have very gentle, shy personalities. *The store is located on Route 8 (4041 Riner Road). It is open daily except Sunday. The farm is located at 5629 Brush Creek Road. Call ahead to sign up for a farm tour. For more information, call 800-382-9764 or 540-381-9764 or visit www.bcbuffalostore.com.*

GRANATELLI PORCELAIN STUDIO

In this hillside studio near the confluence of the Little River and Beaver Creek, Silvie Granatelli displays and sells functional porcelain tableware fired in a gas kiln. Granatelli values the aesthetic her work contributes to the dining table, commenting that it is meant to "bring food to light." Her serving platters and dessert plates, vibrantly colored with a rich palette of glazes, feature unique designs. *Located off Route 8 at 407 Slusher Store Road NE, the studio is open by appointment. For more information, call 540-745-4613.*

MONTGOMERY COUNTY CANNERY AND RINER MUSEUM

The revitalized Montgomery County Cannery and the diminutive Riner Museum are located on the Auburn High School campus. Reviving a rural agricultural tradition, the cannery introduces locals to methods of preserving fruits and vegetables and promotes locally based and sustainable methods of

The Lee Highway intersection with Route 8 South to Riner, Christiansburg
COURTESY OF THE *MONTGOMERY NEWS MESSENGER* PHOTOGRAPHIC ARCHIVES

food production. Adjacent to the cannery is the Riner Museum, which displays photographs and artifacts documenting the community's history. *Both buildings are located off Route 8 at 4613 Riner Road. Hours vary with the season and staffing. For information about the cannery, call 540-382-5194. For information about the museum, call 540-382-5644.*

River's Edge

Situated on 24 acres along the Little River, River's Edge offers elegantly furnished rooms with private baths. The oldest parts of the inn date to 1913. Recent renovations include an enclosed sunroom. The innkeeper is a ninth-generation Virginian, so Southern hospitality is assured. Guests can relax in the two sitting areas, on the grand wraparound porch, and in a hammock under ancient trees. They can also walk through the formal flower gardens, fish the river, borrow the inn's canoe for an afternoon excursion, and trek the Virginia Birding and Wildlife Trail nearby. *At the county line about five miles south of Riner, turn off Route 8 onto the gravel Route 716 (6208 Little Camp Road). The inn is open year-round. For more information, call 540-381-4147 or visit www.river-edge.com.*

From Riner, follow Route 8 South for about 25 miles through Floyd and watch for signs for the Blue Ridge Parkway heading north. The town of Floyd is covered in chapter 2 of this guide.

Stop #10   Blue Ridge Parkway North

This stop covers the section of the Blue Ridge Parkway between Floyd and Roanoke.

Adney's Gap

U.S. 221 departs the parkway at Adney's Gap for a 19-mile descent into Roanoke County. Construction commenced in February 1936 on this, the earliest section of Virginia's portion of the parkway. The gap was named for 18th-century miller Thomas Adney, who processed hemp nearby. Before its production was outlawed in the 1930s, hemp was an important agricultural product in colonial America, used to produce homespun fabric and rope. *The gap is located between Mileposts 136 and 135.*

AMRHEIN WINERY

Amrhein, a family-run enterprise founded in 1995, specializes in wines with a German influence. The vineyard has received many awards, including the 2002 Virginia Governor's Cup for a citrus-infused Voignier. Visitors are invited to tour the tasting center and traverse the vine-covered slopes rising to 2,500 feet. The winery hosts a number of events, including an August celebration of wine and crafts and the September Moonlight Stomp, which includes live mountain music, pork barbecue, and wine tastings. *Exit the parkway at Milepost 136 at Adney's Gap, then follow U.S. 221 South to Route 644 (County Line Road). Located at 9243 Patterson Road, the winery is open on weekends. For more information, call 540-929-4632 or visit www.roanokewine.com.*

EXPLORE PARK

This 1,100-acre living-history and nature park has exhibits spanning two centuries, as well as three historic areas with costumed interpreters depicting life in southwestern Virginia. Those areas are a Native American village from the mid-1600s, a frontier settlement from the mid-1700s, and a small 1850s community. Living-history demonstrations show early skills such as flint knapping, log hewing, blacksmithing, spinning, and weaving. Visitors are free to mountain-bike, to fish, and to hike the six miles of marked nature trails that wind through the property. The gift shop stocks memorabilia and souvenirs. *The park is located at Milepost 115 of the parkway between U.S. 220 and Route 24. Hours vary seasonally. Admission is charged. For more information, call 800-842-9163 or 540-427-1800 or visit www.explorepark.org.*

Floyd County Dry Goods

This shop in a historic commercial building offers a variety of products including outdoor gear, books on local subjects, hand-turned wood items, and pottery. A selection of local baked goods including the store's specialty sourdough bread is also available. *Located at 5121 Franklin Pike near Milepost 150, it is open seven days a week. For more information, call 540-745-7300.*

Hensley-Polseno Pottery Studio

Donna Polseno and Rick Hensley have contributed to Floyd's reputation as an arts center by opening a pottery studio in a restored barn and a showroom in an old general store outside town. Both artists produce richly colored functional pottery. *Their studio is located between Mileposts 157 and 156 at 1643 Starbuck Road SE. It is open select hours and by appointment. For more information, call 540-745-4624.*

Historic Brugh Tavern

The Brugh family immigrated to Virginia from Pennsylvania in the early 1790s. They honored their German heritage by establishing a tavern in Botetourt County that served travelers along the Great Wagon Road. In the late 1990s, the tavern was carefully dismantled, relocated to Explore Park, and opened as a full-service restaurant. It hosts a number of special-occasion dinners. One of them, Indian Summer's Eve, includes Native American music, storytelling, and a candlelit colonial dinner on All Hallow's Eve. *Located near Milepost 115 on Route 658 (3900 Rutrough Road), the tavern is open select hours. For more information, call 800-842-9163 or 540-427-2440.*

Kelley Schoolhouse

Adjacent to this stretch of the parkway is Route 640, which passes the original lot of a one-room schoolhouse constructed in 1877. To accommodate a growing student population, the larger Kelley School was built nearby on the property in 1922. The school building was reincarnated as a country store in the 1940s; the local buyer added electricity and upstairs living quarters. In the 1950s, the Pate Store was a blend of country tradition and technological progress. Local residents still gathered in chairs at the back of the store, but rather than swapping stories, they met to view an evening of television. *Located near Milepost 149, the site is accessible year-round, weather permitting.*

Mill Mountain Park and Zoo

Mill Mountain Park rises to 1,747 feet, a good 1,000 feet above downtown Roanoke. Named after an 18th-century gristmill established here, the park is famous for its all-encompassing view of the city and its giant star. Constructed in 1948, the star reaches almost 89 feet in height and is visible under clear skies from 60 miles away. The picnic area serves as a trailhead for a two-mile hike down the mountain and a three-mile horseback trail leading to the Blue Ridge Parkway. The Mill Mountain Zoo is run by the Blue Ridge Zoological Society. Conceived in 1951 as a children's petting zoo, the facility currently has over 50 species of North and South American mammals, birds, and reptiles. Exotic creatures on the premises include a red panda, a snow leopard, and a Siberian tiger. *Exit the parkway at Milepost 120 and follow the signs. The park is open seven days a week year-round. Admission is charged. For more information, call 540-343-3241 or visit www.mmzoo.org.*

Roanoke Mountain Loop Road

A four-mile loop road travels around and up the mountain. The steep grade permits only passenger vehicles. The seven overlooks along the way offer impressive views of the city, the Roanoke Valley, and Mill Mountain. *Located at Milepost 120, the loop road is accessible year-round, weather permitting.*

Roanoke Overlooks

The Roanoke River Overlook allows views of the Roanoke River and the Niagara Hydroelectric Dam, built in 1906. Picnic tables are adjacent to the parking area. An easy self-guided trail runs less than a half-mile down to the river. Fifteen miles south is the Roanoke Valley Overlook, which, after dark, looks down on the lights of the city. *The Roanoke River Overlook is located between Mileposts 115 and 114. The Roanoke Valley Overlook is between*

Mileposts 130 and 129. Both are accessible year-round, weather permitting.

Smart View Trail

A moderate 2.5-mile loop around a picnic area, this trail descends through a ravine, follows a fast-running creek, and passes through mature woods on its ascent from the creek. After a stretch of moss-covered rock outcrops is a clearing at 2,500 feet considered a prime spot from which to view the North Carolina Piedmont. Situated in this clearing is a preserved cabin built in the 1890s. The trail is known for its colorful display of wildflowers in April and blooming dogwoods in May. *Located between Mileposts 155 and 154, it is accessible year-round.*

Stonewall Bed-and-Breakfast

This three-level log home with a native-stone foundation offers seven guests rooms and two cabins. The guest rooms come with shared or private baths. For the seriously rustic, one of the oak-and-hickory cabins has an

Cemetery, Adney's Gap
Photograph by Anna Fariello

outhouse. Guests have access to a large common area and a library stocked with volumes of Civil War and American history. Some rooms are handicapped-accessible. All packages include a full country breakfast featuring seasonal local produce. *Exit the parkway at Milepost 160 and turn right on Route 860; the inn is located at 102 Wendi Pate Trail. It is open year-round. For more information, call 540-745-2861 or visit www.swva.net/stonewall.*

VALHALLA WINERY

This winery is a success more than a decade in the making. The family-run operation, situated at 2,000 feet, overlooks the Roanoke and Shenandoah valleys. Valhalla produces estate-grown varieties and is famous for its Virginia Valkyrie and its Chardonnay-Voignier blend, called Row Ten. Visitors can sample Valhalla's wines at the newly refurbished Cellar Door, a combination tasting room and event center. Among the several events the winery hosts are the Moonlight Winemaker's Dinner in July and the Blessing of the Vines in August. *Located off U.S. 221 at 6500 Mount Chestnut Road, the winery is open seasonally. Guests should call ahead (540-725-WINE) or visit the Web site (www.valhallawines.com) for a schedule and information.*

WORMY CHESTNUT

Originally Agee's General Store, the Wormy Chestnut is one of the oldest businesses on the parkway. Legend has it that Agee's sold the essential moonshine ingredients—sugar and bottles—to residents of nearby Shooting Creek. Today's shop stocks local gifts and crafts including pottery, metal, woodwork, quilts, photography, handmade baskets, dulcimers, and candles. *Exit the parkway at Milepost 160 to access Route 680; the shop is located at 105 Chestnut Lane SE. Visitors should call ahead, as hours may vary; the number is 540-745-2406.*

Norfolk & Western steam engine, circa 1900
COURTESY OF CHARLES ALIFF RAILROAD COLLECTION,
VIRGINIA TECH SPECIAL COLLECTIONS

The Coming of the Railroad

For nearly three centuries, travelers used overland roadways to move about the continent. The Warriors Path, the Great Wagon Road, the Wilderness Road, and 19th-century turnpikes took travelers through southwestern Virginia. First on foot and then on horseback, some with wagons or wheeled carriages, Americans traveled the Blue Ridge and the Valley of Virginia. A system of canals added options for transporting goods to and from far-off ports. In 1840, the James River and Kanawha Canal reached Lynchburg. Within 20 years, extensions were built to Buchanan and Lexington.

But all of that changed with the construction of a network of railroads in the region. In the middle of the 19th century, the dominance of American road travel began to wane when wagons and horses were replaced by rails as the preferred means of travel. In the 1850s, north-south and east-west rail lines were constructed in Virginia. The Virginia-Tennessee Railroad linked Lynchburg to Bristol, while Virginia Central connected Richmond to Staunton. In the central-eastern part of the state, the Southside line linked Lynchburg with Petersburg. Spur lines reached into the southern counties of the commonwealth. These shorter lines took on colorful local names, like the Dick and Willie, which connected Stuart and Danville. The Virginia Creeper was a name given to the locomotive that traveled the steep grades between Damascus and Abingdon. Such trains hauled lumber, iron ore, supplies, and passengers, relieving the pressure to build additional roads.

Today, Roanoke is a major population center, but in the mid-1800s, Salem was the largest town in the area. A county seat, Salem was home to Roanoke College and was a serious contender for an important rail connection then under consideration. Instead, Norfolk & Western chose the nearby community of Big Lick as its rail hub. Soon, the Roanoke Machine Works opened there to equip shops that built locomotives. With the machine works offering immediate employment, workers flocked to the site. Roanoke earned its nickname, "the Magic City," from its instantaneous growth from a mere 600 residents in 1882 to more than 5,000 just a year later—nearly a tenfold increase.[1]

Although roadways had been a priority for the nascent nation, it looked by the turn of the 20th century as though road travel would be forever eclipsed by rail. And no wonder, since rail travel was efficient, economical, and glamorous. In 1916, when a contingent of Quakers decided to visit the Christiansburg Institute in Montgomery County, they rented a private rail car to carry them from Philadelphia to the graduation ceremonies. When the celebration was over, the Quakers retired to their rented sleeper car and departed for Natural Bridge, where the car was uncoupled and they spent the night. The next day, after they had seen the natural wonder, their car was picked up by a locomotive for the trip home to Philadelphia.[2]

The popularity of the bicycle and the invention of the automobile shifted the balance between rail and road. For 100 years, rail had surpassed overland travel as the nation's preferred mode of transportation, only to have the pendulum swing back with the invention of the automobile at the end of the 19th century. In 1891, New Jersey established the first state highway department. By 1917, all the states had highway agencies. By 1904, there were 2 million miles of roads in the United States, although most of them were still not paved.

There was so much concern about improving roads that a "good-roads" movement became the focus of a national conversation. The idea gained the support of the newly formed American Automobile Association. The demand for good roads received important political support from President Woodrow Wilson, an automobile enthusiast. While Wilson favored a modern roadway system for practical reasons—namely, its effect on commerce and tourism—he, like Thomas Jefferson, expressed his interest metaphorically. Wilson imagined a system of highways "weaving a net of neighborhood and state and national opinions together,"[3] a phrase that sounds more like a description of today's Internet than a plan for a young nation's roadways.

By the mid-20th century, the family car put Americans back on the road in record numbers, commuting to work and traveling for pleasure. But in the ebb and flow of economic circumstances and resource allocation, we can't be certain if American road travel can weather its reliance on fossil fuels. Americans have yet to face the fact that oil is as finite and consumable as our virgin forests once were. At the start of the 21st century, we are a nation firmly planted behind the wheel, traveling at speeds unheard of in centuries past. Hopefully, our innate curiosity and national determination will find innovative solutions to tomorrow's transportation needs that will allow tourism to continue to fuel small-town economies. Whether by road, rail, or some unforeseen invention, we will no doubt travel at ever-faster speeds, bringing city and countryside closer as the 21st century progresses.

[1] John R. Hildebrand, "Triumph and Tragedy: A Railroad Struggle Instrumental in Creating Roanoke, Virginia," *Smithfield Review* 5 (2001): 67-84.

[2] Friends Historical Library of Swarthmore College, *The Freedman's Friend* 9 (1916): 59.

[3] Richard F. Weingroff, "Federal Aid Road Act of 1916: Building the Foundation," *U.S. Department of Transportation Federal Highway Administration*, http://www.fhwa.dot.gov/infrastructure/rw96b.htm (accessed on June 1, 2005).

Historic commercial signage, Roanoke
PHOTOGRAPH BY ANNA FARIELLO

From the Blue Ridge Parkway, follow the exits to downtown Roanoke, taking U.S. 220 at Milepost 121 or Route 24 at Milepost 112. The North Blue Ridge Trail completes its loop at Roanoke, where the sites are grouped into two stops—those within walking distance of downtown (stop #11) and those within a short drive (stop #12).

Stop #11 Roanoke

Settled in the mid-18th century, the Roanoke Valley was home to early farming families who settled near creeks, dormant salt marshes, and historic Indian paths. For nearly a century, agriculture was dominant here. All that changed in late 19th century, when the railroad arrived at the community then known as Big Lick. The town was subsequently chartered as Roanoke, which became a hub for rail travel and commerce, boasting hotels, saloons, and a downtown commercial center. Though today's historic market district overflows with a variety of contemporary shops, boutiques, and restaurants, it retains a feel of the past, thanks to its colorful advertising signs atop original commercial buildings. The city hosts a number of celebrations and festivities throughout the year, including the Festival in the Park, the Henry Street Festival, Strawberry Days, and the Virginia Chili Cook-Off.

Art Museum of Western Virginia

Located in Center in the Square, this open and airy museum houses permanent collections of 19th- and 20th-century American works and contemporary art. Other displays include African tribal art, masks, and weavings. The large wing devoted to regional professional artists offers photography, paintings, sculpture, and contemporary crafts. Art Venture, an interactive children's center, hosts classes and activities on a revolving basis. *Located at One Market Street, the museum is open daily except Monday. Admission is charged. For more information, call 540-342-5760 or visit www.artmuseumroanoke.org.*

Center in the Square

Originally home to McGuire's Farming Supply Company, the Campbell Avenue side of Center in the Square dates to 1914. McGuire's supplied Roanokers with agricultural necessities from seed to horse-drawn buggies. Today, Center in the Square is a cultural center housing museums, specialty shops, and galleries. *Located at One Market Street, it is open daily except Monday. For more information, call 540-342-5700 or visit www.centerinthesquare.org.*

Farmers' Market

Roanoke boasts one of the oldest continuously operating farmers' markets in the commonwealth. The original market building, constructed in 1884 and refurbished in 1922, is now home to a food court serving international cuisine. The interior has original architectural features including pressed-tin ceiling tiles and exposed pipes. Along Market Street, the yellow-and-white awnings shade 70 stalls piled high with fresh produce, cut flowers, freshly baked and canned goods, and locally produced crafts. Customers can meet the growers and artisans responsible for the colorful goods.

Located at the intersection of Campbell Avenue and Market Street, the market is open daily except Sunday. For more information, call 540-342-2028.

FIRE STATION NO. 1

This still-operational red-brick fire station, built in 1906 by the Roanoke-based architectural team of Huggins & Bates, was designed with a Georgian Revival façade that resembles Philadelphia's Independence Hall. The preserved interior includes the original brass fire pole and pressed-tin ceilings. *The station is located at 13 East Church Avenue. A tour can be arranged by calling 540-853-2257.*

GALLERY 108

This gallery is a recent addition to Roanoke's historic farmers' market area. An artists' cooperative, Gallery 108 is staffed by volunteers. The walls and cases are filled with pottery, jewelry, enamels, etchings, and photography. Oils, pastels, and textiles are also on display. *Located at 108 Market Street, the gallery is open daily except Monday. For more information, call 540-982-4278.*

HISTORIC EBONY CLUB

Built in the Classical Revival style in 1923, the Strand Theater stood on First Street. Adjacent was the Ebony Club, constructed the same year. Those two establishments, representative of the far-reaching impact of Harlem's cultural renaissance, provided venues for famous black entertainers and film-makers, including Oscar Micheaux. The cinematographer took up residence at the Hotel Dumas in 1924 and filmed several movies in the Henry Street Historic District. From Roanoke, Micheaux went on to live and work in the Big Apple. He has been honored by the Producer's Guild of American Film with the presentation of an annual award in his name. Twenty-first-century plans for the Ebony Club include physical restoration and the creation of an arts institute. The Henry Street Historic District hosts a number of lively annual festivals. *Located at 109 First Street NW, the Ebony Club may be viewed from the street year-round.*

Historic Hotel Dumas

The Henry Street area developed as the central entertainment and commercial district for Roanoke's African-American population during the Jim Crow era. A narrow bridge extended across the railroad track to connect Henry Street with downtown. The three-story Hotel Dumas, constructed as the Hotel Hampton, is the oldest building in the district. Put up by a local manufacturing company that employed many African-American workers, the hotel had 26 guest rooms, a dining room, an ice-cream parlor, and a ballroom on the second floor. It is best known for its late-night jam sessions featuring such famous guests as Marian Anderson, Duke Ellington, Count Basie, and Fats Domino. The hotel has been restored to serve as a musical and cultural arts center. *Located at 110 First Street NW, it may be viewed from the street year-round. Visitors may call ahead for a tour; the number is 540-345-6781.*

History Museum of Western Virginia

This museum chronicles the history of western Virginia spanning 10,000 years. It has permanent exhibits of early Native American artifacts, Civil War-era implements, and a Victorian horse carriage. Also on view are several intricately detailed dioramas, including a fully furnished Victorian parlor. Once each year, the museum puts on its popular Fantasyland exhibition, a collection of mechanized 1930s toys that once graced area department-store windows during the holiday season. The museum offers frontier, railroad, and World War II displays. Its gift shop is stocked with replica maps, books on local history and culture, reproduction toys and games, and local handicrafts. *Located at One Market Street in Center in the Square, the museum is open seven days a week. Admission is charged. For more information, call 540-342-5770 or visit www.history-museum.org.*

Hotel Roanoke

Built in 1882 by railroad tycoon Frederick Kimball, the original Hotel Roanoke, a frame structure with three dozen guest rooms, was situated on a slight hill overlooking the city's newly established commercial district.

By 1938, the hotel was a multistory Tudor-style building with a distinctive entrance. After undergoing major renovations in the mid-1990s, the hotel now has a period lobby filled with antiques and original chandeliers. Its restored Regency Room is the home of the hotel's famous peanut soup. The hotel, listed on the National Register of Historic Places, offers a wide selection of guest rooms and suites. *Located at 110 Shenandoah Avenue, it is open year-round. For more information, call 800-222-TREE or 540-985-5900 or visit www.hotelroanoke.com.*

MILL MOUNTAIN THEATRE

In 1964, two producers from New York arrived in Roanoke intent on establishing a summer stock theater. They chose the abandoned 25-room Rockledge Inn on Mill Mountain as the site for staging their plays. The theater was an immediate success, drawing regular attendees from Roanoke and environs. When a tragic fire in 1975 resulted in the loss of the playhouse, Mill Mountain Theatre took up temporary residence in a historic movie house, the Grandin, moving down from the mountain. Today, it boasts an impressive contemporary location in the downtown market district. Visitors can pick up reasonably priced tickets for a world premiere or a time-tested classic. The theater also presents daily readings of one-act plays during the noon hour, when admission is free. *The theater is located at One Market Street in Center in the Square. Performances are held seven days a week. Admission is charged. For more information, call 800-317-6455 or 540-342-5740 or visit www.millmountain.org.*

O. WINSTON LINK MUSEUM

Housed in the Norfolk & Western passenger station built in 1905 and redesigned in 1947 by renowned industrial architect Raymond Loewy, this museum is listed on the National Register of Historic Places and is a Virginia Historic Landmark. The O. Winston Link Museum showcases the largest of the famous rail photographer's collections, including almost 200 signed prints and 2,400 negatives. Glass cases in the contemporary gallery display Link's equipment and Norfolk & Western memorabilia. To the rear of the welcome desk is additional exhibit space, as well as a rail schedule posting arrivals and departures up and down the East Coast during the station's last days of operation in 1955. A walking path connects the museum with the city's historic commercial district and the Virginia Museum of Transportation. *Located at 101 Shenandoah Avenue across from the Hotel Roanoke, the museum is open seven days a week. Admission is charged. For more information, call 540-982-LINK or visit www.linkmuseum.org.*

PATRICK HENRY HOTEL

The Patrick Henry Hotel is listed on the National Register of Historic Places and the Virginia Landmarks Register. The Georgian Revival structure was built in 1925 from a design by New York architect William Stoddard. In 1991, it was renovated to its former grandeur. The lobby has 30-foot ceilings, elaborate crystal chandeliers, and handsome wrought-iron and brass detailing. Guests may choose from 117 oversized guest rooms with private baths. Amenities include complimentary shuttle service to and from the airport and morning newspapers. Visitors may dine at the hotel's restaurant and spend an evening dancing in one of the two traditional ballrooms. *Located at 617 South Jefferson Street, the hotel is open year-round. For more information, call 800-303-0988 or 540-345-8811 or visit www.patrickhenryroanoke.com.*

SCIENCE MUSEUM OF WESTERN VIRGINIA

This nationally accredited museum features hands-on exhibits focusing on Virginia's natural history, wetlands and Chesapeake Bay conservation, and regional plant and animal life. A 750-gallon aquarium re-creates a hard-bottomed reef. The museum has five permanent galleries treating such subjects as weather, geology, and human anatomy. The Hopkins Planetarium, a 40-foot star dome, presents shows exploring southwestern Virginia's seasonal skies, lunar and stellar phenomena, and the sky lore of indigenous cultures. *Located at One Market Street in Center in the Square, the museum is open seven days a week. Admission is charged. For more information, call 540-342-5726 or visit www.smwv.org.*

Studios on the Square Gallery

Located at street level in a historic commercial building, this gallery offers a tremendous selection of fine art, contemporary handicrafts, and studio jewelry. An elaborate staircase at the rear of the gallery leads to the 17 artists' studios on the second and third floors. There, local artists in stone, metal, oils, pastels, watercolors, and clay welcome guests to ask questions as they work. *Located at 126 West Campbell Avenue, the gallery is open daily except Sunday. For more information, call 540-345-4076 or visit www.studiosonthesquare.com.*

Virginia Museum of Transportation

As the southern terminus of the Norfolk & Western rail line, Roanoke rocketed from a population of 600 to 10 times that just three years later, defining the city as an important transportation hub. The state transportation museum, housed in Roanoke's historic 1918 freight station, honors the area's rich legacy of rail travel. Exhibits include a reconstructed Main Street lined with carriages, early automobiles, freight trucks, and

Historic commercial signage, Roanoke
Photograph by Anna Fariello

fire engines. A newly constructed pavilion exhibits a rail collection featuring authentic locomotives. The gift shop has unique travel-themed prints and souvenirs. The historic O. Winston Link Rail Walk connects the museum with downtown's historic Market Square. *Located at 303 Norfolk Avenue SW, the museum is open seven days a week. Admission is charged. For more information, call 540-342-5670 or visit www.vmt.org.*

VISITOR CENTER

Situated in the heart of Roanoke's commercial district, the visitor center has a staff that can answer questions regarding local eateries, shops, and attractions. Visitors can browse the selection of brochures and pick up a map for a walking tour of the historic downtown. *Located at 114 Market Street, the center is open seven days a week. For more information, call 800-635-5535 or 540-342-7119.*

Sites included in the following stop are within the Roanoke city limits and within easy driving distance of the town center.

STOP #12   ROANOKE AREA

CRYSTAL SPRING PUMPING STATION

Early Scots-Irish settlers in the Roanoke Valley knew the value of the pure, copious waters of Crystal Spring. A gristmill was constructed there to serve the budding community. Under various owners, the mill was modified to suit the needs of the ever-increasing population of Big Lick, the railway community just north. The year 1905 saw the installation of a magnificent steam pump, delivered in parts by train from Buffalo, New York. Today's site includes a restored pump system, educational exhibits, interactive media, and landscaped walking paths. *From Roanoke, take U.S. 220 South (Franklin Road) to the park entrance, located across from the hospital complex. Visi-*

Henry Street, Roanoke's center of African-American Culture, circa 1910
COURTESY OF NORFOLK & WESTERN HISTORICAL PHOTOGRAPH COLLECTION,
VIRGINIA TECH SPECIAL COLLECTIONS

tors may also call the History Museum of Western Virginia for directions. The site is open Sundays and by appointment. For more information, call 540-342-5770.

FIFTH AVENUE PRESBYTERIAN CHURCH

The original Fifth Avenue Presbyterian Church burned to the ground in 1959. Firefighters and volunteers were able to save a unique stained-glass window commissioned in the 1920s to honor Confederate general Stonewall Jackson. That historic piece was incorporated into the present building. Visitors are invited to call for an appointment to view the saved treasure. *Drive north on Second Street or Fifth Street into historic Gainsboro to see the church, located at 301 Patton Avenue NW. Sunday services are open to the public. At other times, visitors should call ahead; the number is 540-342-0264.*

GRANDIN THEATRE

This historic theater, built in 1932, was popular with local children attending Saturday-morning cartoons, Westerns, and World War II news shorts. The restored Grandin has a vintage marquee, mahogany candy cases, and tiled floors. It shows select first-run films, as well as independent, foreign, and children's films at discount prices. *It is located two miles southwest of downtown Roanoke. Follow Campbell Avenue (U.S. 11 South) as is becomes Grandin Road; the theater is at 1310 Grandin. Visitors may call for a show schedule or stop in to explore the historic structure; call 540-345-6177.*

HARRISON MUSEUM OF AFRICAN-AMERICAN CULTURE

The Harrison Museum is located in a historic 1916 building that was home to Roanoke's first public African-American secondary school. The museum preserves and interprets the achievements and experiences of African-Americans through revolving exhibits of photographs, artifacts, and memorabilia and a collection of African and contemporary art. Its archives contain a collection of local oral histories. The gift shop is stocked with Afrocentric art, books on local and regional history, and locally made crafts and jewelry. *Drive north on Fifth Street into historic Gainsboro. Located at 523 Harrison Avenue NW, the museum is open Tuesday through Saturday. For more information, call 540-345-4818 or visit www.harrisonmuseum.org.*

HISTORIC GAINSBORO LIBRARY

During the 1920s, African-American leaders in Roanoke put out a citywide call for neighborhood branch libraries. The first was dedicated in 1921 in a section of the old Odd Fellows Hall on the corner of Patton Avenue and Gainsboro Road. As early as 1926, the library had a subscription to the *Journal of Negro History*. Over the course of that decade, the collection focused increasingly on topics pertaining to black culture. Virginia Lee Young, who became the librarian in 1929 and served the Gainsboro community for 40 years, assisted in the institution's move to a newer, larger facility in 1940. Designed by a Roanoke architectural firm for the city's then-segregated neighborhood, the brick-and-limestone Tudor Revival building has retained its original doors and book-return slots. *Located at 15 Patton Avenue NW, it is open daily except Sunday. For more information, call 540-853-2540.*

Rosenberg Pottery Studio

Carol Rosenberg's studio features a variety of handcrafted stoneware pottery and decorative items with a unique dogwood motif and other patterns from nature. The artist uses multicolored glazes on her hand-thrown vases and lanterns. *Follow Campbell Avenue (U.S. 11 South) as it becomes Grandin Road. Located off Grandin Road at 3466 Windsor Road SW, the studio is open by appointment. For more information, call 540-774-5297.*

St. Andrews Catholic Church

St. Andrews is one of the finest examples of Victorian Gothic architecture in the commonwealth. The elaborate yellow-brick church dates to 1902. Its striking silhouette with twin spires, inspired by European cathedrals, is visible from many vantage points in the city, including I-581. Its dramatic interior includes extensive ornate woodwork, stenciling, and stained glass. *The church is located at 631 North Jefferson Street. Sunday services are open to the public. For more information, call 540-344-9814.*

To return to I-81 and complete the trail loop,
take I-581 North to I-81 South to Salem or points beyond.

Steam-powered Baldwin locomotive
PHOTOGRAPH BY EARL PALMER,
COURTESY OF RADFORD UNIVERSITY
SPECIAL COLLECTIONS

Suggested Reading

Abramson, Ruth, and Jean Haskell, eds. *Encyclopedia of Appalachia*. Knoxville: University of Tennessee Press, 2006.

Adams, Noah. *Far Appalachia: Following the New River North*. New York: Dell Publishing, 2001.

Anderson-Green, Paula Hathaway. *A Hot-Bed of Musicians: Traditional Music in the Upper New River Valley-Whitetop Region*. Knoxville: University of Tennessee Press, 2002.

Bell, Augusta Grove. *Circling Windrock Mountain: Two Hundred Years in Appalachia*. Knoxville: University of Tennessee Press, 1998.

Berry, Wendell. *The Gift of Good Land: Further Essays Cultural and Agricultural*. San Francisco: North Point Press, 1981.

Biggers, Jeff. *The United States of Appalachia: How Southern Mountaineers Brought Independent Culture and Enlightenment to America*. Emeryville, Calif.: Shoemaker and Hoard, 2006.

Blethen, Tyler, and Richard Straw, eds. *High Mountain Rising: Appalachia in Time and Place*. Urbana: University of Illinois Press, 2004.

Bolgiano, Chris. *The Appalachian Forest: A Search for Roots and Renewal*. Mechanicsburg, Pa.: Stackpole Books, 1995.

Bryant, Bill. "The Civilian Conservation Corp." *Parkway Milepost* (Fall-Winter 2002-3): 11.

Campbell, John C. *The Southern Highlander and His Homeland*. New York: Russell Sage Foundation, 1921.

Caudill, Harry M. *Night Comes to the Cumberlands: A Biography of a Depressed Area*. Boston: Little, Brown & Company, 1962.

· Collins, Timothy. *Native Americans in Central Appalachia: A Bibliography*. Livingston, Tenn.: Appalachia Science in the Public Interest, 1989.

Dane, Suzanne G. *Stories Across America: Opportunities for Rural Tourism*. Washington, D.C.: National Trust for Historic Preservation, 2001.

Davids, Richard C. *The Man Who Moved a Mountain*. Philadelphia: Fortress Press, 1970.

Drake, Richard B. *A History of Appalachia*. Lexington: University Press of Kentucky, 2001.

Dyer, Joyce, ed. *Bloodroot: Reflections on Place by Appalachian Women Writers*. Lexington: University Press of Kentucky, 1998.

Eaton, Allen. *Handicrafts of the Southern Highlands*. New York: Russell Sage Foundation, 1937.

Edwards, Grace Toney, et al. *Handbook of Appalachia*. Knoxville: University of Tennessee Press, 2006.

Eller, Ronald. *Miners, Millhands and Mountaineers: Industrialization of the Appalachian South, 1880-1930*. Knoxville: University of Tennessee Press, 1982.

Fariello, M. Anna. *Movers & Makers: Doris Ulmann's Portrait of the Craft Revival in Appalachia*. Asheville, N.C.: Curatorial Insight, 2005 reissue.

————. "Trail Blazing: A Conversation about Cultural Tourism." *Virginia Association of Museums* newsletter (Winter 1999): 3-5.

Foster, Stephen W. *The Past Is Another Country: Representation, Historical Consciousness and Resistance in the Blue Ridge*. Berkeley: University of California Press, 1988.

Fox, John. *Trail of the Lonesome Pine*. New York: Scribner's, 1908.

Frazier, Charles. *Cold Mountain*. New York: Atlantic Monthly Press, 1997.

Fussell, Fred. *Blue Ridge Music Trails: Finding a Place in the Circle*. Chapel Hill: University of North Carolina Press, 2003.

Giardina, Denise. *The Unquiet Earth: A Novel*. New York: Norton, 1992.

Givens, Lula Porterfield. *Christiansburg, Montgomery County, Virginia: In the Heart of the Alleghenies*. Christiansburg, Va.: 1981.

Glassie, Henry. *Pattern in the Material Folk Culture of the Eastern United States*. Philadelphia: University of Pennsylvania Press, 1968.

Hamby, Setta Barker. *Memoirs of Grassy Creek: Growing Up in the Mountains on the Virginia-North Carolina Line*. Jefferson, N.C.: McFarland Press, 1998.

Harkins, Anthony. *Hillbilly: A Cultural History of an American Icon*. New York: Oxford University Press, 2004.

Higgs, Robert J., and Ambrose N. Manning, eds. *Voices from the Hills: Selected Readings of Southern Appalachia*. New York: F. Ungar, 1978.

Higgs, Robert J., Ambrose N. Manning, and Jim Wayne Miller, eds. *Appalachia Inside Out*. Knoxville: University of Tennessee Press, 1995.

Hildebrand, John R. "Triumph and Tragedy: A Railroad Struggle Instrumental in Creating Roanoke, Virginia." *Smithfield Review* 5 (2001).

Ingles, John. *Escape from Indian Captivity*. Privately published by Roberta Ingles Steele and Andrew Lewis Ingles, 1969.

Jolley, Harley E. *The Blue Ridge Parkway*. Knoxville: University of Tennessee Press, 1969.

———. *The CCC in the Smokies*. Gatlinburg, Tenn.: Great Smoky Mountains Natural History Association, 2001.

Kephart, Horace. *Our Southern Highlanders*. New York: Macmillan, 1913.

Kincaid, Robert L. *The Wilderness Road*. Indianapolis, Ind.: Bobbs-Merrill, 1947.

Koons, Kenneth E., and Warren R. Hofstra, eds. *After the Backcountry: Rural Life in the Great Valley of Virginia, 1800-1900*. Knoxville: University of Tennessee Press, 2000.

Lampell, Ramona. *O, Appalachia: Artists of the Southern Mountains*. New York: Stewart, Tabori, and Chang, 1989.

Lee Highway Association, Inc. *Lee Highway*. Washington, D.C.: Lee Highway Association, 1926.

McCrumb, Sharyn. *The Songcatcher: A Ballad Novel*. New York: Penguin Books, 2001.

Olson, Ted. *Blue Ridge Folklife*. Jackson: University Press of Mississippi, 1998.

Pawlett, Nathaniel Mason. *Historic Roads of Virginia: A Brief History of the Roads of Virginia, 1607-1840*. Charlottesville: Virginia Highway and Transportation Research Council, 1977.

Peters, John O., and Margaret T. *Virginia's Historic Courthouses*. Charlottesville: University of Virginia Press, 1995.

Pine, B. Joseph, and James H. Gilmore. *The Experience Economy: Work Is Theatre and Every Business a Stage*. Boston: Harvard Business School, 1999.

Pudup, Mary Beth. *Appalachia in the Making: The Mountain South in the 19th Century*. Chapel Hill: University of North Carolina Press, 1995.

Ritchie, Jean. *Singing Family of the Cumberlands*. New York: Oxford University Press, 1955.

Rouse, Park. *The Great Wagon Road from Philadelphia to the South*. New York: McGraw-Hill, 1973.

Salmon, John S. *The Washington Iron Works of Franklin County, Virginia, 1773-1850*. Richmond: Virginia State Library, 1986.

Shapiro, Henry D. *Appalachia on Our Mind: The Southern Mountains and Mountaineers in the American Consciousness, 1870-1920*. Chapel Hill: University of North Carolina Press, 1978.

Shareef, Reginald. *The Roanoke Valley's African American Heritage: A Pictorial History*. Virginia Beach, Va.: Donning Company, 1996.

Speed, Thomas. *The Wilderness Road: A Description of the Routes of Travel by Which the Pioneers and Early Settlers First Came to Kentucky*. Louisville, Ky.: J. P. Morton & Company, 1886.

Starnes, Richard. *Southern Journeys: Tourism, History and Culture in the Modern South*. Tuscaloosa: University of Alabama Press, 2002.

Steele, William O. *The Old Wilderness Road: An American Journey*. New York: Harcourt Brace, 1968.

Stewart, Kathleen. *A Space on the Other Side of the Road: Cultural Poetics in an "Other America."* Princeton, N.J.: Princeton University Press, 1996.

Virginia Museum of Fine Arts. *Painting in the South*. Richmond: Virginia Museum of Fine Arts, 1983.

Washington, Booker T. *An Autobiography: The Story of My Life and Work*. Atlanta: J. L. Nichols, 1901.

Wells, John E., and Robert E. Dalton. *The Virginia Architects, 1835-1955: A Biographical Dictionary*. Richmond: New South Architectural Press, 1997.

Whisnant, David E. *All That Is Native and Fine: The Politics of Culture in an American Region*. Chapel Hill: University of North Carolina Press, 1983.

Wigginton, Eliot, ed. *Foxfire* series. Garden City, N.Y.: Anchor Press, 1973.

Williams, John Alexander. *Appalachia: A History*. Chapel Hill: University of North Carolina Press, 2002.

Williams, Michael Ann. *Great Smoky Mountains Folklife*. Jackson: University Press of Mississippi, 1995.

Wilson, Charles Reagan, and William Ferris. *Encyclopedia of Southern Culture*. Chapel Hill: University of North Carolina Press, 1989.

Wood, Curtis, and Joanne Greene. "Origins of the Handicraft Revival in the Southern Mountains." In *Remembrance, Reunion, and Revival: Celebrating a Decade of Appalachian Studies*. Proceedings of the 10th annual Appalachian Studies Conference.

INDEX

Page numbers in italics refer to illustrations